# SLOWHAND
## THE STORY OF
## ERIC CLAPTON

D1065817

PROTEUS BOOKS is an imprint of
The Proteus Publishing Group

United States
PROTEUS PUBLISHING COMPANY, INC.
9, West 57th Street, Suite 4503
New York, NY 10019

distributed by:
CHERRY LANE BOOKS COMPANY, INC.
P.O. Box 430
Port Chester, NY 10573

United Kingdom
PROTEUS BOOKS LIMITED
Bremar House, Sale Place
London W2 1PT

ISBN 0 86276 148 4 (paperback)
ISBN 0 86276 149 2 (hardback)

First published in U.S. 1984
First published in U.K. 1984

Photocredits:
Chris Walter/Photofeatures International
Barry Plummer
Andre Csillag
Ian Dickson
Ace
Michael Zagaris
Alan Messer
Hamish Grimes
Cyrus Andrews
David Redfern
Steve Emberton

Editor: Kay Rowley
Designed by: Adrian Hodgkins
Typeset by: SX Composing Ltd
Printed in and Bound in Great Britain

# SLOWHAND

## THE STORY OF
## ERIC
## CLAPTON

## Harry Shapiro

**PROTEUS BOOKS**
LONDON/NEW YORK

# CONTENTS

IN DECEMBER 1974, ERIC CLAPTON WALKED OUT ONTO THE STAGE OF THE HAMMERSMITH ODEON IN LONDON, HIS FIRST GIG THERE AS A WORKING MUSICIAN IN OVER FOUR YEARS. BUT THE AUDIENCE HAD NOT FORGOTTEN HIM. SOMEBODY SHOUTED OUT *"CLAPTON IS GOD!"* AND THERE WAS GREAT APPLAUSE. THEN A SILENCE FELL OVER THE CONCERT HALL – CLAPTON WALKED TO THE FRONT OF THE STAGE AND SPREAD HIS ARMS – *"I'M NOT GOD,"* HE SAID, *"JUST THE GREATEST GUITARIST IN THE WORLD"*.

# INTRODUCTION

In January 1971, I went to see Johnny Winter at the Watford Town Hall, a venue situated just north of London. Sitting up in the circle, I felt the full impact of the heat rising from the bodies massed in the auditorium below. But I was hotter than most as, unknown to me at the time, I was going down with glandular fever and the sweat was pouring off me. On stage too, the Johnny Winter Band with Rick Derringer were cooking fit to bust when about halfway through, Winter sat down on a stool and picked out by a single spotlight, started a simple country blues. I went cold, the sweat dried on me – that sound was not just spine-chilling, it was freezing. As an emotional force in contemporary popular music, electric blues guitar playing has few peers. One of its finest exponents and probably the best known guitarist in the world is Eric Clapton, a musician who has frozen more sweat on the backs of more packed audiences than any guitarist alive.

Clapton's influence on developments in rock music over his twenty years as a professional musician has been far reaching. The first musician to be tagged a guitar hero, Clapton's example served to switch the focus in many bands from the singer to the guitarist. Sidemen became mainmen and band leaders, and the guitar was elevated from its tinny antecedents in the Fifties and early Sixties to a position of prominence in the new sounds of rock. When Clapton ousted Hank Marvin from top slot in the guitar polls, it was the dawning of a new era for the electric guitar at a time when Cream was changing the whole way rock sounded. Now it was rich, full and loud, headed up by Clapton's rediscovery for a different generation of the Gibson guitar (and thereby saving the company from extinction), plugged into Marshall amplification. Under Clapton's patronage both products became locked together to symbolise high energy, high technology music for the Sixties. Thousands of budding guitarists all over the world went out and bought the gear that Eric played hoping somehow to capture that magic sound.

E.C. has secured for himself a place as one of rock's premier representatives in the pantheon of Twentieth Century musicians, but it has been a battle: not so much to win the place because that happened relatively quickly, but to come to terms with what it all means. Clapton's legendary status has sat uneasily on his shoulders. Rilke has said that "Fame is the sum of the given misunderstandings that gather about a new name" and the pressure resulting from this has driven Clapton into periods of non-communication using drink and drugs as a precarious defence mechanism. His mistakes over the years have largely been a corollary of his insecurities particularly an over-reliance on earthbound illusory prophets and ill-considered public outbursts, but little has really served to dim his star in the eyes of his many fans everywhere. Above all, he has proved himself to be a survivor, coming through a period when many of his contemporaries made themselves ill or even died tilting at the windmill of a granite-faced industry. The music may now tend to reflect the relative safety of Eric's position, but rather that, than a tribute on Radio One and seventy-three miraculously discovered 'live in the toilet' out-take albums.

There are certain things this book is not. It is not a hagiography; Clapton is not God. Neither does being an excellent musician endow him with cosmic vision. Gods are entities that people hang their lives on, objects of adoration and those who regard rock stars as such do themselves and their heroes a disservice. Jesus was a carpenter and Eric laid floors, but that's as far as it goes! Nor is it a definitive biography for two reasons; first (and thankfully) the guy is still with us making records and touring. Although it seems unlikely that he will dye his hair blue or join AC/DC, nothing is certain with Eric, so watch some space, somewhere. Secondly, I was unable to conduct any original interview with Eric, although I doubt whether he will ever be quite as candid again as he was with Steve Turner during the post-heroin confessional period. . . Yet even though Steve included everything – between the lines there was much left unsaid or half-hinted. So what is presented here can best be described as a personal interim report.

But at a deeper level, this book has a special significance for me because it was written during a time of great personal anguish when I think I learnt more about the blues than in seventeen years of record buying back to 1966 when the first blues album I bought was a John Mayall and Eric Clapton album. Listening to Eric's past achievements, his openness as a composer and player and the universality of his simple approach came through very sharply. Sometimes, however, the message was too clear and on occasion, I deliberately skipped tracks on albums because I just couldn't listen to them, returning later when the mood was less black. But don't you chicken out like I did – don't just read the book, dig out those Clapton albums and give them a spin. And if you were one of those who abandoned Eric when Cream broke up, hopefully this book might encourage you to think again. Eric remains an awesome guitarist – don't take my word for it, go to a concert and hear for yourself that E.C. is still here.

In helping to bring this book together, I would like to acknowledge the co-operation of the following:
John Baily, Pete Brown, Jack Bruce, Pete Frame, Giorgio Gomelsky, Hamish Grimes, Alexis Korner, Andrew Lauder, Jim McCarty, Tom McGuinness, John Mayall, Paul Samwell-Smith, Mike Sawin, Steve Turner, Chris Welch.
A big debt is owed to my mother going far beyond the typing of this manuscript; special thanks to John Holmes and John Brady for technical assistance and to Mark Roberty for discographical efforts well beyond the call of duty.

# OVERTURE
# Me And The Devil Blues -
# The Spirit Of Robert Johnson

By the time Eric Clapton was born in 1945, his spiritual ancestor Robert Johnson had been dead for about seven years, after drinking some poisoned whisky in a bar in Greenwood, Mississippi, probably administered by a jealous girlfriend or irate husband.

Biographical information on Johnson is sparse as there are few around to remember or really had much cause to remember – the blues researchers had a hard time finding out about him, even in the years immediately following his death. His stature as a blues player only became apparent years later, through the growth period of electric urban blues and the birth of rock'n'roll.

Born around 1910, his earliest ambition was to be a harp player but soon he yearned to be a guitar player like Willie Brown and his protégé, Son House who, constantly pestered by the young Johnson, tried to teach him a few licks. But the boy couldn't play to save his life and it tore him up. He absconded from his plantation home and disappeared for about six months – nobody knew precisely where he went – but it was the beginning of the Johnson wanderlust that through his life took him not only all over the deep South but to Texas, Chicago, New York and even Canada. When he came back, not only was he a man, but also a musician of awesome quality and power with a guitar technique second to none in the emotion it conveyed. Not surprisingly, among the religious and superstitious black community of his homeland, there were rumours of dark and mysterious happenings. Son House was emphatic "he sold his soul to the devil to get to play like that". One thing was for certain, Robert Johnson did not need any more lessons. Playing a Sears & Roebuck Stella guitar, he was recorded by Don Law for Vocation Records over two sessions in a San Antonio hotel room during November 1936 and June 1937. The twenty-nine sides he laid down represented the total of his recorded output but many of them, like *Dust My Broom*, became blues classics. Elmore James built his career on that song and it was the cornerstone of the whole English blues revival of the mid-Sixties, especially for bands with slide guitar players like Fleetwood Mac. When Johnson played it sounded very full and rich – walking bass lines that heavily influenced the Chicago sound and loud jangling beats overlaid by lyrics of explicit sexuality which can be regarded as prototype rock'n'roll. He also had a remarkable voice. *They're Red Hot* had at least three different vocal intonations and the harmonising of his voice and guitar on many other songs in the upper registers is echoed by Jimi Hendrix on songs like *Voodoo Chile*. An appropriate example, it contains those same basslines and unisons pertaining to what people thought Robert Johnson was – a child of the devil.

His music was full of dark satanic imagery: devils, phantoms and monsters populated his visions – *Hellhound On My Trail* and *Me And The Devil Blues* for example, which metamorphosed into part of rock's own heart of darkness – *Their Satanic Majesties Request* – with its own demons, both real and imagined. Like all Southern blacks, Johnson had to live under the shadow of the Klan and institutionalised racism which prompted the black curfew regulations alluded to in *Crossroad Blues*.

But Johnson's most repeated theme, his most aggravating problem was 'woman trouble' and unrequited love. Described by a blues contemporary of Johnson's, David 'Honeyboy' Edwards, as tall and skinny, he also had one bad eye which must have made him fascinatingly flawed. Johnson was very much the 'ladies man' and he wasn't too fussy whose lady it was. Lyrics like "squeeze me til the juice runs down my leg" and "stuff I got'll bust your brains out baby" had them crowding round the juke joints waiting to find out. No pubescent Osmond-style hysteria here, these women knew what they were after. The additional attraction of Johnson was that he was not, in a relative sense, without money. Many blues artists got a pat on the back and a plate of grits for their recording efforts and that was it, but Johnson was paid several hundred dollars for the songs he recorded and in the time he had left after those sessions, there was much drinking, gambling and womanising. Yet while being confident and swaggering with women, he was shy and diffident about his music. The musicians who watched him record in San Antonio were shown his back and rarely did he face his audience.

Whatever one may think of the social implications of Johnson's songs, whether expressing the American or just the black experience in microcosm, it was their strong autobiographical nature, their intense personal passion, chaos and loneliness, executed so vibrantly that captured the imagination of modern musicians. Johnny Winter was rumoured to have learnt to play slide from Johnson records and the Stones recorded *Love In Vain*, but probably the musician most influenced was Eric Clapton.

No doubt what follows applies to other musicians as well in a biographical sense at least but, without trying to bend history too much, Clapton's career does seem to hold up a mirror to Johnson's life. Both were superlative pioneering musicians in the blues idiom, wanting to get further into the blues than anyone else, having the ability to get there and in the process influencing two generations of musicians. When Muddy Waters saw Robert Johnson playing on a street corner he had to walk away because it scared him to death. But what he heard he took to Chicago, reinterpreted and embellished it and almost singlehandedly gave birth to the Chicago graphy of the soul, belying Leadbelly's comment that the white man cannot sing the blues because he's got nothing on his mind. *Layla* resonates back through the years to Johnson's own *Love In Vain* which appears in the lyrics to *Layla* and *Kind Hearted Blues* (I love my baby/my baby don't love me). In *Come In My Kitchen* Johnson (this time as George Harrison) loses his woman to his best friend, resolved for Clapton and Johnson in the line from that same song "some joker got lucky, stole her back again".

Eric Clapton's career can be interpreted in some respects as the search for the spirit of Robert Johnson. Perhaps even the heroin period was, in a perverse way, a kind of metaphoric death which paralleled Johnson's own: Clapton was twenty-five at the time and Johnson was about the same age when he died. An oft-quoted statement of Clapton's tied in the deaths of Jimi Hendrix and Robert Johnson to the idea of "a few good years, then go". But more positively, Eric Clapton went through years of developing technical brilliance, restating Johnson as the master blues player in faithful cover versions of his songs until there came the realisation that when approached through the narrower perspective of personal anguish, the white man can feel the blues as well as sing and play them. What makes Clapton such a remarkable musician is his ability to transcend pure technical virtuosity, one reason why he has always been reluctant to accept the 'God' tag. He has always seemed to take his ability for granted and never welcomed the praise he received in the early days. Jimmy Page and Jeff Beck, for example, may be technically superior, but Clapton captured the imagination with a true link to the blues tradition – his head with Buddy Guy and Freddie King, but his heart with Robert Johnson.

The main criticism levelled at Clapton during the Seventies, is that all the fire has gone, that he's got nothing more to say or, to put it another way, the search is over. This ignores another side of the blues – its paradoxical role as a music of celebration, entertainment and love. Whatever he does, Clapton will always be a blues player; *Wonderful Tonight* has as much validity as *Ramblin' On My Mind* or *Layla*, as an expression of Clapton's inner feelings, the emotions no less heartfelt, the execution no less tasteful or effortless.

But the impetus for this search, and its progress through to the present day, did not happen in a vacuum. The context for the rise of Eric Clapton as the world's most lyrical and fluent white blues guitarist is the rise of rhythm and blues in Britain and the musical revolution that it generated.

sound that Mike Vernon did so well to capture on the famous Mayall/ Clapton Bluebreakers album years later.

Like Johnson, Clapton became a guitar hero, the first guitarist to whom that title was officially applied, at the same time frightening and encouraging many guitarists by his example. Peter Green switched from bass to lead on hearing Eric, and Mick Taylor stood in the crowd at the Flamingo Club in London's West End making mental note of every Clapton lick. To these two premier musicians one can add hundreds, probably thousands, of other budding blues guitarists, most of whom never made it past the village hop or wistful stares at gleaming Gibsons in shop windows but who were nevertheless inspired to try, by the music of Eric Clapton.

Both have lived 'the rock life', with periods of self-imposed exile, sudden bouts of wanderlust, drinking and gambling. Clapton took this further, merely because he had the money to indulge himself. Fame came early to both and neither appeared to handle it too well, particularly in relation to women. Content to ramble from one casual affair to another, they demonstrated all the immaturity of youth and, beneath the veneer of adolescent machismo were somewhat in awe of female sexuality. Only Clapton was to find an anchor to tie him down in the sea of storms. Yet it was also the intensity of youth that gave them their sense of power. In *If I Had Possession Over Judgement Day* Johnson demonstrated an over-weening arrogance by suggesting that if he did have such power "then the woman I'm lovin' wouldn't have no right to pray". And in a remarkably frank interview during the era of 'what's your favourite colour' style rock journalism Clapton, then 21, stated quite categorically that he was a very lonely person with no real close friendships or women and that furthermore he was "not interested in guitar sound or technique, but in people and what you can do to them via music. I'm very conceited and I think I have a power – and my guitar is a medium for expressing that power".[1]

The legends of both have been enhanced by myths about hibernation and aloofness offering a mysterious (but in reality more balanced and rounded) character perspective. Clapton's 'disappearance' to get his playing together is pure myth and his refusal to face his audience on some occasions was not so much from shyness but more to do with improving his guitar sustain by facing the speakers. Although this indicated a greater concern for musical perfection than the sensibilities of the audience, the very act added enormously to his image of the urban cowboy and endeared him to fans even more. Johnson *did* disappear and *did* turn his back on his audience, even though one can reasonably speculate that Johnson learnt his skill from the doing of it in every bar and on every street corner he could find, rather than from the more romantic notion of seclusion.

More directly, Eric sang Robert Johnson numbers in the early days, but as Greil Marcus has pointed out, Clapton's love for Johnson's music really came to fruition "once Johnson's music became part of who Clapton was (when) Clapton came closest to himself".[2] That happened with *Layla*, a modern Johnson song of unrequited love, Clapton's own personal blues in which he discovered what one part of the blues is all about, an autobio-

# CHAPTER ONE
# From Beale Street
# To Wardour Street

The history of R&B in Britain goes back to the late Forties. And the man who probably deserves more credit than anyone for giving the music its first public airing is Chris Barber, the trad. jazz band leader who one might have thought would have regarded R&B as anathema. His regular working jazz band was going from about 1947 and within it Alexis Korner, a keen blues enthusiast and guitarist, had a blues set.

Born in 1928, Korner came from a strange, romantic background. His father was an Austrian cavalry officer in the First World War who was fifty-eight when Alexis was born, his mother was of Greek extraction. Korner senior wanted Alexis to become a brilliant nineteenth century-style dilletante and a virtuoso violin player but all he did study was classical piano and was saved from a life of elegant uselessness by hearing a Jimmy Yancey record.

Trad jazz bandleader Ken Colyer came back from his pilgrimage to New Orleans around 1948 and teamed up with Chris in a band which included another budding blues enthusiast, Tony Donegan. In 1949, Donegan went off into the army to do his national service, just as Alexis was coming out. Korner returned to the Barber band to play blues in the inter-vals – there was not much point playing at any other time, because unampli-fied guitar was inaudible in a band with two cornets in the front line.

There was a history going back to the Thirties, and carrying on through to the British "blues boom" of the Sixties, of music fans here and in Europe taking up 'lost' black musical causes; New Orleans jazz, Dixieland, bebop, cool jazz and country blues. What this also spawned was the purist ethic whereby you were a staunch follower of one musical form or another with a vehement dislike for anything else. Alexis Korner was an early victim of this, upbraided for having catholic tastes. His problem was that he liked King Oliver and this meant that the beboppers (or reboppers as they were first called) branded him a "mouldy fig" while the trad jazz guys froze him out for saying he thought Charlie Parker was a great musician. In the early Sixties R&B was a label tagged on to many different sorts of bands, ranging from the Rolling Stones and the Pretty Things, Georgie Fame and Graham Bond to Manfred Mann and the Swinging Blue Jeans. This was largely the result of a very worried music press that could not decide exactly what R&B was to its own satisfaction or neatly parcel it up and file it away under "Five Minute Wonder". So the readership was regaled with soul-searching articles like *R&B – What Is It?* and *R&B – Trend or Tripe?* Very much the same articles were appearing on the jazz pages – *The New Wave – Is It Killing Jazz?* – the new wave in this case being John Coltrane, Charlie Mingus and Ornette Coleman.

Chris Barber had been a blues fan for some years and had a substantial blues collection. Having made trad jazz commercially viable, playing to capacity crowds at every concert, he devoted his time and money to actively promoting another kind of music which was dear to his heart. This music was a potential threat to his own career and one that was realised when many trad jazz clubs switched over to R&B in the early Sixties in order to survive. It was Chris who introduced Alexis to another blues fanatic, Cyril Davis, a panel beater during the day and a banjo player in skiffle groups and trad jazz outfits like Steve Lane's Southern Stompers by night. However, a developing interest in the blues led him to harmonica and twelve string guitar. He was famous for his harp playing – Jack Bruce says "I never dared pick up a harp until Cyril had died" but among many musicians he will be remembered as the finest acoustic twelve-string guitarist Britain ever produced. Davies was also co-organiser of the London Skiffle Centre. Skiffle was one of Britain's early attempts at playing the blues, being a pseudo-country folk outcrop of the Fifties New Orleans jazz revival. The centre was upstairs at the Roundhouse pub in London's West End and it was always full, but Cyril in his usual forceful way managed to persuade the other three organisers to introduce a decidedly fringe interest music. In the summer of 1954 the London Skiffle Centre re-opened as the London Blues and Barrelhouse Club with an initial audience of about three, watching the new acoustic blues duo of Alexis Korner and Cyril Davies.

But even more important than bringing Alexis and Cyril together, Chris Barber was instrumental in organising visits to Britain by key American blues musicians. Some of these musicians had been before: Jimmy Cotton was an early visitor, as was Big Bill Broonzy, an early Clapton influence, who played Kingsway Hall in London in September 1951. Alan Lomax, who had done so much to capture Mississippi country blues on record, compered the event and jazz critic Max Jones brought Broonzy to the concert from the airport in his MG sports car. Josh White came in 1952, as did a New Orleans blues and jazz guitarist/singer called Lonnie Johnson who inspired Tony Donegan to change his name.

Barber's first promotion was Sister Rosetta Tharpe at the end of 1957. He paid for her visit, and those of others like Sonny Terry and Brownie McGhee, from his own pocket just because he thought it was important that British audiences should experience this music. He created the demand – there was no large blues audience in this country clamouring for the music – and showed people what they were missing. Probably the most significant visits were by Muddy Waters beginning in 1958. During the 1940–1950 period when Alexis Korner was first getting involved in the blues and Chris

Barber was beginning to introduce the music to the people, Waters, along with over a million of his black brethren, were leaving the rural South for the urban North along Highway 51 in search of work. On the way, he and many of his contemporaries were drawn to Memphis, a crucially important blues centre at this time. Around the bars of the Beale Street area and on the street corners itinerant blues musicians tried to make a living. From the radios blared WDKA Memphis, proclaiming itself the only fifty thousand watt Negro station in America pumping out blues and gospel twenty-four hours a day, seven days a week.

Sam Phillips' Memphis-based Sun label began releasing material in 1950, leasing the masters to the Chicago independent label Chess for whom Muddy had been recording since 1947. He had previously been recorded in 1941 for the Library of Congress by Alan Lomax, who had initially come in search of Robert Johnson. In those days Waters was an electrifying country blues singer, but after having been taken round the noisy, sleazy clubs and bars of urban Chicago by Bill Broonzy, he switched to the electric guitar. T-Bone Walker was, however, probably the first blues guitarist to go electric after the pioneering jazz efforts of Count Basie's guitarist Eddie Durham and Charlie Christian.

Christian had used the first Gibson electric guitar, the semi-acoustic ES150 which appeared in 1935 and made the guitar his own to the point where the pickup was named after him. The first solid electric guitar was introduced by Leo Fender in 1948 and he called it the Broadcaster, but had to change it to Telecaster in 1950 after Gretsch pointed out that it was the trade name of their drum kits. In 1954, however, Fender introduced his *pièce de résistance*, the Stratocaster, with three pick ups and its own built-in tremelo unit. The guitar was an instant success – the thin wailing versatile sounds of Fender guitars were a feature of the Chicago sound and Muddy Waters has always been a Fender man, either the Stratocaster or, more usually, the Telecaster. The Fender guitar was an instrument of danger and threat, there was no way of playing it with delicacy or politeness. But Fender wasn't finished yet for rumbling darkly beneath the guitar was the Fender Precision bass guitar. This was the world's first electric bass guitar, introduced in 1951, and probably more important in shaping the destiny of the sound of rock than even the electric guitar, creating as it did the springboard from which the rhythms and melodies of rock could be launched. The Fender bass was so dominant in the field that for a while Fender became the generic name for *bass playing*, as ubiquitous as Hoover or Biro and the Fender Precision is still the most popular bass on the market. It was not really until the mid-Sixties that Fender, who had previously swept all before it, was challenged by Gibson, largely due to the use of the Gibson Les Paul by Eric Clapton.

So with a line-up including Otis Spann, Little Walter and Jimmy Rogers, Waters had helped create the Chicago sound which was a blues type in its own right, different even to that of Detroit, being very hard and even more aggressive and loud. It was *this* sound that appealed to young white blues enthusiasts – long, sustaining notes using cranked up amplification and Fender guitars, rapid cascading runs, whining, tortured sounds that shook audiences up, causing elation or terror – there was no halfway house. It was not a music that could be ignored, and blues musicians did not have to become quasi-cabaret artists to be heard as some of the great jazz musicians had to do just to get the noisy, inconsiderate club audiences to turn their heads and watch and listen. Thus the Northern club circuit in America provided a generation of 'flash' guitarists who etched out the blueprints from which Eric Clapton would draw his initial inspiration: B.B. King, Albert King, Freddie King, Buddy Guy and Otis Rush.

1958 was a watershed year in the history of British R&B. It was the year that Bill Broonzy, doyen of the country blues elite died – the joke was that Broonzy had been playing electric for years in Chicago and only when he came to Europe did he pay lip service to the easily bruised sense of ethnicity and authenticity among audiences here. It was also the year that Muddy Waters brought his heavily amplified blues band to play the Leeds Music Festival and other venues including the St. Pancras Baths in London and the Free Trade Hall in Manchester – the audiences were horrified.

For jazz and blues enthusiasts 1958 was already a year to forget because raucous and crude rock'n'roll burst on to the British pop scene in a big way. By January Jerry Lee Lewis was at no. 1 with *Great Balls Of Fire*, Buddy Holly was at no. 4 with *Peggy Sue* and by the end of the month, Elvis Presley had gone straight to no. 1 with *Jailhouse Rock*, the first record to do so since the UK chart began in 1952. Chuck Berry and Fats Domino both charted that year and Holly and Jerry Lee both toured, the latter sensationally, when his marriage to a 13-year old cousin was revealed. Questions were asked in the House of Commons and ballad singer Dickie Valentine was calling for the death of rock'n'roll. It was loud, bad music and people still hadn't recovered from the hysteria and mayhem caused by *Rock Around The Clock* and the Haley tour of 1957. And now in small venues around the country, the romantic vision of the Delta blues singer mournfully plucking away at his acoustic guitar bemoaning the 'masser's' whip and the broiling sun, was being rudely blown away by these brash city slickers in sharp suits. People fled to the toilets and words like 'vulgar' appeared in the press reviews. Blues fans had been expecting down home Alan Lomax style recordings because that's all they had heard up to now, but Muddy Waters came on like every white stereotype of the Negro, i.e. sexually voracious. Years later Hendrix played the same game causing Clapton to comment "Everybody and his big brother in Britain still think Spades have big dicks. Jimi came over and exploited that to the limit". One could discern a subliminal racism in the rather condescending and patronising attitude of some to black country blues, and the startled reaction to 'uppity' blacks assailing the ears with strident music, emphasising its inherent sexuality (which was always present even in the 'safest' Delta blues), seeking no favours from nobody – least of all whitey.

None of this came from the musicians, however. They were bowled over by what they saw – the first electric blues, the first electric guitar. For the usual bottle of Scotch or a share of the take, Muddy Waters played the

Barrelhouse, a small venue more used to the mandolin and acoustic twelve string of Alexis and Cyril. All the visiting bluesmen played this club, the only blues venue in London, and in fact it became better known in Chicago than here because bluesmen on returning home would tell other musicians about it.

Even die-hard purists like Cyril Davies, who thought saxophones were the instruments of the Devil and that jazz was a spent force with the arrival of arranged jazz and the Fletcher Henderson Orchestra in 1922, quickly switched to amplified acoustic. Davies was hooked by the Muddy Waters sound, so much so that when Alexis began to introduce horns into their set up during 1962, Cyril left amid a bitterness and rancour that was never resolved to the day Cyril collapsed and died of leukemia in 1964.

But long before this split they laid down their first recordings for Tempo Records. Still a duo then, they added Mike Collins on washboard, Chris Capon on bass and Dave Stevens on piano and on the 1957 EP did songs by Leadbelly, Sleepy John Estes and Maceo Merriweather. To cash in on the skiffle boom of the day, the record label announced the Alexis Korner Skiffle Group. Now Alexis was quite willing to defend skiffle as an important development, because it encouraged people to listen to various aspects of skiffle roots, particularly the blues, and the instruments could nearly all be home-made; it was the first garage music. But it was *not* the blues and Alexis was *not* playing skiffle. The net result was a big row with the company after which the 'skiffle' tag was dropped. Alexis and Cyril also joined the Chris Barber band in 1960, doing the last part of the show as a blues set, with Chris' wife Ottilie Patterson on vocals. This carried on for six months, but there was increasing friction because Alexis and Cyril wanted to do more blues than Chris would permit. At this point Barber's manager stepped in and suggested that they should form their own unit because the audience reaction was so good and, using the name thought up by Alexis' wife Bobbie, they went out as Blues Incorporated in 1961.

The main problem in getting off the ground was their use of amplification – it got them kicked out of venues everywhere, including the Barrelhouse itself, over which Cyril only had a part interest, even if he was the loudest voice. The other hassle was being on the same bill as trad jazz bands – that was *the* music of the day and they had to be where the audiences were. Unfortunately this often spelled trouble. There was a near riot at the Civic Hall, Croydon where they played with Acker Bilk – fists and chairs flew, but it helped put Blues Incorporated on the map and they were further encouraged by the letters they received from Bilk fans apologising for the trouble makers. That incidentally was not the last time that Acker Bilk was upstaged by 'the new wave'. He was top of the bill at one of the Richmond Jazz Festivals, playing on the main stage. Then a group started up in one of the side tents and virtually the whole audience *ran* across the field to see what was going on, leaving poor Acker playing to the birds. What was going on was the Rolling Stones and together with Alexis' band and its various offshoots, they created the force that swept away the trad jazz scene in this country in a very short space of time. So Blues Incorporated had to find a venue of their own and, after much discussion, guitarist Jeff Bradford mentioned a basement club he knew called the Moist Hoist below the ABC tea rooms on Ealing Broadway in West London, Cyril's stamping ground. After negotiations with the manager, whereby he would have the bar takings and the band would have the door money, the Ealing Club opened just a fortnight before Clapton's 17th birthday, on 17th March 1962. Having sought out somewhere of their own so as to avoid trouble, they almost walked into it on the first night. In blissful ignorance, they chose St. Patrick's night to open, right opposite the Feathers, one of the heaviest Irish pubs in the district. But all went well and with minimal advertising, the place was packed with over one hundred people. Sometimes it was anything up to two hundred, which was suffocation level. The band that took the stage that night was Alexis, Cyril, Andy Hoogenboom on bass, Dick Heckstall-Smith on tenor sax, Art Wood on vocals and an advertising trainee on drums called Charlie Watts, who found out on that first night why the place was dubbed 'Moist'. He was sitting directly underneath the pavement light onto the street above which dripped water all down his neck and all over the drums making the skins stretch. Next day the band had to rebuild the stage and suspend a tarpaulin across to catch the water. All kinds of people came in – the audiences from the Barrelhouse club initially, then converted jazz fans, folk lovers and rock'n'rollers. A few came, heard the sound, ran out and never came back. But so packed did the club get, that people were offering a pound to get in, just to hear the last number.

Band personnel fluctuated around a basic nucleus. John Baldry, a refugee from the Barrelhouse Club was a fairly regular singer with the band and there was a procession of young hopefuls appearing side by side with men who had already been playing music for anything up to twenty years. Using what he considered to be the more authentic name of Elmo Lewis, Brian Jones, then living in Cheltenham, would bash out some Elmore James inspired slide guitar. On his way to London through Oxford (no motorways in those days), he would give a lift to a young blues enthusiast called Paul Pond (aka Jones), who also gave his lungs an airing on stage. A renegade Chuck Berry fan from the London School of Economics, Mick Jagger, would sidle up on stage with his school mate Keith Richard and sing a very nervous version of *Around And Around* and Eric Clapton too, got up on the stage from the audience to do the occasional vocal.

Blues Incorporated went from strength to strength, and news of what was happening in Ealing reached the ears of Harold Pendleton, the manager of the Marquee who was wrestling with the problem of how to fill the club on Thursday nights. No matter who was on, the takings were sparse, primarily because it was the day before pay day and people were broke. So, not liking the music too much, but being a businessman, he offered Alexis the Thursday night spot just to see what would happen and Blues Incorporated played the first R&B session at the Marquee on 3rd May 1962. Fortunately, within the next few months, there was something of a tourist boom in London and the beginnings of a changeover to Thursday paydays which all helped, and by Christmas 1962, they were attracting a thousand people, twice a week and breaking every fire regulation in the book.

Blues Incorporated underwent some fundamental changes between May and December 1962. Ginger Baker replaced Charlie Watts, Jack Bruce was on bass and in November, Cyril Davies left to be replaced by Graham Bond on alto sax. Cyril hated Alexis' move away from the Muddy Waters 1956 Chicago sound and sought to perpetuate it by teaming up with Screaming Lord Sutch's Savages and making them the Cyril Davies All Stars. They included a bass player whose real name was Ricky Brown, but who also went under the name of Fenson, being a composite of Fender and Gibson, Nicky Hopkins on piano, Bernie Watson on guitar, (who went on to John Mayall) and John Baldry on vocals.

In the meantime, Keith Richard and Mick Jagger were trying to convince Charlie Watts to leave his secure £14 a week job (for which he had left Blues Incorporated), to join them in a decidedly dicey venture. During the early part of 1962, Mick was virtually the resident vocalist with Blues Incorporated and was giving scant attention to the band he was *supposed* to be getting together with Keith called Little Boy Blue and the Blue Boys. What he didn't know was that, at the same time, Keith and Brian Jones were working together with Ian Stewart on piano, Pretty Things founder member Dick Taylor on bass and Tony Chapman on drums. They had asked Paul Jones to sing with them and it is a favoured story of his that he told Brian he thought it was a waste of time, that nobody would want to listen to that music and that he didn't want to join. Mick eventually did start rehearsing with them and his involvement increased in direct proportion to Cyril Davies' efforts at squeezing him out of Blues Incorporated, a strange reaction, when it was Cyril who encouraged him to sing in the first place!

When Blues Incorporated was booked to play BBC Radio's Jazz Club, the BBC refused to pay Mick who was only the singer, did not play an instrument, and thus, they reasoned, was superfluous to requirements. This, plus Cyril's increasing resentment towards Mick, pushed him towards joining Keith and Brian and the Rolling Stones made their debut at the Marquee on 12th July 1962, deputising for Alexis' band on the night they were doing the radio show.

Though trad jazz was still big through 1962, the success of Blues Incorporated at the Marquee on a Thursday night when all else had failed, signalled the writing on the wall. So too, was the success of another R&B band, Georgie Fame and the Blue Flames, in revitalising the fortunes of another West End club, the main rival to the Marquee, the Flamingo round the corner in Wardour Street. Like the Marquee and the Ealing Club, the Flamingo was a cellar club but there were some crucial differences. The Marquee, both in Oxford Street and when it too moved to Wardour Street in 1964, attracted a younger audience, the art school crowd of which Eric Clapton was one and because it kept early hours, it was generally less convivial, wearing something of a clean-cut, respectable image. This was in stark contrast to the Flamingo which, with its All-Nighter sessions, only really got going when the Marquee audience was on its way home. The Flamingo held a great attraction for black American GIs on forty-eight-hour passes, who preferred the more soul-based, jazzier feel of the music provided by bands like Georgie Fame, who topped the bill of the All-Nighter for the first time in September 1962. As the London R&B scene took off, the differences became more accentuated with the Marquee audiences going for the guitar/harmonica bands like the Stones, the Pretty Things and the Yardbirds, influenced by Chuck Berry and Bo Diddley, while down at the Flamingo, the crowd wanted the organ/horn sounds of Georgie Fame, Graham Bond and Zoot Money. The sharp dichotomy of musical allegiances meant that when Alexis later moved Blues Incorporated from the Marquee to the Flamingo, the switch proved less than successful. The influences here were not Chuck Berry but Mose Allison and James Brown.

Even though it was all called R&B, there were obvious differences. One of the most significant was that many of the early R&B musicians came from jazz, whereas the second wave of young musicians led by the Stones, came from rock'n'roll and with that came the "social" arm of the revolution. Among the advance guard were modern jazz musicians looking for a bit more freedom and spontaneity, others were merely dissatisfied with the dated jazz sounds of the Forties and Fifties. And of course, underlying this aesthetic was the feeling that if you can't beat them, join them. Once things got underway, this was the music that was filling the clubs and a musician has got to eat. Musicians of the calibre of Ginger Baker, Graham Bond and Dick Heckstall-Smith were seasoned players who could see the coming trends but they were also individuals, mavericks, and not part of anyone's revolution.

In the club audiences were many young musicians like Tom McGuinness who, while appreciating what Blues Incorporated was doing, was looking for something tougher.

"Coming from the rock'n'roll side of R&B, I much preferred the harder edged sound of the Rolling Stones. Alexis was too jazzy for me, which was of course part of his background."

There was a terrific empathy between audiences and musicians in those days, both feeling the sense of discovery – often musicians first made their mark by coming out from the audience to play, as happened at the Ealing Club. McGuinness looks back to those days with great affection, "It's hard to visualise now, but then, it seemed like there were only two hundred people in England who knew about rhythm and blues. We ate, lived and breathed music. The audiences were growing, but it was still very tight and it would come back along the grapevine 'hey, there's this band in Newcastle' – and that was the Animals, or 'did you hear about this Birmingham band? They've a young kid playing with them' – and that was Spencer Davis. We knew it was good and that was all there was to it – we had no sense of history about it when we queued up at the Station Hotel in Richmond to see the Stones, it was just a really good night out". Alexis Korner expressed the same feelings, "a tremendous atmosphere developed because we all met up, all digging the blues, but all believing that each of us had been the only one who had been listening to the music before". An example of how homogenous the audience/musician unit was – at the same time that musicians would be queuing with everybody else to see the Rolling Stones, the band would be rushing down to Imhofs in New Oxford Street, where they had an import section of blues albums. Brian Jones even got himself a job in a record shop to enable him to have first pick and play the music. Back in whatever hovel they were staying, the Stones would just play records day and night, caring nothing for studios, contracts, business razzmatazz or anything else, except the music.

When he was not watching the Stones, Tom McGuinness played guitar in a local group in Wimbledon, South London, doing what most other young local groups were doing then, Cliff Richard and the Shadows numbers. "Things weren't going too well. There had been some trouble between me and the lead singer and anyway, I wanted to do other things. I remember saying to them, 'I'm going to form an R&B band' and they all fell about laughing, because we were earning £5 a night doing Shadows dance routines and Johnny Burnette numbers and as far as they were concerned, that was where it was at. After trying for six months and getting nowhere, I began to think they were right and I was mad. Then I saw an ad. in *Melody Maker* – 'piano player wants to join R&B band'. A typical cry in the wilderness ad. of the day. This led me to Oxford and a tremendous Otis Spann-style pianist called Ben Palmer, and also Paul Jones. They had earlier tried to get a band together with Brian Jones but nothing came of it and nothing really came to fruition this time either. About a year later, I saw another ad. saying 'R&B band forming'. I rang the guy up and we chatted, exchanged names like Chuck Berry, Bo Diddley and Jimmy Reed and he suggested I came to their next gig which was at the Station Hotel in Richmond, deputising for the Stones. Just before I put the phone down, I asked him what he played. 'Oh, trombone'." Tom's heart sank, because it sounded like yet another trad jazz band desperate to make the transition or at least desperate to be known as an R&B band to get the gigs letting the confusion over what was and was not R&B become a protective mantle. And that is precisely what it turned out to be – the band was called Dave Hunt's R&B band which had metamorphosed from Dave Hunt's Confederate Jazz Band. But equally desperate to play, Tom went along with his guitar and amp. "When I walked in, I immediately regretted it. There were about thirty people in the place and I felt very conspicuous standing there with my gear. On stage there were *three* trombones, piano, string bass and drums. They were doing Jimmy Rushing, Joe Turner style; nobody could sing and it was awful. The guy spotted me during the interval. I told him I didn't really think it was my sort of R&B, but he persuaded me to go up and play. He asked me what number should they do and I suggested *Kansas City*, thinking of the Wilbert Harrison version. 'Great', he said, 'is E flat okay for you?' Well, coming from rock'n'roll, E flat was just about the worst key he could have chosen. As far as I was concerned, the only place to play E flat was eleven frets up the guitar. Anyway, we got started, but it was all the wrong feel for me. I was doing Jimmy Reed and they were playing swing jazz. After two numbers I unplugged my guitar and walked off.

Afterwards, I was talking to my girlfriend at that time who mentioned this guitarist who was at Kingston Art School playing John Renbourn acoustic folk/blues, (Renbourn lived and played in the same area, Kingston/ Richmond). That was the first I'd ever heard of Eric Clapton."

# CHAPTER TWO
# Slowhand

Eric Patrick Clapton was born at his grandparents home, 1, The Green, Ripley in Surrey to Patricia Clapton on 30th March 1945. The space on the birth certificate for the father's name was left blank. His real mother moved away leaving his grandparents Rose and John Clapp, who was a plasterer and bricklayer, to bring him up. He went to Ripley Primary School and then St. Bede's and Surbiton Secondary Schools. In his early schooldays he was apparently keen and enthusiastic with a particular skill at art. Then about the age of twelve, his mother reappeared and he learnt the truth about his background. 'I was really doing well (at school) – then my real mum came back to stay with us. From that moment they say I was moody and nasty and wouldn't try. We had to go through this whole thing of pretending she was my sister'.[3] Not that Eric can really relate to that situation. He saw it slightly differently, accepting what those around him thought about the way he changed, but telling Steve Turner that despite this 'I definitely had a lovely time growing up'.[4] Even so, to be faced with the reality of that sort of rejection at such an early age was especially shattering – old enough to appreciate what it means, but too young to have the necessary emotional armour to handle it. He seemed to decide albeit subconsciously, that this revelation marked him out as somebody different – an outcast, and at school he began to drift to the fringes of day to day activities with a small group who, for whatever reason, felt the same way. Being of slight stature did not help much either. 'I was the one who used to get stones thrown at me because I was so thin and couldn't do Physical Training very well. . . . I was always the seven stone weakling'.[5] So he hung around with a similar non-participating crowd who were dubbed 'the loonies'. He was assailed from all sides, by teachers as well as kids. 'I was always getting hit on the hand with a ruler, or on the side of the head'.[6]

Eric began then to look for situations of security – the truth of his upbringing appeared to have damaged his sense of belonging and self-confidence, even though his grandparents loved him very much, and he them. 'I never expected to be voted top of anything, (after his umpteenth musical poll award), I thought I'd always be bottom of the pile'.[7] The theme of belonging reoccurs throughout Clapton's talk with Steve Turner in *Conversations with Eric Clapton*, which began life as an article for Rolling Stone. Clapton at his most frank at a time when he had little to lose, in the final stages of a three-year lay-off due to heroin addiction. Clapton said that the outcasts he hung around with at school formed a clique and were the first to buy Buddy Holly records, yet another aspect which had them branded as "freaks" and drew them closer together. Talking about the old days at the Ealing and Crawdaddy Clubs with a select group of blues enthusiasts, "it was like a security in a way" and he called the intense and emotional atmosphere of the Layla Studio where the booze and drugs flowed freely, "a womb" and likened the heroin experience to "surrounding yourself in pink cotton wool. Nothing bothers you whatsoever".[8]

Yet amidst the cliques and closeness, there was loneliness. In a rare interview with Eric's grandmother Rose, she said "I can sit and cry when he plays the blues. He was always a lonely boy and his music still gives me that feeling about him. We all loved him so much, there was no need for him to be lonely".[9] By this time, however, although compounding his inner sense of isolation, it was a different sort of loneliness – the vacuum of the rock star, the void of living life as a personality in the glare of publicity, the sharpened pens of rock critics and gossip columnists poised for your next move. Certainly the Cream experience left Clapton very mistrustful of most people, too many of the wrong sort of people wanted to get close.

But Clapton's initial impetus towards music was not a conscious move on his part to sublimate any despair he may have felt. Most people have fooled around with an instrument of some sort, particularly as a teenager and Eric was no exception. He began to buy the rock'n'roll records that were filtering through on the BBC-dominated airwaves and traced their ancestry back through to artists such as Bill Broonzy. When he was fifteen, he got a Hofner acoustic guitar, played around with it and then lost interest for a couple of years and it could all have finished there, another adolescent whim. In the meantime he had left school and gone to Kingston Art School, ostensibly to train as a stained glass designer, but that only lasted a short while – his heart wasn't in it and it showed in the meagre amount of work he presented at the end of the first term. By his own admission, he got drunk during the lunch hour, played records and was a general nuisance to the Establishment. Clapton E. was removed from the roll. "Actually, I am quite proud of that, not many people are kicked out of an art college".[9a]

After that, he busked around Kingston and Richmond playing for a pint and a sandwich, came to London, missed the last train and slept on Waterloo station, much to the chagrin of his grandparents. He was pressured into being a labourer's mate for his grandfather who was a bricklayer and laid floors but when he wasn't laying down floors, he was laying down licks. As his grandmother said, "he just sat there and practised all day long, it rather annoyed me at the time".[10]

In 1963, he was part of the small coterie of blues enthusiasts, musicians and otherwise, who packed those few venues available like the Ealing Club and the Station Hotel, immersed in the sense of discovery. In those days Eric Clapton was like any other potential R&B musician, fumbling around below the bottom rung of the ladder – they were all in it together. Nobody had to shoulder responsibilities. It was at the Station Hotel that Tom McGuinness finally met up with Eric. After an initial chat, they decided to form a band together called the Roosters. The derivation of the name is lost in the memory haze, but Howlin' Wolf's *Little Red Rooster* and *Rooster Blues* by Lightnin' Slim, are two explanations proffered. Whatever its linguistic antecedents, the Roosters as a group never included Brian Jones or Paul Jones as legend has it, although Rooster members were involved with both in earlier *ad hoc* associations which couldn't really be called bands. Into the Roosters formed in January 1963, came Tom's friend Ben Palmer on piano, Robin Mason on drums (whose big plus point was that he had a car) and Terry Brennan on vocals, one of the few singers in London who just wanted to sing R&B and who, according to Tom McGuinness, "was quite good at impersonating Little Richard". Although noted as a bass player with Manfred Mann, McGuinness was in fact a guitarist, playing a Futurama, and the Roosters never actually found a bass player. 'Bass players didn't want to play R&B because there was no money in it."

Clapton himself was now playing an electric guitar for the first time, despite the doubts of Tom's girlfriend Jenny, that the guy she knew as the Kingston Art School hobo would want to eschew his acoustic playing. The guitar in question was a Kay which was "expensive and flash". The family bought it for him on hire purchase so "it became clear I'd have to make a go of it".[11] It was Alexis Korner's endorsement of the guitar in *Melody Maker* that alerted Eric and, although Alexis said he did not actually remember it, Eric told him that the first time they met was when Eric approached him at the Marquee to ask him what strings he used. The answer in fact, was that Alexis bought whatever strings he could afford and used them until they broke.

Eric, Tom and the rest of the band were obsessive about their music, "you went out on Saturday mornings trying to buy the new John Lee Hooker album from the import record shop in Soho and Billboard to read the R&B chart". But it wasn't all blues. Eric had been an acoustic guitar player and was listening to folk, particularly Bob Dylan whose first album was released in 1962, and says Tom, "We were both knocked out by the Beatles. I can remember walking back from a Roosters rehearsal carrying our guitars, having missed the last bus back to Wimbledon from New Malden and singing songs like *Misery* and saying 'Hey. I wouldn't mind being in a band like that either', because the songs were so good".

When it came to playing though, the Roosters were a broad based R&B band, covering material by Larry Williams, Fats Domino and Chuck Berry. Berry's work was very familiar to Eric, "I was pretty terrible at the start, kept doing the same three licks. I'd learned a whole Chuck Berry album off by heart and I played it one night at the Marquee with terrible feedback. I got a mike and stuck it on a box and did it sitting down".[12] That Eric Clapton did not burst into the world as a fully fledged guitar hero is confirmed by Tom McGuinness, then, as now, a guitar player himself. "I didn't feel threatened. I cannot say that the minute he started playing I knew I was in the presence of a genius. We were just two guitar players scuffling along *trying* to learn how to play rhythm and blues. I felt the same even during the Yardbird days – it wasn't until he started working with Mayall that I started thinking 'Oh God'. I had spent the 1964–66 period playing bass guitar with Manfred Mann because I was offered the gig. I bluffed my way into the group by saying I had played bass before. They already had a bass player, (called Dave Richmond), who was a fantastic jazz musician, but was actually too good – he played solos through every number. But I really regretted those wasted years when I saw Eric again – not that I thought I could have been as good as Eric, because he's far more inventive than me. Nevertheless it took me a long while to get over it".

During the day, Eric laid floors, Terry Brennan did some painting and decorating, while the others did nothing much. In the evenings they rehearsed at the Wooden Bridge Hotel, Guildford and the Prince of Wales, New Malden. Their success as a band was limited. Throughout their eight month existence to August 1963, they played less than two dozen gigs, mainly in the London area at the Marquee and the Scene in the West End, the Jazz Cellar in Kingston and the Ricky Tick club in Windsor. This was largely the experience of all R&B bands – playing the same circuit of London and Home County venues, with occasional sorties into the provinces to play clubs like the Twisted Wheel in Manchester. Some outfits like Blues Incorporated and the Graham Bond Organisation had very strong provincial support and because of their musical style, were not in such direct competition with the Beat bands from Liverpool and Manchester, as were the Yardbirds, for example, who were aiming for largely the same young audience and played few Northern gigs.

Like Blues Incorporated, the Roosters had to contend with trad jazz enthusiasts and venue managers not exactly enamoured of amplification. The audiences complained that it was too loud and the band couldn't hear one another, having no sense of dynamics, merely using power to make everything louder.

Their first gig was at the Carfax Ballroom in Oxford, one of their few out-of-town gigs, apart from an ill-judged appearance at Uncle Bonnie's Jazz Club in Brighton, where the singer got into a fight with some French students who held up handkerchiefs arranged as hangman nooses, to display their disgust at music that was patently not 'le jazz hot'.

The MM publicity for the group which said 'can't be beat' in advertising their club dates, was not reflected in their audiences, who were mostly friends of the band. Apart from the vestiges of a residency at the Jazz Cellar and the odd Marquee date where they scraped a couple of pounds each, they were literally playing for pennies and anyone who had a job during the day, kept it.

Tom McGuinness sums up the Roosters thus: "It was good fun and we got some good reactions, but we never could find a bass player and nobody in the band was strong enough to hold it together". The Roosters didn't so much break up as simply throw in the towel. Whether they could have eventually made it with improved and additional personnel is mere conjecture. The recipe for success was saturated with luck and a myriad of intangible factors that have had record companies tearing their hair out since the very beginning. Within the next couple of years, the music press was to be full of features about who was going to make it big, 'tips for the top' and side by side with groups like the Yardbirds and the Animals would be those who disappeared within months.

The group all went their different ways, the only two members with any career in music ahead of them were Eric and Tom and it was at this point that they both joined Casey Jones and the Engineers and turned professional together.

Casey Jones (real name Brian Casser), was an early figure on the Liverpool music scene, forming several backing bands from about 1961. One of the first was Cass and the Casanovas, which became the Big Three after Casser left. The Casanovas went to Hamburg but the members of the group, John Gustafson, John Hutchinson and Brian Griffiths were getting rather tired of Casser's energetic, almost clownish stage act and they squeezed him out. The Big Three went on to become a highly respected Mersey band, admired by musicians and fans alike. However, Casser's routine was popular in Germany and he perpetuated it in Casey Jones and the Governors, who recorded two albums on the Golden 12 label containing such evergreen R&B numbers like *Talking 'Bout You* and *Too Much Monkey Business*, both done by the Yardbirds and every other rhythm and blues band in Britain. In London around October 1962, he had a backing band called the Nightsounds, which included Clapton band member-to-be, Albert Lee on guitar. In 1963 anyone with a Liverpool ancestry was almost guaranteed a recording contract and he did a single for Columbia called *One Way Ticket*. At the time of recording, he didn't actually have a band, so the search was on. Eric met the drummer Ray Stock, at the Scene, Ham Yard, off Great Windmill Street near Piccadilly Circus, a real dive, which during the height of the Mod era, was populated by the pill-popping younger set. Ten shillings (50p) bought one hundred purple hearts and a blind eye was turned, unless somebody got out of hand, at which point the bouncer, an ex-fairground lad named Dicky who shared door duties with his cousin Derek, would relieve the acned youth of his cache. Said youth would hear the toilet flush, but never dared ask whether his stash really had been swept away. In the sultry atmosphere of the Scene, Eric learnt that Casey Jones was looking for two guitarists, so he told Tom about it. "Eric gave his job up and we drove to Macclesfield for our first gig and it turned out we were supposed to back Polly Perkins, a sort of cabaret artist doing stuff like *Who's Sorry Now*. Neither Eric nor I knew the chords, but it was like 'if you don't back Polly Perkins, you don't get paid'. The same thing happened at the Oasis in Manchester. They too had to suffer the gymnastics of Casey Jones and financially they weren't that much better off than with the Roosters. But travelling the length and breadth of the country, being "on the road", did give the whole venture at least the veneer of professionalism. "We played everywhere. Manchester, London and in Reading with the Undertakers" (one of Merseyside's better groups with singer Jackie Lomax).

However, Eric was soon tired of the whole, slightly farcical, charade; Tom recalls that "one night he didn't turn up and I went looking for him. I ran into Guy Stevens who said 'Oh, Eric was round earlier. He's not doing it anymore'. So I thought, well sod that, I'm not doing it either, because I'm not enjoying it". Eric did seven gigs, Tom did eight, but only because he had to go back for his amp. Clapton said later of his Casey Jones experience, "It was really a very heavy pop show, you know, and I couldn't stand that for very long".[13] About two weeks later Eric Clapton joined the Yardbirds.


Like Tom McGuinness, Paul Samwell-Smith was playing Hank Marvin *Apache*-style numbers in a school band in Kingston – Jim McCarty was the drummer. At the same time, Keith Relf and a guitarist friend, Roger Pearce, were playing around the Kingston/Richmond folk circuit. All members of the drinking/coffee bar 'in crowd', Paul and Keith also played together with another guitarist Laurie Gains and a drummer whose name is forgotten, but is recalled by Paul as "a tyrant who was in and out of jail" and by Jim as "a little squat guy with a beard who was into porny magazines". Jim was swiftly drafted in and they gigged as the Metropolis Blues Quartet (which has appeared incorrectly through the years as the Metropolitan Blues Quartet), a name thought up by Keith. They played local venues, for example, the interval session of a Kingston trad jazz club and a small hall run by the owner of L'Auberge, a Richmond coffee bar. The Rolling Stones were another act who played there, in the days of Ian Stewart and Tony Chapman on drums; on one occasion they rang L'Auberge during the afternoon prior to a gig, threatening not to play unless the fee was raised from £10 to £12.10s. Even a blues purist has to eat and they got the extra money. Chris Dreja came in for Laurie Gains on rhythm guitar, but they were still without a lead player, because in the interim, Paul Samwell-Smith had switched to bass. His first meeting with Eric precipitated the decision. It was at the end of the interval set at the jazz club. "I was still playing lead, all the classic R&B stuff and sixteen bar blues and taking the odd solo. Eric was in the audience and I already knew him from just around Kingston – he could often be seen playing acoustic guitar on Kingston Green. Anyway, he came up to me at the end of the set and said 'Would you do me a favour?' 'Yeh, Eric. What is it?' 'Don't play any more lead guitar'. He was always very assertive. I mean the first thing he ever said to me was not to play. He was right though, and I've never tried since."

The other spur was seeing Cyril Davies' bass guitarist Ricky Brown (aka Fenson) at the Marquee. "I was knocked out by his playing, so exciting, he just floated over the strings. I copied everything he did – and he knew it. My first bass was one that Keith had borrowed from a friend of his. It was horrible, had all these nasty home-made frets hammered into the fingerboard. So I pulled them all out – it sounded great then and I was much happier with it. Keith wasn't too pleased though, because of what I'd done to his friend's guitar."

They went to see another local guitarist, Tony 'Top' Topham who, at sixteen, was three years younger than the others. The inclusion of Topham in the group heralded the true birth of the Yardbirds, another Relf name derived from Charlie Parker's nickname and one who bummed rides on American trains. In retrospect, the name is no more difficult to conjure with than the Beatles or the Rolling Stones, but in the early months, the press had a hard time getting hold of it and contented themselves with near misses like the Yardsticks, a phrase more familiar to English readers. It also signalled a change of direction for the group as Jim McCarty explains. "The Quartet were playing slow, ethnic blues, but we decided to jazz the whole thing up and get into the R&B scene".

An early venue for the band in their South West London heartland was Eel Pie Island at Twickenham, one of the most unlikely club spots in the London area. When it hosted trad jazz, a chain ferry would take musicians and audience across, but with the arrival of more prosperous R&B days, a bridge was built on the other side of which sat two little old ladies waiting to take the toll money. Structurally, the place was falling apart and through the floorboards of the dressing room above the stage, one had a clear view of everything going on directly beneath. It was tough getting work. They played the interval for Cyril Davies at Eel Pie Island and also at the Railway Hotel, Wealdstone (where the Who started out). Even though Cyril got a little upset because he thought the Yardbirds were stealing his audience, it was to Cyril that the band looked to for their initial inspiration. Paul Samwell-Smith puts it like this, "We all went to the Marquee to see Cyril play. Watching him made me think 'I want to do that' – we all felt the same, so we all went off and did it".

The Yardbirds also went to see another band that Davies had encouraged who were doing their first headlining residency at the Station Hotel, Richmond – the Rolling Stones. 1962 was an up and down year for the Stones. They lost the gig at the Marquee, apparently through not being authentic enough with Chris Barber, Harold Pendleton of the Marquee and Cyril Davies all being 'credited' as the hatchet man. Then in December, drummer Tony Chapman introduced Bill Wyman to the band and then left himself to be replaced by Charlie Watts, finally prised away from the world of design by Mick and Keith. Bill came in to replace Dick Taylor who carried on at Art School before switching to lead and forming the Pretty Things in September 1963.

Earlier on in 1963, just as the Roosters were forming, Sunday R&B sessions began in a small room at the back of the Station Hotel in Richmond which became known shortly as the Crawdaddy Club, instigated by one of the legendary figures of British rock, Giorgio Gomelsky. He was born in Italy in 1934 and, like Alexis Korner, had a cosmopolitan upbringing in France and Switzerland. "My first exposure to music was through my father, who would play classical records, but during the war as a teenager, I got into jazz, particularly bebop, by hearing it on American Forces Network Radio in Europe". His interests spread to blues and also into film and it was as a jazz band and film critic that he moved to England around 1954–1955. "I became interested in the idea of promoting authentic blues music, trad jazz was beginning to die and the pop scene was just a third hand imitation, so I felt that those young musicians trying to play a more authentic and exciting music should be encouraged".

The club had only been open for a couple of weeks when Gomelsky met a young graphic designer named Hamish Grimes at a party. "I arrived with some Bo Diddley records under my arm which Giorgio immediately spotted and he told me about the club. The first time I went, there weren't many people there – the Stones got £1 each and at 2/6d. a head, all the take went to them. Hamish took over the promotional side, adverts, posters and so on. "Just by word of mouth, the numbers doubled every week. A journalist from a local paper rang up to find out what was going on and asked the name of the club. It didn't have a name then; I just thought it up on the spur of the moment. I think it was a Bo Diddley song". As the Sundays went by, the queues down the street were getting longer and longer and so they moved to new premises with a capacity of nearly seven hundred, double that of the old place. Hamish remembers "a bouncer we had from the Saracens Rugby Club – he was built like a barn, but always held doors open for ladies". The Crawdaddy became a very popular venue, attracting those welcome and those not so welcome. "You could tell the pill pushers" recalls Hamish, "they were the ones wearing purple suits".

In April, Giorgio left the country to travel to Switzerland to attend his father's funeral, and arrange a jazz festival. Among the hordes cramming their way into the Crawdaddy to see the Rolling Stones play the most anarchic, raw and anti-social music ever heard in Britain at that time, was a failed teenage pop star and publicist named Andrew Oldham. He got to talking with the Stones, giving them all the *spiel* about how they needed new clothes, new equipment, new image and, armed with the financial muscle of Eric Easton, he signed the Rolling Stones to a contract, something they never had with Giorgio. As well as being an ideas man, Gomelsky was also something of an idealist and did not want anybody to be tied down by bits of paper. The value of verbal agreements in the music business, he was to find out when he got back.

Meanwhile, Hamish Grimes was faced with the task of finding a replacement for the Rolling Stones. "I visited all the clubs and thought about several bands including Them (with Van Morrison), but after seeing the Yardbirds at Ken Colyer's Club off Leicester Square, I approached Keith who jumped at the chance".

Giorgio was very hurt over losing the Stones in that way "I realised that it was business we were talking about; I would have been happy with no contracts, but obviously verbal agreements weren't working out".

Possibly as an over-reaction to his experience with the Rolling Stones, Giorgio tied up the Yardbirds lock, stock and barrel – everything was signed over to him and wages were paid through the Marquee management who came to handle the band's bookings. Not that they weren't grateful –

in those days musicians were grateful for anything. The Animals said 'thank you' when they got £5 each as the standard session fee for *The House Of The Rising Sun*, or so the story goes. It was only in later years when numerous Yardbird compilations were released over which the individual band members had no rights or control, that some of the implications of Sixties business practices became apparent.

There were some early problems for the band. The first was gaining acceptance from the large contingent of Rolling Stones fans at the Crawdaddy. While failing to make the Top Twenty with their first single *Come On* released in June 1963, it did get the Stones onto a national package with the Everly Brothers, Bo Diddley and Little Richard. As the touring increased, so they appeared less and less frequently at the Crawdaddy and the Yardbirds stepped in. Initially numbers dwindled as the fans realised that they had lost their heroes and those that came made disparaging comments about the Rolling Stones look-alikes, with a lead singer who had long hair and played harp and maraccas. In the same way that bands felt betrayed when they lost individual members on this tight, passionate music scene, so fans too did not take kindly to new faces until they had proved themselves. What happened to the Yardbirds, happened to many individual group members, such as Peter Green and Jon Hiseman when they replaced Clapton and Ginger Baker in John Mayall's Bluesbreakers and the Graham Bond Organisation respectively. For Green it was "we want God" and Hiseman "you've got two bass drums, let's see you use them".

The second problem was internal and was focused on Tony Topham. As he was only sixteen, his parents were becoming increasingly concerned about his travelling with a band, being up all night and says Jim McCarty "messing around with people like us". They wanted him to go to art school and began pressurising him to pull out. There was the beginnings of pressure from inside as well. As the band's commitments increased, it was frustrating to have somebody who could not give his all because of domestic hassles, his guitar playing was only average and being a bit on the plump side, he didn't fit into the developing lean, mean and moody persona of the Yardbirds which became their trademark.

It was a painful business cutting Topham loose from the band, but everyone including Topham knew it had to happen and by October 1963 he was out. He faded out of the music business apart from a solo album and a stint with Christine Perfect's band. At the time of Topham's departure, Keith already had in mind who he wanted as the replacement. Keith had been to art school with Eric and began what Jim McCarty calls a "selling job" to get Eric into the band. "We already knew him as a guitarist in the area, but Keith also said he'd be good for the girls and the image – that's how it was sold to us". Later on in an interview with *Melody Maker* in 1966, Eric said rather harshly that he had heard the Yardbirds wanted him to join and so he'd gone to see them play, summing them up in his own mind as R&B puppets – a pushover to play for. And indeed, after a rehearsal with Eric at the Great Western pub in Richmond, it was obvious to Jim and the others that he was somebody a bit special "musically it went up a step right from the word go". Eric took a step up as well, switching shortly to an instrument of classic distinction, the Fender Telecaster, beginning his love affair with the best guitars money can buy.

Musically Eric fitted in very well. He did not try and impose his own ideas on the band but picked up instantly on what they were doing, largely the same repertoire as the Roosters. Playing with the Yardbirds never presented Eric with any technical problems and he was easily the best instrumentalist in the band, Keith Relf harp playing notwithstanding. And as Jim McCarty admits, "he had a far wider blues knowledge than any of us".

Temperamentally, however, the adjustment took a little longer. Eric and Jim did not hit it off at first, "he seemed very quiet and moody at the start, with very set ideas, very much the individualist. We'd got used to thinking as a band and here was somebody who was thinking on his own". Eric and Paul Samwell-Smith had their problems too; "yes, there was quite a lot of conflict; we were both young and very uptight and both rather difficult to work with, I suppose, and there was the thing about Eric's background, which we never talked about because we were so young – although Keith's father (also the Yardbird's road manager) was always very good to Eric and understood that situation well. But I was always prepared to go with Eric because he was so good".

Many of these underlying tensions remained throughout Eric's time in the band; a similar cauldron of volatile chemistry pervaded Cream and the results were the same – wonderful music, sharp-edged, raw and aggressive. Therefore, the tensions with the Yardbirds were not altogether negative, nor were they all-pervading. Eric, Chris and Keith shared a flat in Kew and the whole band virtually lived in each others pockets, apart from times when they would all try and supplement their meagre earnings right at the beginning, by working during the day – Eric doing labouring, Jim in a stockbroker's office, Paul in his father's electrical firm and Keith assisting Paul with an interest also in the antiques business. There was always a very good feeling on stage between Eric and Keith and even as Eric's own personal following grew they worked with, rather than against, each other. Keith's admiration for Eric was based on his own aspirations as a guitar player, which although never fulfilled, he had more passion for than singing which he considered a secondary activity. Eric and Paul found some common ground as well: "the only area Eric and I could ever relate was the manic joking session – we went through a phase of spraying each other with beer when we were in the van and laughing hysterically about it". These were the two faces of Eric Clapton – on stage and sometimes offstage, shy, diffident and moody, other times fairly outrageous, rumoured to have demonstrated the evils of Nazism by parading down Oxford Street in full German uniform and purchased wind-up toys for the delight of smashing them to bits. Jim thought Eric's humour difficult to pin down – "he had a funny sense of humour; all these characters that he'd worked out, that he had special faces for, that seemed quite well defined".

Dogmatic about his music, Eric was also very involved in fashion.

During the time that Paul Samwell-Smith knew of Eric on the Kingston scene, when he told him not to play guitar anymore, "he was always wearing very advanced fashion, long scarves and the college boy look, everyone else was about two years behind". Jim McCarty, too, recalls his self-assuredness on this point "when he came into the band, he had all his style worked out, his clothes, his hair. We were quite relaxed about what we wore, but Eric was different. Wearing something was quite important to him. He got Chris (Dreja) very much into the same style, all that Ivy League stuff. And he had all his set shops; Austin's in Shaftesbury Avenue for his clothes, Dobells for his records, a certain shop for his strings and so on. He also knew the West End club scene much better than we did". Contemptuous of management's idea of band uniform, he was not really bothered about ideas of group identity either as Paul Samwell-Smith demonstrates "he came to one gig with very short hair. When we were fighting the frontier battle for long hair – we were being thrown out of hotels because of it and there was Eric, over all that and into seersucker jackets and ties. He was staggeringly *avant-garde*, he really was".

So although the songs remained the same when Eric Clapton joined the Yardbirds, the band was very different. Hamish Grimes states, "he really got that band going" while Paul Samwell-Smith reflects that "we relied on Eric to hold the front of the stage for long periods of time". Into the set-up came a paradoxical figure; his initial shyness, interpreted as aloofness and arrogance, was just the right demeanour for the Yardbirds and set the tone for their whole stage image. His fashion was distinctive, he was good looking and above all the guitarist of a new age. As Chris Welch, formerly with *Melody Maker*, who has taken a keen interest in Clapton's career over the years, asserts "up to Eric the instrumental group being talked about were Sounds Incorporated and it was the tail end of the Shadows era. The Beatles weren't rated as good players and nor were the Stones". It is necessary to meld all these factors together in any attempt to grab the nebulous entity of the Clapton mystique as it attracted the club-goers of the day, which, explains Jim McCarty was immediate, "he seemed to have this aura about him straight away, a certain magnetism and it was not totally due to his playing – the clothes, the way he looked, was all part of it".

It wasn't too long before the crowds at the Crawdaddy were back to capacity, Eric's personal following beginning to grow from the hard core of friends amongst whom he had originally watched the Rolling Stones from the audience – 'Clapton Is God' stemmed from 'Local Boy Makes Good'. Another Gomelsky venue, The Star in Croydon, hosted the Yardbirds on Saturdays, they took over the Stones residency at Ken Colyer's club where Hamish Grimes had found them, headlined at Eel Pie Island on Wednesdays and gigged around all the other R&B circuit venues in and around London – the Ricky Tick in Windsor, the Toby Jug Hotel, Tolworth, Guildford Plaza Ballroom, Pearce Hall, Maidenhead; the St. John's Ambulance Hall in Reading and the Cooks Ferry Inn, Edmonton, destined to be the venue for Cream's first London club date.

The Hamish Grimes publicity machine began to roll; he designed the

Yardbirds logo and created a series of increasingly outlandish adjectival slogans to advertise the band in the music press, starting with 'the fabulous blueswailing Yardbirds' and moving on to 'Great Twitch Inspiring', 'Crawdaddyfying' and in preparation for their first single in May 1964, 'Great Happenings with Recordyfying Yardbirds'. He compered the shows and roused the crowds with a variety of publicity stunts like dancing on the tables and getting people to monkey climb across the beams of the club roof – whipping up the atmosphere as Andrew Oldham did for the Rolling Stones.

Some credit Grimes with coining Eric's nickname 'Slowhand' which began to be heard towards the end of 1963, others (including Eric himself) say it was Giorgio, and the derivations of the name are as many as there are people to tell the story, but it seems to have emerged as a synthesis of three elements – a joke because Eric played so fast – a play on the name 'Clapton' as in Slowhand Clap-ton and the good natured slowhand clapping from the audience and the stage when Eric broke yet another string. Wherever it came from, it stuck and was resurrected by Eric for his album title of 1977.

Shortly after Eric joined, he got his first chance to play with the real thing when Sonny Boy Williamson (Rice Miller) came to Britain as part of an American Blues Festival package that Giorgio helped to arrange which also included Muddy Waters, Lonnie Johnson, Big Joe Williams, Memphis Slim and Willie Dixon. The Festival played the Fairfield Hall in Croydon in October 1963 and the reception for Sonny Boy was so good that he stayed for another six months supported at venues all over the country by Cyril Davies, Georgie Fame, the Animals, Gary Farr and the T-Bones (with Keith Emerson and Lee Jackson) as well as the Yardbirds. It was Sonny Boy who originally dubbed them 'blueswailing', a harp playing metaphor, and he was as impressed by the enthusiasm for the blues in Britain as audiences and musicians were enamoured of his majestic blues playing, "in the States you don't have no white boys sing the blues". His drinking was as legendary as his wailing. He stayed at Giorgio's house where Hamish Grimes was also in residence acting as Sonny Boy's 'gofer'. "He used to call out to me at nine o'clock in the morning, 'Hey, youngblood, go get me a fifth of scotch from the pub' (sic). Eric too, has memories of Sonny Boy's love of whiskey.

> 'There was one night where we were all on stage with the lights out and there was this curtain to the side where he was to walk through and the spotlight would hit him as he came across the stage . . . and this night they announced, 'And now . . . Sonny Boy Williamson', and this figure collapsed through the curtain and all these harmonicas fell out of his coat or somewhere . . . he just lay there in a heap and the spotlight hit him. We just didn't know what to do".[14] The organisers did – they cancelled the gig.

He was putting away a bottle of scotch a day and, before the Sixties were out, he was dead, immortalised in a song by Jack Bruce which appeared on the Al Kooper/Mike Bloomfield live album of 1969. For Eric, playing in the presence of, and encouraged by, this awesome blues master was an education – and urged on by the dire threats issued by Sonny Boy if the music wasn't right, Eric was tested, probably for the first time since picking up a guitar.

Gomelsky persuaded a friend and record producer from Germany, Horst Lippman, to fly to Britain especially to produce an album with Sonny Boy and the Yardbirds. The decision was taken to record a live album at the Crawdaddy as the best way of showcasing the blues show, drawing from the charged atmosphere of a hot sweaty club crammed to bursting point. Once the club was packed, it was sweltering, but on the afternoon of 8th December 1963 in an unheated and empty club room, rehearsals went on in sub-zero temperatures. In the evening it was recorded live, engineered by Keith Grant. Released originally in 1966, it has been reissued on at least three subsequent occasions including one with Jeff Beck on the cover. Presumably this was done because Beck was in the band at the time, but it was a cheap deception nonetheless. The album consisted solely of Sonny Boy numbers, and not surprisingly was unrepresentative of the Yardbirds' usual stage act. Clapton's playing was illuminating – although his guitar sound was thin and the approach one of awed hesitancy, on tracks like *Mr. Downchild* and *Twenty-Three Hours Too Long* are the seeds of Clapton the lyrical, tasteful guitarist with an embryonic interpretation of B.B. King's 'ringing tone' on *Take It Easy*. He played deft, economic solos against Williamson's harp in the tradition of Hubert Sumlin's work with Howlin' Wolf. Eric's natural empathy for harp sounds and the symbiotic relationship between those sounds and that of Eric's guitar was also in evidence with Keith Relf and to a lesser extent with John Mayall and Jack Bruce. Steve Turner noted that many of Clapton's albums featured harmonica over guitar. Clapton pointed out that harp players were bending and sustaining notes in an acoustic blues idiom before the discovery of feedback allowed electric guitarists to do the same with equal effect. Thus although he was taking from B.B. King and the other blues guitarists, he was also copping licks from Little Walter and Sonny Boy Williamson.

That same evening, more tracks were laid down which did not surface until 1981 on a German label as *The Yardbirds London 1963 – The First Recordings*, six of the nine tracks being live cuts from the Crawdaddy on 7–8th December. The sound is pure Yardbirds – rough and ready, bread and butter R&B, Eric doing good Chuck Berry impersonations, but no better than anybody else (Keith Richard for example) on *Let It Rock* while on the evergreen *You Can't Judge A Book By Looking At The Cover*, he goes for frantic chord freak outs that don't quite make it. The longest track is a six-and-a-half minute version of *Smokestack Lightnin'*, probably the archetypal Yardbird song and as the vehicle for Keith's harp playing, it was the basis of the epithet 'blueswailing' which meant harp and that meant the Yardbirds. In this context, Eric veered from unrestrained rhythm and blues showman to the platform from which the Yardbirds launched their famous marathon 'rave ups' heavy, pulsating, rapid fire, rhythm-oriented music

35

dominated melodically by the harp and lasting anything up to half an hour, an indirect precursor of the extended solo flights of Cream. Indirect, because Bruce and Baker came from the world of jazz improvisation and because Eric arrived at Cream from a different route, abandoning chord-based barrage guitar playing and developing the skills that began to emerge when he was playing with Sonny Boy Williamson.

Those Crawdaddy sessions and the crowd excitement that they generated guaranteed the Yardbirds a spot at the Marquee. Their first gig there was with Sonny Boy in January 1964 and they backed him on his final gig in Britain on 13th March 1964, also at the Marquee, but this time at the new venue in Wardour Street where they played the opening night – 6/- for members, 7/6d. for non-members. By April they were headlining there and the print in all the adverts was getting larger each week.

They were also gathering some press coverage. More concerned with fashion and pop stars than music, the music press of the day gave scant attention to reviewing live concerts. In fact it was the local press that gave the Yardbirds one of their first puffs; the *Surrey Comet* headlined their report of January 1964, from the Toby Jug Hotel, Tolworth, "Yardbirds set fans shaking ... three hundred mods, rockers and beats who piled into the hall . . . and the two hundred who did not get nearer than the door assured instant success for Surrey's latest Rhythm and Blues Club and its young residents, the Yardbirds". What happened at the Toby Jug was a classic example of how the music scene was beginning to change in Britain. The reporter on the *Comet* spoke to the club manager, Len Fletcher, who said that only weeks before they had tried to introduce trad jazz into the club, "by the sixth week they were down to sixty" – and here were five hundred kids going ape to see the Yardbirds. True to form Eric broke a string, " 'these things happen even to the Beatles' announced Keith Relf singer and 'harp' player, and the group one guitar short, romped through the finale to the obvious and complete satisfaction of the audience".[15]

January 1964 was a fairly momentous month in the history of British rock, something of a watershed, because the Rolling Stones reached the Top Ten at the second attempt with *I Wanna Be Your Man* on the 6th and the next day, their mentor, the unpredictable, explosive genius of Cyril Davies was extinguished forever when he collapsed and died of leukemia. In a radio interview his drummer in the All Stars, Carlo Little recalled that after one gig the band had heard a tremendous breaking of glass from the dressing room. They rushed in to find the mirror broken and Cyril with bleeding hands, 'I don't know what he saw in that mirror, but a year later he was dead'.

The Stones did even better in March when *Not Fade Away* reached number 3, but the band that had stepped into their shoes at most of the major R&B venues had yet to release their first single. Before that was to happen, the Yardbirds recorded some more live material, this time at the Marquee in March 1964, emulating the first recordings of Blues Incorporated and Georgie Fame and the Blue Flames, both live albums. It made sense – live music was not reported nor heard on the radio, word of mouth as a means of drawing in crowds had its limitations and so it was logical, if rather cheeky, to debut with a live album. Not that the band were having any trouble getting dates – hit records were less important in club work – if a group got a good reception and filled the place, they asked you back and that's how you filled up the diary. By the time that *Five Live Yardbirds* was recorded, they were working virtually every night of the week – the only places which presented problems were those like the Klooks Kleek in West Hampstead, a venue they never played because the club was licensed premises and the Yardbirds attracted an audience too young to be admitted. But at the Marquee, it was soft drinks only.

Another reason for doing a live album was that it was the best way to present the band at that time and despite the rice pudding production, *Five Live Yardbirds* remains one of the quintessential British R&B albums, encapsulating a whole era of music. Songs like *Too Much Monkey Business* and the Isley Brothers' *Respectable* are shot through with an incredible adrenalin surge. It is the energy and immediacy rather than the technical virtuosity of the album which comes through even now that makes this such marvellous music. Clapton does a vocal duet with Chris Dreja on *Good Morning Little Schoolgirl* throwing in a solo of swooping incisiveness which was recorded at a louder volume than the rest of the track. It served to emphasis a feeling that the solo is almost out of place in a song with a distinctly pop-oriented vocal backdrop and that perhaps Eric was out of place as well. His playing had lost a lot of its tentativeness and the sound was less twangy and thin, in fact it had the gutsy, rich sound of a Gibson, suggesting that on these live tracks, as he did for the Toby Jug gig reviewed in the press, he was using Chris Dreja's Gibson 335, Dreja himself possibly using a Futurama.

But whatever the merits of doing a live album, the success of the Rolling Stones in the singles market was a clear signal that if any R&B band wanted to break out of the enthusiastic but limited local club scene and find a national audience, then it had to be done through the charts. The period March–May 1963 saw debut singles by the Pretty Things (the double A-side *Big Boss Man/Rosalyn*), the Spencer Davis Group (*Dimples*), the Animals (*Baby Let Me Take You Home*) and the Graham Bond Organisation (*Long Tall Shorty*). Added to that list was the Yardbirds debut offering *I Wish You Would/A Certain Girl* released on 1st May 1964, recorded at Olympic Studios as early as November 1963. Even earlier, just as Eric joined, Giorgio had taken the group to the R.G. Jones Studios in Surrey, where they laid down at least three tracks under the supervision of Mike Vernon, then a Decca staff producer.

The first was Jimmy Reed's *Baby What's Wrong* which surfaced on Sire's *History Of The British Blues Vol. 1* (1973) among a myriad of other long lost gems. Clapton dominates the track which has no harp but a sharply defined guitar solo in the middle, picked up again in the fade out right at the head of the mix. The purity and clarity of this studio solo, and those on the B sides of the three Yardbird singles with Clapton, can only make one regret that the Yardbirds did not record a studio album during this period. His guitar work from this period has not been highly rated in retrospect, and it is true that there was an over-reliance on Berry/Diddley constructions, which Clapton has readily admitted since. But that was what the Yardbirds live show was all about and so that's what he had to play. However, whenever the opportunity arose outside that milieu, he demonstrated how much of the blues idiom was already in his grasp, and it was far beyond variations on *Johnny B. Goode*. The other tracks recorded at the Jones Studios were John Lee Hooker's *Boom Boom* and Billy Boy Arnold's *Honey Hips*. They were issued as a single in Holland by mistake and withdrawn after two weeks, appearing only recently on the *First Recordings* album mentioned previously. Given that it has taken nearly twenty years for those tracks to come to light once more and that nobody can actually remember *what* was done in the Jones Studios, it would not be surprising to see more material released from this session, and no doubt many others, now lying in vaults, basements and packing cases. The demos were taken to Decca who already had the Stones but who weren't too sure about them, so they certainly were not going to compound the risk by signing the Yardbirds. Eventually they were signed to EMI on the Columbia label, ostensibly as EMI's answer to the Rolling Stones. They cut *I Wish You Would* (also on the *First Recordings* album) the third of the three studio cuts.

Apart from the Animals single, none of the R&B oriented releases of Spring 1964 made the top twenty, including *I Wish You Would*, but the band was still very busy. They now had a Friday night residency at the Marquee whose manager, John Gee, was tipping them for the top and there were TV appearances and more interest from the press. In a *Record Mirror* poll of April 1964 they were voted the third best group behind the Stones and Manfred Mann. This was based solely on their live performances because at that point no records had been issued. They were also spotlighted in a *Melody Maker* article, *The Beat Battle Is On – a guide to the beat groups set for the big breakthrough*. Favourite artists were listed as Matt Murphy, T-Bone Walker, Jimmy Reed, Bob Dylan and Bobby Bland; the sound was described as "very clean with bass and drums predominant – a highly-rated lead guitarist". There were fan letters in the music press: "Let Me Proclaim The Gospel. The Yardbirds Are Coming. The chart isn't big enough for the Stones and the Yardbirds. The Rolling Stones will have to go"[16] – and others in a similar spiritual vein. For some, the Yardbirds were gods before Eric was singled out for deification. There were plenty of grounds for optimism in the summer of 1964, culminating in a triumphant appearance at the 4th National Jazz and Blues Festival on their home territory in Richmond. The only incident that marred the occasion was Keith's reoccuring laryngitis and Mick O'Neil of the Authentics and Mike Vernon stepped into the breach. The September *Melody Maker* poll placed the Yardbirds third behind Lulu and Zoot Money in the 'Brightest Hope' category and the September issue of *Beat Instrumental* gave them an ecstatic write up, proclaiming them as the next band to follow the Stones to international stardom. It announced the release of the band's second single *Good Morning Little Schoolgirl* on 4th September, but the problems with Keith's voice delayed release until October, appearing at the same time as *Five Live Yardbirds*.

The single was launched in a typical Sixties madcap fashion. One morning the band went down to a local girls' school near Keith's home and told all the girls that the Yardbirds would be outside after school. The band arrived as promised in the van and when school was over, hordes of hysterical schoolgirls streamed out of the gates and chased them down the street while cameras flashed frantically. However, the publicity failed to shove the record higher than forty-four in the charts. Yet from the point of Eric Clapton history, that record was to prove highly significant, not for the A side, but the flip side, *I Ain't Got You* featuring arguably Eric's finest piece of playing with the Yardbirds. The B side of *I Wish You Would* also contained a fine solo but that was just the *hors d'oeuvre* to the main dish, a mean, dirty, down-home blues solo, startlingly aggressive with which they opened their set reviewed by *Melody Maker* in October 1964, back in London after a tour with Billy J. Kramer and the Dakotas.

"The most blueswailing Yardbirds made a welcome and power-packed return to the London Marquee. A large, very enthusiastic crowd supported them throughout from their bluesy opener *I Ain't Got You* to the marathon raver *Here It Is*. In their second stint, their current disc release *Wish You Would* (sic) demonstrated . . . the accomplished playing of lead guitarist Eric Clapton".[17]

That the reporter didn't even know they had a new single out was indicative of their problems as they entered what could be described 'a winter of discontent'. The crowds were still coming in, but the band was still in the clubs. In trying to break out, they had to face the dilemma of isolating loyal fans. As Eric explained in an interview in November after the tour, "club audiences are very possessive and when records start selling the kids come up to you and say 'we've lost you'. We had that feeling at the Crawdaddy. Then we left for a while and when we played (there) last Sunday it wasn't quite the same".[18] This affected Eric more than the others. Notwithstanding a rather hopeful letter in the *Melody Maker* which said that the Yardbirds would show everyone how you could get to the top without selling out, there was a growing belief in the camp that without chart success, the band would stay on the club circuit until people got fed up with them, which would probably have happened to the Rolling Stones, but for Andrew Oldham. *Schoolgirl* was a compromise – an attempt by Giorgio to be commercial while still retaining the vestiges of purist integrity – it didn't work. This was the central problem of the band. They played some of the heaviest R&B around but like the mythological two-faced god Janus who looked both ways at once, they too wanted pop success like the Rolling Stones. *Schoolgirl* and the B side summed up their approach perfectly, pop songs with blues/rock guitar solos, destined to fail in 1964. Individually there were problems as well. Paul Samwell-Smith was veering towards the commercial, caught somewhere in between with ambitions of being a producer, both strong willed and persistent and also beginning to tire of the endless gigging and life on the road. Eric, too, was very restless, not happy with playing endless Chuck Berry riffs and very uneasy that the band were being frog-marched to success in suits, each minute of their lives planned out – no physical or musical freedom – the straitjacket of pop. And it was no over-night sensation. Chris Welch saw the band playing during the summer at the Bromel Club in Bromley, Kent which had just opened. "They were playing *Smokestack Lightnin'* which was their big number where Eric got to freak out and play a lot of chords and after that he came off stage with a face like thunder and I said 'you look a bit fed up' and he said 'Oh, it shows, does it?' Even then he didn't want to be in the Yardbirds any more and wanted to get out which was a bit embarrassing for the others, because they were rather in awe of him too".

Chris' first formal interview with them was for *Melody Maker* in August 1964 "I met them in a coffee bar in Fleet Street," Eric was subdued and everybody else did the talking, he seemed to be outside of it all, distancing himself from what was going on. In the interview Eric did talk rather mutedly about the music, "we're a sort of R&B band, I suppose", but left Paul and Keith to talk about commercialism and success. "He was a purist at the time, resenting attempts to expand and develop the blues more commercially, although he did it himself later on. Everyone thought he was mysterious and aloof, but really he was just shy, talking in a well modulated Home Counties accent". It wasn't that Eric didn't want to be successful, he did enjoy many of the good things, buying clothes, records and so on, but he wanted it all on his own terms. He left the band briefly for about two weeks while he visited his real mother in Germany – Roger Pearce stood in. The Yardbirds played the Beatles Christmas Show and it was then that the surface tension that had held the band together began to break up. Their music publishers, Feldman's urged them to do a song called *For Your Love* composed by a young songwriter called Graham Gouldman. Paul Samwell-Smith wanted to produce it. Eric, on the other hand, wanted to do an Otis Redding number. It was agreed that they would do both and then decide which song would be the next single. Paul took charge of *For Your Love*. "Eric was getting quite tense about this because the Yardbirds only played the middle section – the rest was bongos, double bass and Brian Auger on harpsichord. The band hardly appeared, it was my fault because I was the producer, but everybody loved it. If Giorgio had had his way, we'd have still been trying to go for the singles market with songs like *Good Morning Little Schoolgirl*, but it just wasn't making it". So much did everyone like the song that they didn't even do Eric's choice as agreed. To cap it all, Gomelsky sent round a typed memo informing the band that Paul was now the musical director and his word was law. To be completely upstaged by his main 'rival' was the final straw for Eric, and he went to see Giorgio. 'He came to my office, it was obvious he wasn't happy – he had a problem with the music and he also was not happy with Keith's singing and the fact that *For Your Love* didn't need a lead guitarist'. The band had regular meetings at Giorgio's flat and it was at one of these that Eric announced his departure.

The previous Yardbird singles had both featured excellent Clapton guitar work symbolically relegated to the B sides and the B side to the new single was no exception, Eric's swan song rather ironically titled *Got To Hurry* and credited to one Earl Rasputin. The number, an instrumental, came about by chance in the studio as Paul Samwell-Smith explains, "we shouted up to Giorgio in the engineer's box that Eric had this instrumental worked out and he said something like 'great lads, why don't you let me have the rights, we'll say I wrote it and just for a joke we'll put down Earl Rasputin as the writer', which was our nickname for him, because of his accent." It was also typical of the naivety of young musicians of the period and it was partly this kind of manipulation that Eric was rebelling against. As he later said, he got brainwashed by the whole R&B circus, the promotions and the deals and the general paraphernalia of the grubby race for pop stardom.

Announcing Eric's departure just two weeks before his twentieth birthday, Keith Relf told the press, "he loves the blues so much I suppose he didn't like it being played badly by a white shower like us".[19] The 'I suppose', in Keith's statement, underlined the distance between Eric and the rest of the band. Eric had been in the band for a year and a half, Keith had even shared a place with him, yet the exact nature of his motivations was not known. Paul reflects from a distance that "Eric had a totally different idea and he went into this completely non-commercial scene with John Mayall – a few years later, Eric was singing along with the best of them – I'm glad he did. He did right to stay with the blues proper". In the same month as Cream was formed in June 1966, Paul left the Yardbirds to become a successful producer for Cat Stevens and Paul Simon, among others.

*For Your Love* did in fact prove to be the breakthrough that the Yardbirds had been searching for – it went to no. 2 in Britain and no. 6 in the USA, when it appeared in March 1965, the first of five hit singles for the band. Jimmy Page, one of the hottest young session musicians around at the time, suggested Jeff Beck the guitarist from the Tridents and another renegade art school student from South London as Eric's replacement. Page himself later joined when Paul Samwell-Smith left and Chris Dreja switched to bass.

Eric stuck to what he believed in – he wanted to play the blues and not some glossy pop mutation and for that there was literally only one band he could play for – John Mayall's Bluesbreakers. "None of them (the Yardbirds) knew the blues from a hole in the ground, that's why he joined me".

# CHAPTER THREE
# Steppin' Out With
# John Mayall

When Eric left the Yardbirds, he headed for Oxford to stay with Ben Palmer, the former Roosters pianist who was now a sculptor. Like many musicians new to the business, Eric had few musician friends and with Ben and poet Ted Milton, Eric soaked up some of the Oxford culture, catching up on lost education. His desire to plough his own furrow, however lonely that was, had led him to quit a band on the verge of pop stardom. It was a concrete decision on his part, but still the Yardbirds experience left him rather confused and disoriented, uncertain of what to do next.

"I was all screwed up about my playing. I decided that I was not playing well and was really brought down. Playing with the Yardbirds had put me in a very strange frame of mind. I had lost a lot of my original values. I was really going to go off and paint or do something else".[20]

Amid all the doubt one thing was certain, the paucity of outlets for playing the blues in this country and the hiatus in his life caused by the brief period of exile away from the London music scene, prompted him to travel further afield.

He was thinking of America, and in particular Chicago, home of his heart music, where white musicians, soul brothers like Paul Butterfield and Mike Bloomfield were following a similarly lonesome road, but being in Chicago, were right in the middle of all the action. And it seems that had he gone, he would have been warmly received. He played informally with Muddy Waters during the blues package tour of 1963 and on 4th May 1964 played his first studio session, laying down two tracks for *The Blues Of Otis Spann* album, *Pretty Girls Everywhere* and *Stir It Up* (the latter only finally appearing as a single), with Otis Spann, Muddy Waters, Ransome Knowling on bass, Willie Smith on drums and Jimmy Page. In September 1964, Beat Instrumental reported that Muddy Waters had asked Clapton to come to the States to record. However, the idea was buried (but not forgotten) when he got a call from Mayall.

"I'd seen Eric playing before our paths had crossed and when I heard that B side of *For Your Love*, it confirmed my belief in his abilities. I'd seen them at the Flamingo. I wasn't that keen on them because I never really thought that John had a lot of control over his voice. He seemed to know what he wanted to do, but not exactly how he wanted to do it. But, I mean, there were very few people around that could do anything properly".[21]

Mayall convinced the rest of the band, bass player John McVie and drummer Hughie Flint, when he played the record to them as they stood around a jukebox in Nottingham. Roger Dean was still the official guitarist with the Bluesbreakers, but once Mayall had tracked Eric down and persuaded him to join, Dean was out. "I had to dispense with his services". So soon after leaving one band, Eric was initially hesitant about leaping into another, back into the grind of one nighters, seven days a week and the claustrophobia of tight tribal living in the bandwagon, but if he wanted to play the blues in this country, then he didn't have a lot of choice. "He didn't take too much persuading, he was a blues player and I ran a blues band" – in fact he ran just about the only band sufficiently authentic to interest Eric.

Eric joined Mayall in April 1965, by which time the first wave of interest in authentic R&B had run its course. Most of the early adherents had either been diverted into soul or, like the Yardbirds, were caught up in the pop mainstream eagerly and successfully producing hit singles in a milieu more akin to Tin Pan Alley than Chicago. But like Eric, Mayall refused to compromise his music. (Already thirty by 1963, even if he had so wished, his chances of becoming a pop star were fairly limited.) In retrospect, Mayall can be regarded as the grandfather of what became the second R&B movement, or more correctly, a purist and modernist Chicago movement devoid of many of the jazz and soul elements evident in the early Sixties. Although initially inspired by Alexis Korner, Mayall was instrumental in changing the emphasis of the blues sound in Britain away from rhythmic chord playing and horn lines to one closely identified with the electric guitar style of B.B. King, Freddie King and Buddy Guy among others, utilising finger vibrato, string bending, distortion, clipped phrases and fluid soloing. And it took Mayall two years and any number of guitarists to find the one player who could recreate the excitement and breathless virtuosity of that style for a white audience.

John Mayall was born in Macclesfield, Cheshire in 1933, his father a semi-pro dance band musician, whose American jazz records first captured Mayall's imagination. Mayall, too, went through the art school dance, but stuck with it rather longer than Eric, eventually working as a draughtsman in the design office of a department store and then with an advertising agency. While he was at college, he formed the Powerhouse Four, his first band and gained a reputation as the 'neighbourhood nutter' by constructing his own tree house, decorated, furnished and complete with running water, where he played records and practised guitar. The northern excursions of Blues Incorporated to the Twisted Wheel in Manchester, encouraged Mayall to form a new band, the Blues Syndicate with Hughie Flint. It was on Alexis Korner's insistence that there was a living to be made playing the blues in London, that Mayall came South in 1963 to play music by night and be a draughtsman during the day.

Early Mayall line-ups were very transitory, one included the famous Ricky Fenson on bass and folk guitarist Davy Graham. But by July 1963, Mayall had a relatively stable band featuring John McVie, ex-Powerhouse drummer Peter Ward, Bernie Watson on guitar, with Mayall handling keyboards, vocals and harmonica. Now backed by the all powerful Gunnell Agency who had many acts like Georgie Fame and a large slice of the Southern club scene, the Bluesbreakers were booked into the perennial stream of one-nighters up and down the country. They cut one single for Decca, a rather limp attempt at social commentary called *Crawling Up A Hill*, (although the music itself was good). Released in April 1964, it appeared just prior to the departure of Bernie Watson and the arrival of Hughie Flint to replace Peter Ward. Previously with the Savages and Cyril Davies, Watson went on to become a classical musician.

After a number of false starts with several guitarists, Roger Dean joined, appearing on Mayall's second single *Crocodile Walk/Blues City Shakedown* (February 1965). Alexis Korner, Georgie Fame and the Yardbirds had already demonstrated the value of showcasing their work on record before a live audience and Mayall followed suit in March 1965 with *John Mayall Plays John Mayall*, recorded live at the Klooks Kleek in West Hampstead right next door to West Hampstead studios, so close that the cables were slung over the rooftops. Engineered by Gus Dudgeon and produced by Tony Clarke (who later worked with the Moody Blues), it was a fair representation of the Bluesbreakers at the time, but it was also clear that Mayall had yet to find the guitarist he sought. Roger Dean was a good player, but his main interest was country music and sometimes he played his Gretsch guitar sitting down. As Eric had realised, Mayall had a clear idea of what he was striving for without the technical ability to execute it himself and became very frustrated trying to explain it all to one guitarist after another. Clapton was therefore manna from heaven.

The first time the rest of the band met him was in the van on the way to the first gig – there were no rehearsals. Eric went straight in and played the music that was in John's head. Mayall had always garnered a good club following but Eric's impact was immediate. As with the Yardbirds, he was again by far the best musician in the band to which he brought a studied cool, and a self knowing sense of excellence. In June 1965, the Raver column in *Melody Maker* proclaimed "Eric Clapton – a knockout with John Mayall's Bluesbreakers" and a letter the following month lauded the band's purist approach, hoping against hope they wouldn't sell out, declaring that "Eric Clapton is the best blues guitarist in Britain".[22] Not only did Clapton win over existing Mayall fans but brought along his own substantial following and Mayall began to realise that there was a sizeable and growing proportion of the audience who had come primarily to see Eric. Sometimes, however, they didn't see him. Truth to tell at that time, Eric was not one hundred per cent reliable. There was a slightly perverse, quirky side to his character (which he shared with Jeff Beck) that seemed to feel it owed no allegiance to anybody or anything – a kind of outlaw, rebel streak which, on occasion, determined whether or not Eric was going to turn up for the gig. He sometimes went AWOL to jam with other bands and it was not unknown for him to be seen playing at the Marquee with Stevie Winwood in the Spencer Davis Group, when the Bluesbreakers were booked to appear down the road at the Flamingo. When this happened, the Bluesbreakers appeared as a three piece – like one night in Welwyn Garden City. A young guitarist called Mick Taylor was in the audience. "Some friends and I had gone along to see the Bluesbreakers but Eric never showed up – his guitar was there, but he wasn't. They played the first set without him, just the three of them and then after much persuading by friends, I went to see John in the interval to see if I could play the second set. I'd seen Eric at the Flamingo and knew all the songs, what key they were in and everything. John was a bit sceptical at first, but he let me do it". Two years later when Mick answered John's advert in *Melody Maker* after Peter Green left, John remembered him and offered him the job on the spot.

Mayall ran a very tight ship – he had his own bed built into the side of the van while the others sat in the seats and froze – a finely tuned sense of discipline and ideas about progression in music which was rarely static. This meant that most of the musicians who worked with Mayall were eventually fired because they couldn't or wouldn't accept the discipline, adapt to changes or because Mayall felt that a new idea needed new musicians. He would think nothing of dumping a roadie or a musician in the middle of nowhere if they'd had too much to drink, but Eric was so important to the band that virtually no questions were asked of his absences and certainly no explanations were forthcoming. So probably it should have come as no surprise, when early in August 1965, Eric suddenly announced, full gig lists, packed audiences and the blues notwithstanding, that he was going off on a mad jaunt round the world with a bunch of amateur musicians.

He had spent odd nights on Mayall's floor, but was actually living with blues writer Charlie Radcliffe in Redcliffe Gardens, spending a lot of time in LongAcre with Ted Milton mixing with a group of Oxford friends, which numbered Ben Palmer in its ranks. The original idea was cooked up between a doctor and tenor sax player Bernie Greenwood and a psychology student cum singer called John Baily, now a lecturer in ethnomusicology. Their plan was to make an overland journey to Australia in a double decker bus, combining living quarters and a stage area – this was eventually scaled down to a more modest American car. Ted Milton was enthusiastic about this naive, even insane project, initially proposing to go himself as drummer. Because of Ted, Eric and Ben decided to go as well and the band that finally set out consisted of, Ben, Eric, John, Bernie, a trumpet player who switched to guitar and bass en route, Bob Ray and Ted's brother Jake on drums. Ted himself didn't go, but if it hadn't been for domestic commitments, Hughie Flint would probably have followed Eric out of the Mayall band out into the wide blue yonder. After an inordinate length of time, the happy wanderers, calling themselves the Glands, reached Greece, by which time Jake Milton decided to turn round and head for home. He later joined Quintessence.

The first thing they found out was that in Greece, musicians were regarded as the dregs. They were held in no higher esteem than waiters and the fact that they were ENGLISH MUSICIANS at a time when the Beatles were riding high, cut no ice whatsoever with club managements whose methods were autocratic. They had gone out there as an R&B band, but it wasn't really working, as John Baily explains. "Eric and Ben were not too happy at seeing the music they loved being decimated and so Eric took over musical direction, suggesting we play rock'n'roll instead and it was much better". What never changed, however, were the raw deals they were getting – treated like servants and rarely paid. The situation was not unlike the bad old days of the Hamburg club scenes, bands playing for hours and hours on end for peanuts. The Glands were only second stringers in any case; they were support to a Greek band called the Juniors who played British pop songs. Things took a turn for the worse when the Juniors were involved in a serious car accident; one member of the band was killed and another very seriously injured and the club where they were playing closed down. As a friendly gesture, Eric agreed to play for the Juniors to help them out and the club reopened. He soon realised what he had let himself in for – playing for both bands meant about six to eight hours a night and he was wiped out. He was spending a lot of time with the Greek band under pressure from the club owner, who it appears, took a liking to Eric and wanted him to stay. This caused growing resentment from the English contingent whose situation was made even more complicated when they were busted for not having work permits, the result of being 'grassed on' by a rival club owner. Eric, on the other hand, avoided this run-in with the Greek police, as his interests were being looked after by the club owner. So the merry band had no money and couldn't work and the best plan was to leave the country. Unfortunately, they still had some expensive Vox equipment at the club, over which the management were willing to go to some lengths to retain, particularly as it was the type of gear the Beatles used. Eventually agreement was reached. Eric volunteered to stay with the Greek band to allow the others to get away with the equipment – he was a hostage and escape was going to be even more tricky because his boss and the rest of the band were fully aware of who they had in their midst as Yardbirds music was well known to the Athens pop music audience. However, the longer Eric stayed, the more dangerous the situation would become. Plans were hatched for the great escape. The main problem was Eric's Gibson guitar which was still at the club along with the Marshall amp. which it seemed would have to be sacrificed. Having gone to pack their gear at the hotel where they were staying, Ben and Eric went on to the club in a taxi. When they got there, Eric went in on his own and nonchalantly approached the manager to ask permission to take his guitar in order to buy some new strings. He agreed and Eric, plus guitar, but minus amplifier, fled in the taxi to the railway station and thence home. The whole venture collapsed, but John Baily and Bernie Greenwood did make it to Australia and then back via the Americas – he later sang briefly with McGuinness Flint. John Baily has a detailed diary of the saga of the Glands, but he is not showing it to anybody.

Meanwhile back in England, the fact that Eric was the star of the show was revealed by his absence – there was an almost tangible air of disappointment in the clubs when audiences realised that Eric wouldn't be playing. It was panic stations for John as one guitarist after another came in virtually off the streets for one night, never to be seen again. Jeff Kribbets from Doctor K's Blues Band played and so did Peter Green, "I'd always told Eric that the job would be open for him when he came back. After all that time spent looking for a replacement (about two and a half months), Peter turned up, just a week before Eric returned – it was a real shame, but I'd promised Eric and that was that".

Another interesting development took place while Eric was away. John McVie had been sacked in typical Mayall style for alcoholic over-indulgence and his place taken by Jack Bruce. Bruce, in turn, had been sacked from the Graham Bond Organisation as part of rock's bitterest feud which rumbles on even today – the war between Jack Bruce and Ginger Baker.

Jack Bruce was born in May 1943 at Bishopbriggs, Lanarkshire, in Scotland and he studied at the Royal Scotland Academy of Music on a scholarship in composition and cello from Bellahouston Academy in Glasgow. He was, however, totally dissatisfied with the musical conventions that he was expected to follow, where initiative and innovation were frowned upon. He began playing double bass with a variety of Glaswegian modern jazz groups in clubs and pubs and was continually being sacked for wanting to play long ambitious solos. He then spent some time in Italy with an R&B offshoot of a Coventry trad jazz palais band, returning to commence a brief career with Jim McHarg's Scotsville Jazzmen, during which time Jack found himself playing at a 1962 Cambridge University May Ball. With time on his hands, he wandered past a Cambridge dive and heard some music that immediately grabbed his attention. He went down to investigate. The Bert Courtly Sextet were on stage, a band that included Dick Heckstall-Smith, Ginger, John Hockridge, Maurice Salvat and Kathy Stobart. Courtly himself wasn't playing that night. Jack went up and asked Dick if he could have a play. Thinking he was a jumped up student off the streets he was told to get lost, but Jack persisted and they told him to come back at the next interval. He came back and was then told that he could not play because they were doing arrangements. So then, just to get rid of him, Dick selected their most difficult arrangement, a ballad with a complex chord sequence. Jack played through it note perfect and did not mess up a single change. Then he disappeared and Dick spent the next two weeks trying to track him down for an audition with Alexis Korner's Blues Incorporated, of which Dick and Ginger were already a part.

That Cambridge session was Jack's first sight of Ginger.

"He looked like a demon in that cellar, sitting down there with his red hair. He had this drum kit that he had made himself out of perspex or something. . . . I never heard drums sound as good. I'd never seen a drummer like him and I knew then that I wanted to play with him. That night was amazing".

Money was very tight in those days which meant that musicians often played for more than one band. As R&B and blues evolved into rock, and bands became much tighter and wrote their own material, this became much more difficult but it was different in 1962 and the cross-over musicians like Graham Bond, Jack Bruce and Ginger Baker were playing R&B with Alexis Korner and more jazz-oriented material with pianist Johnny Burch and his Octet.

The more Bond, Baker and Bruce played together, the more they felt like cutting loose from Alexis and John Burch and going out on their own. They had already played an experimental gig in Manchester, just the three of them. It went down a storm and they got paid the unprecedented amount of £70, recalls Jack Bruce, "We'd thought we'd won the pools". Originally a first rate alto sax player and pianist, Graham Bond switched to Hammond organ, the powerful L100 as used by Georgie Fame, Brian Auger, Zoot Money and later Keith Emerson, Vincent Crane, Jon Lord and Rick Wakeman, but used first by Bond, who also pioneered the idea of splitting it in half to ease transportation. The trouble was that just as Cyril Davies and Alexis Korner argued about horns, so Bond and Korner disagreed about the Hammond. It drowned out everyone else and Alexis regarded it as Graham's power trip. He also objected because Graham was never around to help carry the Hammond up and down stairs. Therefore, in February 1963, the three of them left Blues Incorporated and formed the Graham Bond Organisation with a young mild mannered jazz guitarist from Yorkshire named John McLaughlin. He left for the Brian Auger band in September to be replaced by Dick Heckstall-Smith. The full story of one of Britain's most remarkable R&B bands and its equally remarkable leader Graham Bond is as yet unchronicled but one aspect of the tale is significant for the Clapton story and that is the personality clash between Bruce and Baker, which Jack has philosophically ascribed to the fact that "He's a Leo and I'm a Taurus". As a band, the Organisation thrived on arguments, rows and chaos, much of its greatness came from these elements, but it reached a peak of intensity which became counter-productive, fuelled by the frustrations created by lack of commercial success.

The main combatants were Jack and Ginger. On the surface, tensions arose due to their opinions of each others playing – Jack thought Ginger was too loud and Ginger did not go for Jack's counter melody lines which he thought much too fussy. "Ginger really got through to me psychologically, that I was no good as a bass player. I was going to give up. Then we backed Marvin Gaye on television and he really flipped about my bass playing. He told me that there was nobody in the States playing bass like me and he said he wanted me in his band."

Bobby Wellins, the tenor player, also encouraged Jack not to be 'psyched out' by Ginger. It was independent acclaim like this from other musicians that kept Jack on an even keel, which is more than can be said for the bandwagon which nearly overturned once, so violent was the row that was going on in the back. And on another occasion, Jack was driving the van from a gig in Ipswich and a row was in full flight. There were no street lights due to a blackout, but Jack refused to turn on the headlights or ease off the gas pedal and they went through the town via several yards of pavement, weaving in and out of lamposts. But the worst trouble came at the Golders Green Refectory, in North London. Jack had been going on at Ginger throughout the set, because he thought the bass drum was too loud. Ginger did nothing, but during Jack's solo, he started bouncing sticks off Jack's head with unerring accuracy, at which point, Jack spun round, hurled his bass at Ginger, which demolished the drumkit and a mighty brawl ensued. When it came to fisticuffs, Jack was unlikely to get the better of Ginger. "If it hadn't been for two quick moving bouncers, that would have been it".

Jack was very independent, very private, shy, but with a mercurial temper. Ginger had the temper to match, but he was naturally very dominant and it was in his nature to want to take over; he had a tremendously competitive spirit, but Jack wanted to resist this and the inevitable result was conflict.

Matters came to a head in September 1965. The band had not had the success that was its due and Graham was sinking deeper in the morass of a heroin habit. As virtual leader of the band by now, Ginger took the decision to sack Jack. There was nobody to appeal to; Graham's attitude was that Ginger's word was law and Dick Heckstall-Smith wisely watched from the sidelines. Jack, however, continued to come to gigs and set up, until Ginger pulled a knife on him saying, "If you turn up again, this goes in you". Jack stayed away.

Although a very busy player, perhaps too much for the Bluesbreakers in 1965, John Mayall had no qualms about asking him to join – "Yes, he did overplay a bit, but he was a blues player, so there was no problem". When Jack and Eric got on stage, there was controlled anarchy. What Mayall did for Clapton was to give him his freedom both spiritually and musically but he had a hard job holding it together when Jack Bruce started improvising with Eric. It was a playing experience that neither would forget. "There was a great thing between me and Eric even then. He knew of me before. He'd seen me with Graham a couple of times and he dug my playing". Right from the start Eric knew how good Jack was. "A natural first choice in any group I might dream of forming".[23]

This first association was to be brief. Jack was asked to join Manfred Mann, by then a successful pop band with two hit singles to their credit. Having just got married, the lure of money was too great, so even if it meant wearing white roll neck sweaters, Jack sacrificed all and left the Bluesbreakers much to Mayall's disgust. Jack Bruce played bass on their next hit *Pretty Flamingo*.

Just prior to Eric's return, his first recording with Mayall was released in October 1965: *I'm Your Witchdoctor/Telephone Blues*. Another track *On Top Of The World* was recorded at the same session. Both this and the A-side of the single have inventive single note feedback solos, early examples of a technique in controlled feedback first demonstrated by Jeff Beck. On the single, the end note of each twelve bars is sustained progressively longer through the song. The single was produced by Jimmy Page and was well received, in a somewhat quaint MM review, "a knockout up tempo number written by singer-organist Mayall. Hums along with some gas parts of unison and the blues guitar of Eric Clapton. A superb disc which deserves to be a hit" – which it wasn't.

Clapton's other recording session with John Mayall that year was for Mike Vernon on his independent Purdah label, two tracks later released as a single, *Lonely Years* b/w *Bernard Jenkins*. The music was rough-hewn Chicago style, wonderfully captured by Mike Vernon whose limited edition of 500 sold out rapidly when the record appeared in August 1966. Clapton's guitar work on both tracks had the feel of early Chicago recordings in the Fifties, rather than the slicker, more contemporary blues guitar style of *Telephone Blues*, and *Bernard Jenkins*, in recreating the Forties duo work of Tampa Red and Maceo Merriweather, looked back even further. Mike Vernon had an instinctive feel for this music; the sound was primitive because the equipment was primitive by modern standards, so there was a danger of making virtue out of a necessity.

There were other jams and sessions for Clapton outside the context of the Bluesbreakers during 1965. There was some loose and fairly dispensable jamming with Jimmy Page which has appeared on British blues anthologies, *Choker*, *Miles Road* and *Long Hard Road*. More interesting were some embryonic 'supersession' recordings in the same vein – *Draggin' My Tail*, *Snakedrive*, *Tribute To Elmore* and *West Coast Ideas* with Clapton, Page, Mick Jagger on harmonica, Bill Wyman, Ian Stewart and either Chris Winters or Tony Chapman on drums. *Snakedrive* is the pick of the bunch, beautifully fluid phrasing from Clapton overlaying some pulsating rhythm guitar from Jimmy Page, in those days a hot session musician. Some of the other tracks represent the blues as dirge, with dull, ponderous playing from everyone, the sort of droning which gave the British blues scene a bad name and prompted the ironic Liverpool Scene song *I've Got The Fleetwood Mac Chicken Shack John Mayall Can't Fail Blues*.

One encounter which, while it did not exactly change the course of rock history, was interesting nonetheless, was the first meeting of Eric and Bob Dylan on his first UK tour. It happened at the CBS studios in Bond Street on 12th May 1965. Dylan had been frogmarched in there by his management to record a sales message for a CBS conference in Miami. Snatches of the tape still exist; he managed a trite message something along the lines of "thank you for selling so many of my records – keep up the good work", as the alcohol went down in some quantity. Then he attempted a boozy rendition of *Go Now*, with the Bluesbreakers. His efforts provoked totally disrespectful cries of "Do it in tune", and from Hughie Flint, "you haven't worked much with bands, have you?", at which point Dylan shouts "FADE IT OUT!"

During his second stint with Mayall from November 1965 to the Spring of 1966, the legend of Eric Clapton began to gather momentum – the dreaded slogan 'Clapton is God' which Eric has worn like a crown of thorns ever since, began to appear on walls around London. The adverts in the music press now read John Mayall's Bluesbreakers featuring Eric Clapton. Briefly eschewing conscious fashion, Clapton stood on stage, mutton chop sideburns, cropped hair, jeans and T-shirt (which itself became the standard blues band uniform) and let the blues flow from his fingers – his name and his music fast becoming synonymous with virtuoso electric guitar. So effortless was his style that, at times, one did wonder just where this astonishing music was coming from. In a packed club during Mayall and early Cream days, his guitar playing was almost spiritually uplifting, florid and pretentious though that may sound and, in temperatures over 100°F, anyone who can make an audience go cold just through playing a musical instrument, is in possession of an ability and a power which has to be experienced to be believed.

On stage, his physical presence was unique – he refused to put on any sort of show. He stood stock still, often with eyes closed in a world of his own, seemingly oblivious to the band and not relating to the audience at all in the way Hendrix, Alvin Lee, Pete Townshend or Stan Webb did. Even less was he like American blues guitarists B.B. King and Freddie King, who had a very traditional sense of showmanship, or Buddy Guy (followed by Stan Webb) who used a very long guitar lead to enable him to move freely among the audience. Of Clapton's mentors, perhaps only in Otis Rush, more reserved and introverted than his contemporaries, could one see the Clapton stance, and of course, Robert Johnson, who hardly ever faced his audience at all. A reader sent an enquiry letter to *Melody Maker*, asking why Clapton faced his amps – and the answer was much more pragmatic than the retrospective glamour of cerebral isolation would allow – it was to increase the sustaining power of his guitar, by ensuring that the pickups were as close to the speakers as possible – and if that meant turning away from the audience, then so be it. But rather than alienating the audience, it endeared him to them even more, because here was someone who was even closer to the blues than they were – even more passionate, even more committed to blues power. Through sheer ability and inspiration, he was tapping into a stream of emotional response that audiences could only dream about. But this did not happen in isolation. The sense of crusade about the blues in Britain ran the whole length of the Korner-Mayall axis – the musicians and the fans were together at the same clubs, listening to the same records, arguing and debating together. With the second wave of interest in the blues, as before, there were pockets of interest all over the country. In schools and colleges, small groups of young fans sat around record players during the lunch hours listening to music condemned by outsiders as "old wogs making 'orrible groaning noises". But it was these groups in the clubs that created the aura of shared experience, from which came the elevation of Eric Clapton as the embodiment of that experience, and the recognition of his abilities as a musician of world stature. Voters in two music polls in the mainstream pop press during 1965, failed to find a place for Eric in the top ten guitar section, but in the Beat Instrumental Poll of 1965, a more music-oriented magazine, Clapton came in at no. 6 on the heels of those destined to be looking at his back in future years, Hank Marvin, Keith Richard and

George Harrison. In March 1966, Eric was voted lead guitar in a "group's group" (precursor of the supergroup!) poll, conducted by *Melody Maker*, together with Ginger Baker, John Entwistle, Brian Auger, Stevie Winwood (vocalist) and Shadows' rhythm guitar Bruce Welch.

This group was hypothetical, but at about this time Eric did play with Stevie Winwood in a curious studio-only band called Eric Clapton and the Powerhouse with Jack Bruce, Paul Jones on harmonica and Spencer Davis' drummer, Peter York. They recorded three tracks for a compilation album released by Elektra in 1966 called *What's Shakin'* with the Lovin' Spoonful, Al Kooper, Tom Rush and the Paul Butterfield Blues Band. The Powerhouse played *I Want To Know*, a debut airing by Eric of Robert Johnson's *Crossroads* (much slower than Cream's version but similar in pace to the excellent version on the Blind Faith bootleg), plus a rather light-weight rendition of *Steppin' Out*.

Clapton also had another workout with an American blues artists, this time it was pianist Champion Jack Dupree for his album *Blues From New Orleans To Chicago* produced inevitably by Mike Vernon with Eric, John Mayall, another excellent blues guitarist Tony McPhee, Malcolm Pool on bass and Keef Hartley on drums, both then with the Artwoods. Clapton's playing was generally muted throughout, apart from one track *Third Degree*.

Through average production, the Powerhouse's attempt at *Steppin' Out* had none of the harshness or brightness of the version that Clapton recorded with Mayall during the same period. One of twelve tracks which went to make up one of the most important albums to come from the mid-Sixties purist blues boom in Britain simply, but significantly titled *John Mayall's Bluesbreakers with Eric Clapton*. Under primitive conditions, Dudgeon and Vernon had created the sound of *Lonely Years* and *Bernard Jenkins* at Wessex Studios in Soho and circumstances were no more propitious when the Bluesbreakers went into West Hampstead's undersized no. 2 Studio with its Heath Robinson equipment. In later years, Mike Vernon was often asked how he got the sound on the album, particularly the savage raw ebb and flow of Eric's guitar. His answer was always the same – in 1966, that's all you could have done. In fact everyone, whichever side of the desk they were on, was pretty inexperienced in the studio – Eric and engineer Gus Dudgeon for example, simply had no conception of each other's requirements. Gus put the mike in front of Eric's amp, Eric picked up his amp and took it across the studio, as far away as possible. Gus told Eric to turn down, which Eric wouldn't, because to get the feedback, distortion and sustain that Eric wanted on his guitar, he had to be turned up full as he was on stage. Much of Eric's guitar on the album was actually picked up by Hughie Flint's drum mike.

In rock writing, the word 'seminal' is over-used but there is every justification for using it about the Bluesbreakers and the band's importance for the future of British rock in the Sixties is hard to over-estimate. If the blues temples were the Marquee and the Flamingo, the prophets Mayall and Korner, and the god Clapton, then this album was the bible. It made Eric

Clapton a star and, featuring some of his finest recorded blues solos, became a textbook for a generation of aspiring rock musicians, many who began as blatant and self-confessed Clapton copyists.

Clapton laid out some of his most important influences at the time with Otis Rush's *All Your Love* and Freddie King's *Hideaway* and his first recorded solo vocal appears on the album, Robert Johnson's *Ramblin' On My Mind*. His use of a Gibson Les Paul introduced to many for the first time, introduced a guitar and a sound that came to dominate the rock music scene alongside the Fender Stratocaster.

Virtually singlehanded, Clapton hauled the Gibson guitar company, whose fortunes were flagging badly, into the world rankings as sales of their guitars soared through his example. Probably the only comparable endorsement success story involved Ringo Starr and Ludwig drums, who had almost gone out of business before the Beatles came along. Eric bought his first Gibson in Lew Davies' shop in the Charing Cross Road, which eventually became Selmer's where Mick Taylor bought *his* first Les Paul, sold to him by a young salesman called Paul Kossoff, who said he'd have bought it himself if he'd been able to afford it. One of Clapton's favourite guitars later on was a black Gibson with white piping round the edges which Kossoff gave him in an exchange deal. In contrast to the piercing, bright clear sound of the Fender Strat, the Les Paul has a rough, gritty sound. The humbucking pick-ups (designed to counteract unwanted hum), make it twice as powerful as the Strat but it is less sensitive in the upper registers, which means it is best played at full volume to pick up what high register sensitivity there is – one reason why Eric refused to turn his guitar down in the studio during the recording of the Bluesbreakers album.

Electronics expert, inventor, singer and guitarist, Les Paul (real name Lester William Polfuss) lent his name to Gibson in an endorsement deal in 1952, the year the company introduced their first solid electric guitar. Les Paul's design started off as a prototype in 1941 called 'the log', literally a four by four wooden log with strings, a pick-up and a plug, and it took him nine years to convince Gibson before the Les Paul Standard made its first appearance. By 1961, Les Paul, Juniors, Specials, Customs and SGs were also on the market but the guitar was waning in popularity: the Beat bands mainly using Gretsch (George Harrison), Burns (Hank Marvin), Vox (Brian Jones) and Rickenbacker (John Lennon). That was until Clapton (and Jeff Beck) started cranking a basically dance band guitar through 100 watt amplifiers.

The album was shot through with superb blues guitar work like *Double Crossin' Time* written by Mayall as an expression of his disgust at Jack Bruce's departure to Manfred Mann "Leaving bands was dirty in those days", said Clapton of his departure from the Yardbirds. The rest of the band and the guest horn players like Johnny Almond played well enough, (apart from a totally unnecessary Hughie Flint drum solo apparently forced on him by Mayall against his wishes), but the album was really a showcase for Eric, exemplified by Mayall's unprecedented decision to put Eric's name prominently on the cover together with a group photo with

Eric reading a copy of Beano.

The album was released in August 1966 – one reviewer called the album "joyless and savage", but paid it the ultimate compliment "No British musicians have ever sounded like this before on record. It is a giant step. It is a credit to John and his musicians".[24] There was no mention of chart potential, but the reviewer in Beat Instrumental prophetically stated "It's Eric Clapton who steals the limelight and no doubt several copies of the album will be sold on the strength of his name".[25] In fact the incredible happened – *Bluesbreakers* went into the top ten three weeks after its release and stayed there for about another eight; probably one of the earliest examples of album success without a chart single to boost sales.

There were two ironies about this album. The first was that, despite Eric's awesome playing, he had to do it in a studio and that meant that, even on this album, he was not at his most free and unrestrained. This only happened in live performances when the pressure was off and, if there is cause for regret that the Yardbirds never recorded a studio album with Eric, then the same applies to the Bluesbreakers. Only fragments of Clapton's live work with Mayall remain. On Mayall's *Looking Back* album (1970), there is a track called *Stormy Monday* recorded in March 1966. Clapton may not have been a visual performer but he could certainly be flash if he wanted, throwing in licks just for effect as he does here. The tape from which that track was recorded was lost in a fire some years back, in which much of Mayall's past life memorabilia also went up in smoke. A later compilation album *Primal Solos* (1977) devoted the whole of side one to a live recording at the Flamingo in April 1966 of the Bluesbreakers playing *Maudie, It Hurts To Be In Love, Have You Ever Loved A Woman, Bye Bye Bird* (previously done by Clapton with Sonny Boy Williamson) and a rock version of *I'm Your Hoochie Coochie Man*.

The second irony was contained in Neil Slaven's sleeve notes "A lot of people wondered why Eric left the Yardbirds just as they were hitting big. But Eric had an inevitable course to follow and at the time it led him to the Bluesbreakers, as no doubt it will lead him elsewhere in the future". And by the time the 'Beano' album was released, the Bluesbreakers was indeed past history.

# CHAPTER FOUR
# Cream - A Strange Brew

March 1966 saw Clapton in a rather depressed state of mind – thoughts about leaving the country for the romance and excitement of an America he had only heard and read about began to surface once more. He told *Melody Maker*, "I don't think there will be room for me here much longer. None of my music is English – it is rooted in Chicago . . . the only way is to go to America. Forming a blues band in England is like banging your head against a brick wall".[26] Later in the interview he spoke of his sense of being an outsider, his sense of the power he wielded by being an exceptional guitarist and his annoyance (even before Cream), at those who kept on telling him what a wonderful guitarist he was. Generally Clapton has been almost painfully modest about his talent in interviews, but this was one of the earliest and at twenty-one his youthful bitterness and intensity swept modesty aside. He just said he knew he was great and didn't need anyone else to tell him so. Although he wanted to play Chicago blues, he was bored with the Bluesbreakers format. He looked ahead to a future in the British music scene that was bleak and unfulfilling. If he was going to stay, he would have to create his own environment.

One night in May 1966, Ginger Baker arrived in Oxford to see the Bluesbreakers and asked if he could sit in. Eric and Ginger had played together once before when Clapton had jammed with the Graham Bond Organisation at one of the Richmond Festivals. At Oxford, the chemistry between them was immediate, and in the bar afterwards they talked about the possibilities of working together. Ginger, too, was increasingly frustrated with his situation as the vital break into the big time had so far eluded the Graham Bond Organisation and they were making no real progress. The discussion came around to bass players and Eric said "Get Jack Bruce and you can count me in". This was obviously problematical as Ginger and Jack were hardly the best of friends, but Ginger felt from the start that such a line up could be the incentive they needed to try and resolve their differences. He drove to see Jack in his new Rover car, bought with the proceeds of a song he had written for the Who. About three weeks later, the car was in pieces, a victim of Ginger's exuberant driving, but it was still gleaming outside Jack's flat as Ginger told him about the idea for a new band. That very month, Manfred Mann had a number one hit with *Pretty Flamingo*, but all the same it was patent nonsense for a musician of Bruce's calibre to be confined by the strait jacket of formula pop music: after resisting the idea for about five minutes, he fell in with the plan.

Everything was kept secret while the three extricated themselves from their current commitments, but the news leaked out. In fact, Ginger told Chris Welch at *Melody Maker* and Jack especially was very annoyed to read that "a sensational new Group's Group starring Eric Clapton, Jack Bruce and Ginger Baker is being formed". The report went on to say they hoped to be gigging in a month's time and that "it is expected they will remain as a trio with Jack Bruce as featured vocalist".[27] In the very early stages, there was some discussion as to the wisdom of going out as a trio. One of the great 'might have beens' of rock is that if Stevie Winwood had not been so heavily committed to the Spencer Davis Group whose *Keep On Running* was a hit in the January that year, he could well have been the fourth member. Graham Bond, too, had some idea he might have been asked – but in the end it was just Jack, Ginger and Eric who thought up the name Cream – confirmation of the "Group's Group" press label.

John Mayall was no less annoyed than Jack to read the news – it was *Double Crossin' Time* all over again, only this time it was the star of the show. But he had a replacement, Peter Green, waiting in the wings who, because he started by trying to out-Clapton Clapton, quickly subdued the cries of "We Want God". This is clearly shown on one of the Mayall retrospective albums, *Looking Back* (1970). After Clapton's work out on *Stormy Monday* comes Green with *So Many Roads* complete with gushing guitar style. Side two and six months later, Green was his own man: *It Hurts Me Too* and *Double Trouble* have that special Green magic. Instead of torrents of notes, each one seems carefully selected, his playing is much more restrained and distant. The effect was to drench a song, rather than to stab into it at oblique angles with vicious licks. Some have preferred Green to Clapton as a blues guitarist, mainly due to this restrained style, but each have played the blues in their own inimitable and devastating fashion. As Muddy Waters once said, there were only two guitarists who made him sweat – one was Peter Green and the other was Eric Clapton. John Mayall is unequivocal "Eric was easily the best musician I ever worked with. Quite remarkable".

Two weeks after the official leak came the formal announcement by their manager Robert Stigwood, together with an enigmatic hand-out, "the first is last and the last is first, but the first, the second and the last are Cream. They will be called Cream and will be represented by me for agency and management. They will record for my Reaction label and go into the studios next week to cut tracks for their first single. Their debut will be at the National Jazz and Blues Festival at Windsor in July, when their first single will be released".[28] From these clipped, precise statements, it was clear that Cream was going to be launched on a serious business footing, the deal with Reaction being a five year contract worth £50,000. Via the Clapton-Mayall connection, Rik Gunnell was trying to make his voice heard as a prospective manager of Cream, similarly Giorgio Gomelsky, but Ginger convinced the others that the former Graham Bond Organisation manager and producer was the man for the job. Ginger in fact was very much involved with the business side of Cream in the early days, handling the bookings with Stigwood's right hand man, Robert Masters. Cream was Ginger's idea and he really has not received the credit he deserves for using his strength of character and enthusiasm in getting the whole project off the ground. He had already proved himself one of Europe's finest drummers through his work with Graham Bond and now he quite rightly believed that it was about time he saw some material benefits for all his hard work. Already by the formation of Cream, he had been playing non-stop since the mid-Fifties.

He was born on 19th August 1939 in Lewisham, South London and his musical career started when he was fourteen, playing trumpet with the local branch of the Air Training Cadets. But his first love was bike racing, flashing around the Kent countryside on a bike that he had saved for from his meagre earnings as a trainee commercial artist. His attentions then switched from trumpet to drums and he bought a second hand kit for £3.

"I thought, good God. At last here's something I can do".

A band was immediately formed featuring banjo, trumpet, trombone and drums. Dire as it was, the band still managed to get a Soho gig and Ginger's thoughts began to turn towards the giddy heights of professional musicianship. His decision to throw in his job and hit the road was precipitated by the demise of his one and only bike – flattened beyond all hope by a taxi. He bluffed his way into a job with Bob Wallis' Storeyville Jazzmen and from there he played with just about everyone around, and had rows with all of them. There was Acker Bilk and his Paramount Jazz Band and Terry Lightfoot's band, during which time Ginger made his first album appearance on Terry's *Tradition In Colour* album released in April 1958. He was with Terry for about six months before they had a row and Ginger left to go to Hamburg. He never got there. Instead, he signed with the Diz Disley band for a tour of Germany and Denmark that left a trail of broken toilets in its wake. Ending up broke and hungry, Ginger went home and unloaded lorries during the day on the insistence of his parents who were bored with him, practicing all day on his home-made kit in the empty house next door. He stuck it for a few months then gave up, got married, and found his way into the Ken Oldham Showband which required him to learn to sight read inside two weeks. With that particular skill under his belt, he played for two years anything and everything – 3/4 dance music, ceilidh music and big band arrangements.

He had another go at the continent of Europe, this time with Les Douglas, playing the American bases in Germany. It wasn't long before his wife Liz realised that they had just enough money to get home and that if they stayed much longer they would be owing the band leader money. The hot dog that they consumed on Cologne Station turned out to be their last sight of food until they reached their maisonette in Braemar Avenue,

Neasden in North London. As it was, Liz's parents had to meet them at the station because they had no money for fares.

He began playing in small modern jazz combos with Ronnie Scott, Bert Courtly and Joe Harriott but failed an audition with John Dankworth – when half the band wanted him in and the rest did not. Eventually Ronnie Stevenson got the job, which was a major disappointment for Ginger, because the Dankworth spot was reckoned to be one of *the* top jobs, as well as being one of the only ones. There were occasional gigs with the jazz/poetry band New Departures and the John Burch Octet and an eight month stint with Blues Incorporated, when Ginger, Jack, Dick Heckstall-Smith and Graham Bond became the first jazz musicians to 'cross over' to R&B. During Ginger's Organisation days, he kept an earnings chart on his wall and, until Cream, it had made dismal reading.

Stigwood too, was looking for an upturn in his fortunes. He grew up in Adelaide, South Australia, the son of a Protestant engineer and a nurse. His parents were divorced when he was twelve and apparently attracted by the 'mystery' of Catholicism, was converted at fifteen, almost becoming a priest three years later. There was a big party to celebrate but he changed his mind next day and had to give all the presents back. After spending a further three years writing copy for an ad. agency, he embarked on a Sixties hippy trail in reverse, via India and Aden, ending up in Britain in 1956. From 1958, he ran a half-way house for delinquent boys in Cambridge, before entering the world of show business in 1962 with one Stephen Komlosey, in a talent agency specialising in actors for TV adverts. Stigwood also got together with a renegade genius called Joe Meek, an engineer and one of Britain's first independent record producers to co-produce an actor client of Stigwood's, John Leyton, as a singer. Together, Stigwood and Meek helped to break the mould of British pop process by making a record independently and trying to convince a record company to distribute it, something which had never been done before but nowadays is commonplace. They scored a massive hit with *Johnny Remember Me* and Stigwood went on to five more chart successes in the early Sixties, building up a management, publishing and recording empire, to earn him the title of Britain's first music tycoon.

But it was not all wine and roses and his attempt to promote a Chuck Berry tour in 1965 proved his undoing. The tour was plagued with problems, epitomised by one particular concert in London. During it, Star Wars broke out, as Berry demanded cash in hand not only before, but during his act, actually coming off stage to ask for money. The less than full house booed him, he in turn abused and finally abandoned them altogether, throwing down his guitar and storming off. His back-up musicians were dreadful and the sound system was worse ruining the Organisation support act during which Ginger broke two bass pedals. Finally, singer Winston G was injured as he was pulled from his stool by a hysterical fan.

With debts of £39,000 including £16,000 to the Rolling Stones, he went into liquidation. EMI, to whom he also owed money, offered to bail him out but he refused knowing that his main man there, Roland Rennie, was moving to Polydor and Stigwood wanted to continue their association as Reaction was distributed through Polydor. Signing Cream was Stigwood's first salvo as the Empire struck back. It was also an important step in his business war with the Who's co-manager Kit Lambert with whom he shared an office. Stigwood was the booking agent for the Who, who recorded for his Reaction label – now he had his own heavy pop group to compete with them.

Cream first got together in Ginger's house in Neasden and played 'something in D' for hours on end, after which they were all convinced that magic could be created. They switched venues to a scout hall in Willesden – Jack drove the van himself and Chris Welch was present along with Stigwood, the caretaker and a troop of dispossessed Brownies. They did not set all the gear up, Ginger just used a snare and bass drum, but recalls Chris, "They were playing this wonderful blues with Ginger doing a simple Baby Dodd's style New Orleans military snare pattern. It was marvellous". In public, Stigwood was saying that as soon as he heard them, he knew they were going to be big, but says Chris, "He came over to me at that rehearsal and asked me if I thought they were any good – he really wasn't sure".

Clapton's personal vision of Cream at the outset was Buddy Guy with a rhythm section, but apart from that rehearsal and isolated numbers like *Lawdy Miss Clawdy, The First Time I Met The Blues, Steppin' Out* and the occasional blast of *Hideaway*, Cream rarely featured straight Chicago-style blues numbers. Cream was formed as a co-operative band and neither Ginger nor Jack were going to be content with operating solely as Eric's rhythm section. Jack's experience to date was probably the most broad-based of the three taking in modern jazz, free jazz, R&B, blues and pop and he was writing material for Cream beyond the scope of purely blues modes. At the back stood Stigwood, concerned with mainstream pop promotion, not minority interest backwaters. But to be fair, this idea of Eric's lasted only a short time and as Cream began to slowly map out some kind of musical coherence, Clapton developed his guitar playing within the parameters of a new kind of pop music that he himself helped to design. But at the start, there was no clear ideas to precisely what Cream would be going – frontier busting and experimentation were in the air – Cream was new because they had to be, as Clapton said three years after Cream broke up, "Putting it together was hard, because we had no idea what we wanted to play. We just knew we wanted to play together. We had no idea of what material we wanted to do and for a long time it was hard to find a real direction". The band had not grown up together developing their individual interests and influences into a coherent whole from which a musical policy could develop naturally, and the musical gulfs were almost as wide as some of the personal ones. The audiences were expecting a supercharged version of the Bluesbreakers, while Eric, possibly to diffuse some of the expectations and to realise some of the more surreal aspects of his offbeat sense of humour wanted to introduce bizarre, pseudo-dadaist elements into the act – dry ice, bubbles, turkeys roaming around the stage, a transparent top hat with a frog in it that he would wear. But this all died within weeks, with

Clapton admitting later that they didn't have the wit or imagination to pull it off. The only manifestation of this nod towards the baroque was a stuffed bear which stood on stage, part of what Cream lyricist Pete Brown good naturedly calls 'Great British Rubbish' – "that old moth-eaten bear they carted around, was part of that heritage plus a dose of pop imagery, which had nothing to do with the blues, but everything to do with being bizarre. We are the British eccentrics – now we've got the money, let's be mad. It was more like James Robertson Justice than Buddy Guy. You won't see B.B. King with a stuffed bear on stage".

Ten days after their Willesden rehearsal, Cream played a warm up gig at the Twisted Wheel in Manchester away from the glare of London publicity. The reception was less than ecstatic but this didn't bother anyone. After all, despite the personnel, they were a new band and seasoned enough musicians to know they had to build up a following over a period of time. Yet the writing was on the wall as soon as they played their first official gig on 3rd July at the National Jazz and Blues Festival in Windsor. Ten thousand people turned up to stand ankle deep in mud, as the rain lashed down and went wild – screaming at Clapton to play more while he was still playing. Eric stood there with his Gibson Les Paul standard, Jack creating mayhem on his Fender six string bass (before the switch to the Gibson EB3 which became his trademark), and Ginger battering away on a seven piece double bass drum Ludwig, the first rock drummer to use such a set up. They played numbers like *Spoonful*, Ginger's solo *Toad* and Jack's harmonica *tour de force* adapted from a Forest City Joe piece, *Traintime* – songs which became the core of the Cream extended soloing repertoire but which were still in their shortened format at this time. Their appearance was a resounding success, they came off rather shocked and dazed by the reception, but pleased nonetheless – at least Jack and Ginger were. The elation carried over to a party that evening at Stigwood's flat near Regents Park, to which Chris Welch was invited.

"Jack and Ginger were very happy, but sitting on the floor in a corner, was Eric, looking very glum and miserable and Stigwood said, "Could you go over and speak to Eric? He's very upset and I don't know what's the matter with him. Find out what's wrong". It turned out through a very mumbled conversation that he wasn't happy with what Cream were doing right from the start.

Certainly they were not a blues band; Windsor proved that, but they did go straight on to the blues club circuit, starting off at the Cooks Ferry Inn, North London. It was a rather hesitant club debut; they were obviously nervous, under rehearsed and the crowd only really warmed up later on, as the individual soloing got under way. On 16th August, they broke the house attendance record at the Marquee, on their first appearance, the queue forming seven hours before the doors opened moving on to the Cellar Club, Kensington, the Manor House, the Ram Jam Club and the Flamingo. On each occasion they were billed as "Cream featuring Eric Clapton" at a time when the Bluesbreakers album was riding high in the album charts. The album's success coming when it did, contributed much to the enhancement of Clapton's reputation and his status as the media-perceived star of the show, although as the lead instrument, this was probably inevitable in any event.

It was a point raised with Jack Bruce during an interview for *Beat Instrumental* in November. If the drive of Cream was Ginger Baker, then it's vision was Jack Bruce's. Apart from *Sweet Wine* written by Ginger, all their original material at the time was his and he often spoke on behalf of the group about their music. Eric had not written anything, but was against doing Junior Walker's *Roadrunner* because he felt they could not do a version that was sufficiently their own, something they all felt was necessary for any non-original material. "Whatever we do, it must be our own". The interviewer asked if Jack had any reason to believe "that people looked upon the Cream as "The Clapton Group". He replied "I know Eric has this legendary thing about him, but I don't think that the people who come to see us as a group, are the type of people to follow him exclusively. Ginger and I have played around a lot and we are very well known on our own scene".[29]

As if to emphasis that Cream was not just a vehicle for Eric Clapton, their first single *Wrapping Paper* released on 7th October, featured hardly any guitar at all. It was the first product of the songwriting partnership of Jack Bruce and Pete Brown that was to prove so successful, although this first offering had little to commend it. Laid down only weeks after Cream had been formed, it was a rather low-key twelve bar blues song, which one reviewer suggested would drive Cream fans to suicide. What it didn't do, was drive them to buy the record which crawled no higher than 34 in the chart. In the *Beat Instrumental* interview, Jack Bruce had denied that Cream were purists, "there's so much more going on in pop, I think we would like to be a part of it" and to *Record Mirror* in January 1968 he said, "when the group started out, it was me who wanted us to be commercial, because I had been with a commercial group Manfred Mann". The hand of the manager can also be discerned. He knew they each had a tremendous following and together they would be dynamite, but he also believed that the only foundation for success was a hit single. Stigwood had done the same with the Graham Bond Organisation – their single *Tammy* was as unrepresentative of their music as *Wrapping Paper* was of Cream's.

The Bruce-Brown connection emerged from the *demi-monde* of the London music/arts scene. Jack played a few gigs on string bass in the New Departures jazz/poetry band, backing poets like Pete Brown and Michael Horowitz in recitals. Pete knew Jack's flatmate of the time, trombonist John Mumford and he also knew Eric through another poet, Ted Milton. They all became friends, "Ginger (or it may have been Jack), phoned me up and said, "look, Pete we've formed Cream; we've got this backing track and we'd like you to try and write a lyric to it". I went to the Chalk Farm studios, heard the track, wrote the lyric and that was *Wrapping Paper*.

Between that first gig at Windsor and the release of *Wrapping Paper*, Clapton began to rethink some of his ideas about playing. As Cream were finding some kind of direction, so Eric's confidence in his own playing reasserted itself; while still acknowledging his debt to the American sources, he was no longer simply interested in recreating their sounds. "My whole musical attitude has changed. I listen to the same sounds and records, but with a different ear. I'm no longer trying to play anything but like a white man. The time is overdue when people should play like they are and what colour they are. I don't believe I've ever played so well in my life. More is expected of me in the Cream – I have to play rhythm guitar as well as lead. Jack Bruce has had a tremendous influence on my playing and my personality. It's a lot easier to play in a blues band than in a group where you've got to play purely your own individual ideas. You have got to put over a completely new kind of music – this needs a different image. Jack, Ginger and I, have absorbed a lot of music and now we are trying to produce our own music. . . . It's hard. It's also original. It's also more satisfying and a lot more worthwhile".[30]

Even allowing for the perennial need for showing to the Press the face of complete contentment with whatever you are currently doing, Clapton seemed genuinely pleased the way things were going, rising to the challenge of working with such fierce musicians as Jack and Ginger and being influenced by them. From the outside, too, there was another challenge to be met, one which may have helped Clapton to reassert his racial integrity – the arrival in England during September, of Jimi Hendrix.

Three days before the Clapton interview quoted above, the Jimi Hendrix Experience was formed; their first gig was supporting Cream at Central London Polytechnic. Prior to that, Chas Chandler had brought Hendrix to a London Club where Cream was playing and he jammed with them; for Clapton, the experience was a revelation. "My God I couldn't believe it! It really blew my mind. Totally". After that, Clapton, usually in the company of Pete Townshend saw every Hendrix jam session in London during 1966, bar two, where he couldn't get in, not being exactly world famous then. Not unnaturally, both Clapton and Townshend regarded themselves as the top of the pile in the fields of lyrical and rhythmic guitar playing respectively and to find someone who could do both with such staggering virtuosity and presence was quite a shock. Later Clapton said that seeing Hendrix made him feel "shattered and very, very pleased. It was a great relief that someone had got there".[31] Hendrix showed Clapton that there was a new realm of guitar playing to strive for, fed by sources not solely reliant on the blues, a new aggression and a new feel for the pop age, but also it was a situation tailor made for the press and the fans to make comparisons – one of those manufactured conflicts favoured by the media. Once when compared to Clapton by an interviewer, Hendrix responded "but like, the blues is what we're supposed to dig. But you see, there are other things we can play too. And we just don't think alike. Sometimes the notes might sound like it, but it's a completely different scene between those notes".[32]

Clapton and Hendrix did not meet formally until Clapton walked into a restaurant where Hendrix was with his current lady, Chrissie Charles who had left John Mayall. According to David Henderson through interviewing Chrissie for his book on Hendrix, *'Scuse Me While I Kiss The Sky*, "they immediately clasped hands and joy shone in their eyes – at that point they were blood brothers", and then they got wasted together. They rapped about how long they would be in the business, what they wanted out of it – Clapton said he wanted to be a millionaire and buy lots of cars. Hendrix kissed him, "I kissed the fairest soul brother of England".[33] There was some disagreement about playing however. Inspired by the example of Cream, Hendrix had formed the Experience as a three piece band, but Hendrix, because of his early days in soul bands, attached far greater importance to rhythm than Clapton, who regarded the guitar as a virtuoso solo instrument. Throughout their association, Hendrix could never get Clapton to feel the same way as he did about rhythm playing and it annoyed him quite a lot. There was no doubt that standing on the same stage as Hendrix or watching him from the audience precipitated Clapton's changed attitude to playing. Hendrix opened up new vistas of sound possibilities and dynamic structures; for Clapton to compete, he would have to change and that was immediately apparent on Cream's next single *I Feel Free/NSU*. It provided them with their first top twenty hit reaching number 11 in the chart and a spot on Top of The Pops, dressed rather unimaginatively as convicts, arrow suits and all.

The most significant feature of the song, with its lilting South American feel, again written by Jack Bruce and Pete Brown, was the first appearance on record of Clapton's distinctive sustain technique, adapted from the ringing tone which B.B. King wrenched from his own guitar (named Lucille) but coined by Clapton 'woman tone'. This was achieved by removing all the treble from the tone controls and turning either both pick ups full on, or just using the rhythm pickup. In a way, the use of woman tone was a musical expression of Hendrix's more physical representation of the "guitar as woman", as part of his stage act. But in contrast to Hendrix, Clapton was never heavily involved in guitar electronics and effects – he used a fuzz box on *I Feel Free* and later, a wah wah pedal and reverb (using all three on *Disraeli Gears*), but in the main kept his guitar sound pure, preferring to experiment with different guitars to obtain new sounds rather than distort the sound of one or two.

Through the winter months leading up to the release of *I Feel Free*, Cream worked tremendously hard on the club circuit, gradually burying earlier beliefs inside the business that they couldn't work together, just by the doing of it night after night, which in turn served to tighten up their playing considerably, confirmed by this review of a gig at the Klooks Kleek in West Hampstead – "Any doubts about the Cream's ability to perform as a group and not just three star soloists, were dispelled by their sensational set. In fact one of their main strengths proved to be the fantastic empathy that exists between them. Reports have been filtering in of bad performances by the Cream, but they were seen to be obviously enjoying each other's playing tremendously and working together like a team of bomb disposal experts. Eric Clapton played one of the most outstanding solos of his career on *Steppin' Out*, which he sustained for minutes on end. Ginger

Baker battered fill-ins and off-beats with frightening ferocity . . . Eric sang with feeling and Jack's bass playing was as fast and powerful as the Flying Scotsman. Here is one of the most rewarding and fascinating groups making it today, and if anybody should record a "live" LP, it's the Cream".[34] That the reviewer should say Cream looked as if they were enjoying each other's playing, was very significant, but it was their prime motivation – they wanted to see if they could strike sparks off each other and make some money at the same time. By and large the battle for the audience was won as soon as they stepped off the stage at Windsor – Clapton was already at the point where he could probably have walked in front of an audience played paper and comb and got a standing ovation. What was crucial, was how Cream themselves felt about the music, the organisation of the band and each other. When the spark died, so did the band.

Cream's tight working schedule took them to France, Germany and Scandinavia, far more exotic than some of the English venues they played outside London during the same period, like Hoverton Town Hall and Sutton Public Baths. Despite the fanfare of their arrival and the uncritical nature of the reception wherever they played, six months later they were still playing the equivalent of the village hop – and that for a band who were only officially together for two years.

The collapse of Ginger Baker twice on stage at Sussex University and the Birdcage club in Portsmouth and a period of illness for Jack Bruce, delayed the release of their first album from October to December, meaning that *Fresh Cream* was not quite so fresh. Even in that short intervening period, the band had progressed and Jack Bruce's comment notwithstanding that "we have made a conscious effort to avoid lengthy, boring passages of improvisation",[35] the Klooks Kleek review and their radio concert on 9th December, both showed early signs that Cream were beginning to embellish on the main themes of the songs featured on *Fresh Cream*.

The album (UK version only – see discography), was split equally between original material and Cream interpretations of classic American blues songs – *Spoonful* (Willie Dixon), *Cat's Squirrel* (Dr. Ross), *Four Until Late* (Robert Johnson), *Rollin' And Tumblin'* (Muddy Waters) and *I'm So Glad* (Skip James). Bruce contributed most of the original material, like the opening track *NSU* which usually kicked off their live set as well; other writing was credited to Jack's wife Janet Godfrey, co-writer on *Sleepy Time Time* and co-writer with Ginger on *Sweet Wine*, his first contribution to Cream's repertoire which later metamorphosed into an extended work-out.

The hard gutsy feel of Clapton's playing on the Bluesbreakers was gone, to be replaced by licks that both in tone and structure were razor sharp, clearly defined against the thunderous rhythm section, fast and slick on *Cat's Squirrel* and *Rollin' And Tumblin'*, looping and swirling on *Sleepy Time Time* and his harmonic improvisation of the melody line on *I'm So Glad* had few peers. The tightly constructed, no frills solo on *I'm So Glad* contrasted sharply with the version he was performing by the time the album came out – more free ranging and inventive with jokey passages, the

1812 overture and the theme from a popular Pepsi Cola advert of the day (You're in the Pepsi Generation). To their enormous credit, Cream made sure that Skip James received his royalty payments for *I'm So Glad*, probably unprecedented in the shameful history of the plundering of black musical heritage by the white music industry. The money gave him some comfortable last days and covered funeral expenses when he died in 1969. Jack Bruce received a letter of gratitude from his widow.

*Fresh Cream* had all the hallmarks of Cream's studio work to come – superb song dynamics, cleverly paced passages of light and shade, intelligent use of harmony and overdubbing and, of course, individual musicianship of the highest calibre. Some of the overdubbing was solo guitar, as on *I'm So Glad*, but much of it was rhythm guitar, highlighting the limitations faced by a trio in the studio, although there were never any 'holes' in their sound, which on stage was always rich and full. It was a commonplace for critics and reviewers to pose questions about the 'schizophrenic' nature of Cream on stage and in the studio. But it was no great mystery – they wanted to keep all their options open with the flexibility to experiment in the studio while at the same time exciting audiences with that part of the programme suitable for live performance. Audiences were beginning to accept that Cream was not John Mayall re-visited and interviewed at the end of the year, top venue managers like John Gee and Rik Gunnell agreed that Cream were the biggest club draw of 1966.

But one problem area for Cream, however, on this and future albums, was the mediocrity of some of their studio material. *Fresh Cream* suffered through the absence of Pete Brown material, owing to his 'indisposition' at the time. It has been a beef of Ginger's that the co-operative nature of the band was undermined by the unbalanced share of royalty payments in favour of Bruce and Brown, because most of the original material used was theirs, to the detriment of contributions by others. This was true, but only because they had material ready for the studio, even though the band were on a heavy touring schedule, quite apart from the fact that they wrote the lions share of Cream's most important and enduring material. It was only pressure from within the band that prevented more material from being used. One song for example, *Theme For An Imaginary Western, the* finest song ever written about rock music and bands on the road, was rejected as not being good enough for Cream. In the light of some of the songs deemed 'good enough' for Cream albums, one can only smile through gritted teeth.

Ironically, *Fresh Cream* did precisely as well as the "Beano" album, reaching number six in the album charts. In America, the album just made the top Forty, which was commendable with no personal appearances to boost sales. When Cream did get to America in February 1967, it was something of a damp squib, failing to match up to the big UK music press built over the previous months. Cream were offered a spot on Murray the K's show in New York. Murray was a big name disc jockey on New York's Radio WINS, an American institution like Alan Freed and who, as far as Americans were concerned, discovered the Beatles *and* the Rolling Stones. The show took place in the RKO theatre; the idea was to present as many acts as possible to the largely teenage audience, within the hour and then change the audience. The show started at ten in the morning and went on until midnight to catch the movie crowd. Artists like Wilson Pickett, Simon & Garfunkel, the Who and Mitch Ryder, got about five minutes each. Cream did *I'm So Glad* and *I Feel Free* half a dozen times a day for ten days, using either the Lovin' Spoonful's equipment or the Who's. Anarchy ruled; everything overran by hours; the hall was half empty most of the time and Cream did not go down too well because the audience wanted to see them smash up all the equipment like the Who. At the end of it all, Eric planned to do what he enjoyed most of all – making a mess. Stashed away, were 14-lb bags of flour and eggs in preparation for a massive stage fight. But Murray got wind of it and threatened not to pay them if they went through with it. Instead, it all happened backstage. Murray had hysterics and Pete Townshend had to swim for it when the shower in his dressing room overflowed. Eventually the show was abandoned, leaving Murray $27,000 out of pocket. A very influential figure on the Sixties American rock scene, he died of cancer in 1982.

But the trip was by no means wasted. Clapton soaked up some of the American atmospheres he had dreamed about; everything seemed to live up to his expectations, "the best musical times we had were in Greenwich Village where it was more like the English Musical Appreciation Society. I sat in with a couple of the Mothers of Invention and Mitch Ryder at the Cafe Au Go Go, where Jimi Hendrix used to play. I made a lot of friends there, including Al Kooper, who played organ on Dylan tracks. New York is incredible. I'd love to live there. Everybody is so much more hip to the music scene – taxi drivers talking about James Brown. Can you imagine that here?"[36] Eric was much taken with Frank Zappa and his band. Through their combination of music with sharp wit, they demonstrated how one could play exceptionally well, respect musical form and discipline, without taking the business or life in general, too seriously. Zappa was more than willing to send up the very milieu he was working in, the psychedelia scene at this time, a working philosophy which seems to have been close to Clapton's heart throughout his career; a commitment to high standards (with the odd lapse) in conjunction with having a good time. Why bother if you're not enjoying it?

Eric also sampled some of New York's burgeoning flower power scene. He astutely recognised that bar the committed handful, most people just went for the clothes, "but I don't see much harm in this as long as people don't prostitute it. (Young people) are having a gas time with people and not objects. I went to a Be-In in Central Park and there were 20,000 people just having a good time. There were no stages or admission fees. It was a reaction against materialism". Apparently the kids got the cops stoned on acid-laced popcorn and by the end of the day, the cops were just lying back listening to the music. He was asked about LSD as an integral part of the philosophy, "they are still using it happily. (It was banned in America in October 1966), but no one seemed worried about it. Nobody I saw was flipped out with acid and the people I got to like, didn't even use it".[37]

His own LSD experiences were fairly limited; one bad trip killed his enthusiasm for it, even though he believed it was conducive to creativity. He first dropped acid, as he later told it, early in 1967, at the foot of Ben Nevis during work on the cover of *Disraeli Gears*. Then followed an acid summer, sporting his newly permed Afro hairstyle à la Dylan and Hendrix, in the company of George Harrison and John Lennon, both heavily into LSD.

The music industry was very coy about the drug scene within its ranks (and still is) – few musicians ever owned up in public to even *knowing* someone who took drugs, let alone admitting to personal indulgence. Confessions were bad for business. US immigration laws meant any drug conviction for English musicians put lucrative American tours in jeopardy. But much of it came to the surface in 1967 through a series of almost daily busts by the police of any stray Rolling Stone they could lay their hands on. However, when reporters were outside Mick Jagger's Chelsea flat even before the *police* arrived, liberal ire was roused, the resulting court cases prompting the famous *Times* editorial "Who Breaks A Butterfly On A Wheel?" Quite obviously, the drug squad boys were looking for star busts to get them on the front page to satisfy the Establishment lust for social revenge against pop musicians, and although Eric was never busted in Britain, he had some narrow escapes. A legendary London rock scene nemesis was Detective Sergeant Norman Pilcher, who began at Chelsea Station in the thick of the action, rising eventually to be head of the drug squad at Scotland Yard. The intercom buzzed at Eric's studio flat, a large room in part of a warren of artist and musician domiciles off the King's Road known as The Pheasantry, which he shared with Australian artist Martin Sharp. "Postman – special delivery" and bounding up the stairs, through the narrow passage came Pilcher and Co, shouting "Where's Eric Clapton? Where's Eric Clapton?" Fortunately for Eric, he was out.

The tabloid press were in their element. The *News of the World* ran a four part serial DRUGS AND POP STARS, naming names, including Ginger Baker, "credited" with using everything in the pharmacopeia. And in truth, Ginger did go through periods of heavy drug involvement. Coming from a jazz period, narcotics especially circulated within the working environment, but although there were difficult times during Cream days, he remained in control of the situation and was one of the fortunate ones to survive.

It was in the heady environment of a New York warming up for the summer of 1967, that Cream, with only a few days to spare at the end of their visit before the visas ran out, dashed into Atlantic studios to record their second album, *Disraeli Gears*. Originally due for release under the scintillating title *Cream*, they started playing around with puns like Elephant Gerald (Ella Fitzgerald). One of the roadies was spouting at great length about racing bikes, with an air of authority, totally out of proportion to his actual knowledge. Instead of calling the gearing 'derailleur gears', he came out with *Disraeli Gears*, so they used that.

One weakness with *Fresh Cream* was Robert Stigwood's production.

He was more at home in the theatre than the studio and Cream were not happy at the way he handled their music. In turn, Stigwood was having problems with Cream, because they were not malleable, dewy-eyed young pop stars – they were grown men, seasoned self assertive musicians; Ginger was 28. When Stigwood signed up the Bee Gees in 1967, none of them were out of their teens.

So "by arrangement with Robert Stigwood", as the cover said, this album (and all future Cream albums), was produced by Felix Pappalardi, a highly respected producer/arranger and skilled musician, specially brought in by Atlantic to work with Cream, as the studio had no experience of handling rock music. Tom Dowd engineered the album and Pappalardi left all the technical production to him, but studio boss Ahmet Ertegun wanted somebody down there on the studio floor, sympathetic to the music, able to generate ideas and act as the link between musicians and engineer. Dowd was amazed by the tons of equipment wheeled in just for three guys and by their musicianship and professional approach. "They were incredible. I never saw anything so powerful in my life and it was just frightening".[38]

In contrast to *Fresh Cream*, there were no direct cover versions; Pete Brown was back in harness and material written by Eric was featured for the first time. The opening track *Strange Brew* was co-written by Eric, Felix Pappalardi and his wife Gail Collins, (who was later to shoot him dead in a domestic argument). Adapted from a traditional song, formerly included in the Cream set, *Lawdy Mama*, the song was a stated tribute to Albert King, to the point where the solo bore an uncanny resemblance to King's own *Crosscut Saw*. It set the tone for the whole of Clapton's playing on the album, an amalgam of heavy blues guitar and Hendrix inspired electronic guitar effects, primarily wah wah pedal, but also greater use of fuzz tone and reverb.

Clapton had periodically used fuzz boxes over the years, but the wah wah pedal offered infinitely greater possibilities. Introduced in late 1966 and first heard on record when Hendrix used it on *Burning Of The Midnight Lamp*. The movement of the pedal by the guitarist's foot, electronically recreated the sound of the tone controls on the guitar being switched from full bass to full treble each time the foot pedal moved up and down once. By giving a considerable boost to the volume in the treble position, the wah wah also assisted sustain. At the time, Clapton revealed other factors contributing to the changing sound and style of his playing. Of debatable significance, was the removal of the covers from the pick-ups of his Les Paul. But he did change his strings. Earlier in his career, it was said he substituted a 5th string for a 6th, and 4th for a 3rd and so on, using a banjo string as top E. Now he was using Clifford Essex light guage strings, realising as many had, that it was easier to bend a light string, but discovering later, that slightly heavier strings were preferable, because their tone quality was superior. Clapton brought this constellation of innovations to bear on *Disraeli Gears*, most noticeably on *Tales Of Brave Ulysses*, co-written by Eric and Martin Sharp as a celebration of the Greek Islands, which featured wah wah but also on *Sunshine Of Your Love*, Bruce/Brown's hypnotic rock classic largely responsible for fixing the ostinato bass figure or "riff" into the bedrock of the heavy metal vocabulary and *We're Going Wrong* written by Jack Bruce, based on the fade-out to *Summertime* from *Porgy And Bess*.[39] Of the less famous songs, this one was a killer. Ginger sent tom tom patterns tumbling across his kit against a simple chord figure, with Jack's vocals at their most poignant and dramatic. Then quite late in the song, Eric delivered a devastating configuration of plaintive distorted notes, hanging in the air to haunt the soul like a bitter memory. A realisation of the guitarist as poet. *SWLABR* (*She Walks Like A Bearded Rainbow*), was another Bruce/Brown composition with a fuzz tone solo, while *Take It Back* and *Outside Woman Blues* were both straight blues tracks; Clapton's solo on the latter the more memorable for its timing. *World Of Pain* was written by Felix about a tree in his back garden, while *Dance The Night Away* was an elegant, hard driving tribute to the Byrds, complete with jangling mandolinesque West Coast 12-string electric guitar, reminiscent of *Mr. Tambourine Man*. Ginger, unfortunately, did not sustain the promise of *Sweet Wine* with *Blue Condition*, on which he sang the lead vocal. The most dispensable track, however, whose inclusion defies logic, was a horrible pre-Chas and Dave bar-room dirge called *Mother's Lament*. But that aside, it was a marvellous album, full of excellent songs, shot through with some uplifting guitar work – licks to make the heart sing.

As well as writing lyrics, Martin Sharp designed the day-glo cover for *Disraeli Gears*, the complexities of which proved a nightmare for Hamish Grimes who had to produce the finished cover. By then Grimes was working for Paragon, the public relations arm of Polydor UK and he was also responsible for the design and production of the *Fresh Cream* cover. Sharp went on to work for the underground magazine *Oz*, and design rock posters like the famous multi-coloured 'Hendrix Explosion' poster.

*Disraeli Gears* was a symbol of the artistic self-consciousness of the mid-Sixties, psychedelic mixed media initiative where talented musicians working in modern idioms smashed the concept of an inimitable synonymity between popular music and chart muzak. They identified with romantic artists of all creative genres – and *Disraeli Gears*, a pop/rock record, was the result of a combined effort of musicians, a poet and an artist.

The album was not released until November 1967, but *Strange Brew/ Tales Of Brave Ulysses* came out as a single in June accompanied by a Top Of The Pops promotion, this time dressed as Vikings (or it may have been monks!), but the song did not do as well as *I Feel Free* reaching only number 17 in the chart.

Cream came back to Britain enthusing over their American experience, especially the attitude of American studio personnel. So fulsome was their praise, that by the end of an interview given to *Beat Instrumental* on the subject, CREAM: AMERICAN BUG? there was a hint of desperation on the part of the interviewer at finding any reason why they bothered to come back at all. "The Cream liked the States; they liked the studios and the musicians. But the fans? Says Eric Clapton, 'they like pop. They aren't as appreciative as the blues fans in Britain, although they have the music right under their noses'. So as long as Clapton loves his blues, it seems that Cream will stay with the British scene".[40]

Certainly Cream were well received wherever they played and on their night they were matchless. At the back were ranked the banks of Marshall amps and speakers, their red lights glowing in the gloom like the back drop of a science fiction movie. Clapton's 50-watt Marshall amp and 4 × 12 speaker cabinet of John Mayall days, had now given way to a 100-watt treble stack with a split lead from the guitar to each amp. In front, stood Ginger's double Ludwig kit, the engine room of Cream, from which he powered the band remorselessly. To the left of the stage, Jack Bruce, head cocked to one side as he delivered one of the most distinctive vocal sounds in rock, a driven searing wail that floated above the immense sound and to the right, Eric Clapton, fine-tuning Cream's rhythm machine, a picture not only of musical, but sartorial elegance as well, wearing the mantle of the fashion conscious rock star. From the earliest days of Cream, he dispensed with the blues credibility outfit of denims and T-shirt – Clapton now hardly ever appeared in the same gear twice. As an early devotee of the military jacket, Clapton was a trendsetter in the psychedelic fashion movement, spearheaded by the Victorian and military extravagances of boutiques like "I Was Lord Kitchener's Valet", purveyors of sharp threads to the rich and famous. Cream concerts became a sea of military jackets. Like Bowie audiences later on, a Cream audience would have any number of Clapton clones in its midst. Eric's attire created a lot of interest and many followed his ideas. Even his guitar caught the mood of the times. Towards the end of 1966, his first Les Paul was stolen and one of its replacements was a stunning multi-coloured Gibson Standard (and not a Special as often stated). The guitar was a Series I model made between 1961–1965, incorporating two humbucking pickups as on the Les Paul model. A small bodied, double cutaway guitar, it was designed to replace the Les Paul which had been discontinued in 1960 due to poor sales. But almost entirely due to Eric's patronage, Gibson were able to re-issue the Les Paul in late 1966. Although wrongly dubbed a Gibson Special, Eric's guitar *was* special, because it had been custom painted by two Dutch designers, Simon and Marijke (pronounced Mar-i-yika), who went under the name of the Fool. Beatle protégés, they were responsible for the mural outside the Apple emporium, the painting of Lennon's piano and other Beatle *objets d'art*. Eric later gave the guitar to Todd Rundgren. Virtually in bits, Rundgren rebuilt and used it.

But more than once in Britain, the sheer inappropriateness of the venue mitigated against Cream giving of their best. In May, they played the Oxford University ball. Many of the rock fraternity were there, including Pete Brown. "Cream played at some ridiculous time. Nobody was listening. All the Hooray Harrys were out of their skull and had turned into pumpkins by then. But in front of about nine people, they played all the songs like *Dance The Night Away*, rather than the big show pieces, which they'd never done before and never did again". The 'show' over, Cream set about leaving their mark on the halls of academia. Ginger rode a bike through the bar scattering the dinner jackets to the four winds. Jack left a bucket of something disgusting in the Dean's office and when the floodlights were turned on outside, a well known perm was caught enjoying the fruits of passion on the lawn with a nubile student.

*Melody Maker* fans showed a more conventional appreciation of Clapton's talents when they voted him top British musician, the first time he had won a poll outright; Cream were voted fourth group, a good showing behind bands like the Beatles and Jimi Hendrix Experience, considering the comparative paucity of Cream's chart success to date. They topped the bill at the Windsor Festival in front of 20,000 cheering fans, but they were really only marking time during the summer of 1967 while Stigwood was arranging their first proper American tour. It was a dangerous time for Cream. During these few months they began to reflect on their achievements so far; average chart successes, still basically a ballroom and blues club cult band, with one disastrous American visit behind them and no reason to believe that the next one would be any better. There was some serious talk of breaking up the band altogether.

How wrong they were about their American reception became clear on the opening night of the tour at Bill Graham's Fillmore West in San Francisco, August 22nd 1967. The place was packed to the rafters. Cream got into their set, but soon found they were running out of numbers for encores. Up to then, the playing times of the songs performed on stage corresponded fairly closely to the performance times on record, but the audience was screaming for more. "The audience we had that night was the best we ever had – fantastic. They really appreciated what we were doing. That was the first time that we started to play the really extended things. We were more together and had a good climatic repertoire. It was at the Fillmore that we began to get a really strong reaction".[41] The last threads of reservation that Eric had expressed about America had snapped. The fans loved them and their music. The Fillmore was sold out for five straight nights, at the end of which Bill Graham gave each band member a gold watch. They could not have timed it more perfectly. San Francisco in the summer/fall of 1967 playing innovative, mind blowing heavy psychedelic blues, which had no American counterpart within light years – the right music in the right place at the right time. When everyone was looking for the ultimate head trip, they found they could get it from three guys playing extended, improvised rock music with such power and passion as to leave audiences physically and spiritually drained. There was the musical trip as Cream blew hard against each other on stage, Clapton being driven from behind by Baker and Bruce, as he raced at the head of the melody. The Jimi Hendrix Experience by contrast, was led from the front, Hendrix pulling and goading his musicians to follow, daring them to compete.

Cream reacted to one another and the audience reacted to the sparks flying on stage. And then there was the drug trip, the acid scene which affected the music and everyone involved, both on the stage and amongst a large section of the audience. The tour was extended to October 15th as they repeated their triumphs across the Continent and all three members of the band agreed with hindsight, that this tour produced some of Cream's finest moments. Their power of invention was at its peak so that occasionally they played more than one version of a number in the same set. So varied was their approach the audiences hardly noticed but this was also an indication of how shallow was their reservoir of material.

Cream flew back to England but almost immediately on landing, turned round and flew back again for an extraordinary 'one-off' gig. A business magnate had asked his daughter who she wanted to play at her 'coming-out' party and she said Cream. So for some vast amount of money, Cream it was.

*Disraeli Gears* was released in November. It reached number five in the UK album charts, but coming on the heels of a successful US tour, it did one better in the American charts, reaching number four. Their acceptance in America turned their musical thinking around and, in particular, the deliberate policy of making singles specifically for the charts. Clapton felt most strongly about this and in one of the first interviews he gave on his return, he declared Cream's war on singles. "To get any good music in a space of two or three minutes requires working to a formula and that part of the pop scene really leaves me cold. I hate all that rushing around to get a hit. The whole music scene in Britain is ruled by the charts and people are brainwashed into thinking that the number one record represents the best music available".[42] When asked what the Cream management had to say about such an iconclastic outburst, Eric briskly replied, "our management has come to realise that unless we are allowed to do what we want to do, we can kick up a bigger stink about it than them". And true to their word, Cream released no more singles, other than those culled from albums by the record company.

Cream continued to work through the winter of 1967, including a TV spectacular in Holland and a memorable concert at Brian Epstein's Savile Theatre, London, in January 1968. Supported by the Bonzo Dog Doo Dah Band, a successful amalgam of music and bizarre humour, Cream put on a champagne performance. Eric was well into being a rock star and in a rare display of visual presentation, suspended his guitar on a chain hung from the ceiling and swung it backwards and forwards to get feedback. It was a curious, slightly perverse gesture to those with elitist views about music, who regarded him still as a great blues crusader – Clapton's way of staying one jump ahead of public opinion by throwing up a smokescreen of confusion.

Cream's second tour of America started in February 1968 and lasted until mid-July – five and a half months of one-nighters – no British band had ever embarked on such a colossal touring programme before, nor earned so much money. Again they kicked off at the Fillmore West in San Francisco. There were two thousand people inside, some freaking out, some sitting cross-legged on the floor. At the back were smart college students, evening suits and storm troopers come to see the hippy oiks at play. Electric Flag were the support band and a light show danced across the walls. "Cream trickled on to the stage in bright shirts and piped clashing pants. The gods were there and as the first number exploded into the auditorium, it was as though we were witnessing the explosion of a musical megaton bomb . . . a musical thrill of rare vintage . . . (the music) burned so much, that when at last the Cream retired from the stage, there could have been no one who had not felt some message from a realm beyond normal understanding".[43]

> "There were no antics – no planned trouser splitting from Eric Clapton, Ginger Baker or Jack Bruce, just great cataleptic hunks cut from the aged blues and pummelled out, slit up, re-shaped and thoroughly examined by violent guitars and drums".

Not all the publicity was quite so welcome. On 20th March, Clapton was busted on a marijuana charge at a house in Topanga Canyon, North Hollywood, along with three members of Buffalo Springfield – Neil Young, Richie Furay and Jim Messina. Clapton got off but not before spending a night in jail. All four got stripped and hosed down and Neil Young had an epileptic fit. Wearing prison denims, but still in pink boots, Clapton was slammed up with three Black Panthers, who he had a hard job convincing that he was a blues guitarist interested in American black music.

Nor was the American music press unanimous in its acclaim for the band. Jon Landau from Rolling Stone, for example, took a different line from his colleagues. There was no question that he admired Cream, and his was the first major interview in the American rock press with Clapton during May 1968. Clapton unfavourably compared the British music scene with that in America, complaining that in England there was too much jealousy among musicians and not enough encouragement, at the same time reiterating his negative feelings towards the record charts. He was also aware that because he was a world famous musician, he was bound to be misquoted and misinterpreted, (he speculated that this very interview would be headlined somewhere 'Clapton slams England') and that people expected him both to exercise responsibility because of his power to influence, *and* be an open book for their probings – something he has always resented. "You don't have to be that intelligent to play music; you don't have to have moral responsibility. There's no reason why they (musicians) should have, they're only there to play music and people should leave them like that. Because so much responsibility is attached, it's too much, a drag, too much public opinion placed on a musician . . . if they dig my music, that's great, but they don't have to know what's going on in my head".[44]

The same issue of Rolling Stone that carried the Clapton interview also featured a concert review and analysis of Cream by Jon Landau. Much of what he wrote should be regarded as a deliberate antidote to the eulogies of other rock journalists, rather than an attack on the integrity of band. However, in the process he laid bare the truth of where Cream were at by May 1968 – a band that had lost their enthusiasm after playing the same songs night after night for months on end.

"Cream has been called a jazz group. They are not. They are a blues band and a rock band. Clapton is a master of the blues clichés of all of the post World War II blues guitarists, particularly B.B. King and Albert King. And he didn't play a note that wasn't blues during the course of the concert . . . the specific reason why I discount Cream as jazz is this; in jazz, the focus is always on improvisation. Improvisation means the creation of new musical ideas spontaneously. It does not mean stringing together pieces and phrases of already learned musical ideas. A rock guitarist who improvises in the manner of a jazzman is Larry Coryell. Clapton's problem is that while he has a vast creative potential, at this time he hasn't begun to fulfil it. He is a virtuoso at performing other people's ideas".[45] Pretty damning stuff and not a little unfair. Despite the jazz backgrounds of Jack Bruce and Ginger Baker, Cream never regarded itself as a jazz group, nor did Clapton claim himself as an original – he always honoured his sources. To imply that improvisation is created in some kind of discreet vacuum with no reference points, or to deny improvisation in a rock rather than a jazz context, was dubious and Landau went right off the rails in suggesting that Larry Coryell was basically a rock guitarist. However, his final comments on Cream as a big scale touring band hit the nail right on the head.

"Cream live as on record, are clearly in a transitional stage. Having mastered the rudiments of their instruments, they are rapidly approaching the point where they have to ask themselves where they want to go with it. Currently, their live style and their record style, reveals both their talent and their aimlessness. The whole is not equal to its parts. And the greatest pitfall that stands before them, is that an over-accepting audience in the United States will lull them into a complacency in which they increase their virtuosity at the expense of their own involvement. It would not be difficult for a group of this calibre to start making it all sound like scales. Yet the Cream, even now, are so much more than simple masters of their instruments. When they get over their virtuosity hang up, we may really see something. At the moment they're just warming up".[46]

In fact Cream was ahead of Landau all the way. Easy adulation, boredom, fatigue and the resurrection of the old Bruce-Baker conflict had all pushed Eric to decide that he had had enough and being called a master of clichés was the final nail in the coffin. If America made them, it also broke them. The egos of all three musicians rose to the surface and they began to play for themselves as individuals rather than as a group to the point where, on one occasion, Eric stopped playing and the others did not even notice. They were never great friends socially, so when they got tired of the music they called it a day.

While the American tour was on, however, rumours of a split were strenuously denied, even though Clapton had told Chris Welch in May and Chris had sat on the news as requested. By July, it was confirmed, followed up with news of a farewell tour of America, claimed as an act of faith for those American fans who had not seen them, but in truth a purely money-making exercise. This was shown by the crumbs thrown from the table of Mammon to British fans – just one solitary concert. This was a blow to the hordes of new Cream fans, many of whom had never seen the band at all, and vitriolic letters along the lines of "thanks for the kick in the teeth, lads", landed in the offices of the British rock press.

By way of mollification, a double album, *Wheels Of Fire* was released in August, which went gold in America even before it was shipped. Recorded half in the studio and half live, it was in many respects Cream's definitive album, a panoramic view of all their strengths and weaknesses. The studio album was recorded in New York and the whole package was not unlike the Beatles double white album, an aggregate of individual effort rather than a rounded and fully integrated co-operative venture. Bruce/Brown songs dominated the studio album. They managed to keep their songwriting partnership together despite the arduous touring schedule and four out of the seven original numbers were theirs including two Cream classics, *White Room* and *Politician*. Ginger's name was attached to the other three, *Passing The Time*, *Pressed Rat And Warthog* (based on Vaughan Williams' *Cutty Wren*) and *Those Were The Days*. The music for all these was composed by a British *avant-garde* musician, Mike Taylor, a true genius, who deserves a book of his own. He wrote literally hundred of pieces of music for all types and combinations of jazz instrumentation, including a complete suite for percussion and horns. But he was a tortured spirit obsessively introverted, and racked by a legion of personal problems. For a time he lived with drummer Jon Hiseman and during this time tried to set fire to his music, some of which Jon managed to rescue from the flames, but life conspired to overwhelm Mike and he drowned himself in the sea in 1969.

Significantly, Eric contributed no material and left all the lead vocals on the studio album to Jack, coming to the fore primarily on the two blues standards *Born Under A Bad Sign* written for Albert King by Booker T. Jones and Howlin' Wolf's *Sitting On Top Of The World*. Overall, Clapton had revised his approach, dispensing with 'woman tone' and going for a harder edged feel. Wah-wah featured on *White Room*, a song similar in construction to *Tales Of Brave Ulysses*, although his solo was faded out just as he got underway, and he cut loose with ferocious power on *Those Were The Days* and *Deserted Cities Of The Heart*, the latter solo ringing with the metallic vibrancy of a sitar complete with bottom string drone. On *Politician*, one of the few basic guitar/bass/drums tracks on a heavily overdubbed album, Clapton nevertheless played two solos which were both double-tracked, creating a miasmic haze of sound melding with Jack's rumbling Gibson bass. All the original material was of a high standard, even the much criticised *Pressed Rat And Warthog* – a slight song but nonetheless endearing.

Yet good though those songs were, they were eclipsed by the tracks on the live album, recorded during Cream's halcyon days on the first American tour. Clapton came into his own, particularly on the astonishing six minute version of Robert Johnson's *Crossroads*, prompting John Peel to comment as he introduced the track on his radio programme, "If you thought Eric Clapton was human, you'd better listen to this". His vocal and guitar work were outstanding – freed from the constraints of the four minute studio song, Clapton's playing was positively manic. Unlike Beck or

Hendrix, Clapton has never been that bothered about electronic experimentation, his forte being the way he actually handles the guitar and the fluid emotionalism of his playing which was perfectly demonstrated on *Crossroads* (and also on the live version of *I'm So Glad* from *Goodbye*). With Willie Dixon's *Spoonful*, he took the audience on an apocalyptic journey of nearly seventeen minutes duration. It was a classic example of Cream's neocontrapuntal approach, after the basic harmony and rhythmic patterns of the song were established, *Spoonful* launched into free improvisation, almost breaking the link with the main theme. It was a journey however, during which he got rather lost, when the links were at their weakest before he clawed his way back.

Clapton was side three. Bruce and Baker shared side four, six minutes of Jack's *Traintime* and then straight into Ginger's *magnum opus, Toad*. A wondrous spectacle live with Baker such a frenzied blur of action but, although he was a very lyrical drummer who could weave intricate percussive patterns through pulsating combinations of triplets, ruffs, paradiddles and flams, *Toad* does not stand up to repeated listenings whereas his recorded solos with Graham Bond and Blind Faith, do.

At the same time as *Wheels Of Fire* was being recorded, Cream undertook a curious session for a film soundtrack, *The Savage Seven*, recording two tracks, one of which *Anyone For Tennis?*, was released as a single. Written by Eric and Martin Sharp, it was a vague stab at social commentary, sung and played by Eric on acoustic guitar. An early stereo single, it appeared in May 1968 with *Pressed Rat And Warthog* on the B-side. It only reached number 40 in the UK chart and not even the top sixty in America. Eric hated it as soon as he'd done it but, almost inconceivably, there is a rumour that buried in Atlantic's vaults somewhere is a twenty-minute version recorded on 15th June 1968 at the Ak-Sar-Ben Coliseum, Omaha.

While British fans were busy voting Cream into every available top slot in the music polls both as a band and as individual instrumentalists, (Clapton topped the *Melody Maker* poll in the British and World musician section) a shocked music world learned why they had decided to call it a day. Unlike so many bands since who have trudged on regardless, Cream quit while they were ahead, but the other side of the story, was that they now had different ideas as to what they wanted to play. Jack wanted to move more into a jazz-oriented environment, while Eric was listening to Bob Dylan and his musicians – the Band.

In an interview given at his flat to Chris Welch, Eric played him a tape of Dylan and the Band which eventually emerged as *The Basement Tapes*. "I've got another tape here of Bob Dylan's band. I think this music will influence a lot of people. Everybody I have played it to has flipped. The band is releasing an album called *Music From Big Pink* by the group. Since I heard all this stuff, all my values have changed. I think it has probably influenced me".[47]

But there was still a final tour to do. Meeting again after a break of nearly three months, was tense and at the first rehearsal, they ended up in opposite corners of the studio staring at the floor. Yet even at this late stage, when the band was officially dead, they turned in some inspirational performances. In the run-up to the tour which began in Oakland during the first week of October, *Sunshine Of Your Love/SWALBR* was released. It fared much better in America than in Britain, reaching number 5 thanks to some very heavy regional support, especially in the Cleveland area. After Oakland they visited fourteen American cities, winding up at Madison Square Garden on November 2nd and Baltimore the next day. They earned $25,000 a night and the tour grossed more than half a million dollars. Twenty-two thousand people packed the Garden to see Cream presented with the first ever platinum disc for selling two million dollars worth of *Wheels Of Fire*, number one in America and number three in the UK. The quarterly royalty cheque that went out from Atlantic in October, was in excess of $400,000. Small wonder that grown men wept into their wallets when Cream walked off an American stage for the last time.

Cream played two shows in London at the Royal Albert Hall on 26th October, both of which were sold out within two hours of the box office opening. Two then unknown bands, played support, Yes (doing extracts from West Side Story) and Taste, but for the audience they were merely a tedious interlude. John Peel announced "Cream" and the walls came in – one of the most emotional concerts of the Sixties in Britain. Many just sat there dazed, while Cream played, unable to believe they were actually seeing their distant heroes in the flesh.

For the first show, Eric used a rare limited edition 1963 Gibson Firebird, produced to try and appeal to a larger market than its 1958 predecessor, the Explorer. But for the second and best show, he switched to his favourite Gibson ES335TDC. In the old Rooster days, Clapton's relatively cheap Kay Red Devil guitar was, whether consciously or not, a copy of Gibson ES335-TDC. Now, one of the finest guitarists in the world, he could afford any guitar he wanted. Jon Cott of Rolling Stone reviewed that second show under the headline GOD SAVE THE CREAM.

"What was exhilarating about the sell-out farewell concerts was each member of the group's affirmation of his special gifts – Bruce's subtle whirlwind bass figurations. (Bruce's bass technique is as refreshing and perverse as it is because he plays bass on lead guitar – perhaps this is one reason why the group broke up), Baker's plateaued drum sectionings and textural clarifications, and Clapton's Apollonian elegance and control.

Clapton had his hair short, clean shaven; Baker and Bruce looked rested. But I suppose these were merely physical manifestations of the musical clarity. Each musical line was almost hyperesthetically precise (this especially holds for Baker's drumming), and each line fitted tightly against the other – parallel lines.

Many persons missed that raunchiness and fuzziness of effect which Cream often used to express – a strained indulgence, I thought. What revealed itself at Albert Hall was the poised quality of the performance, the detachment, the structure looked down upon from the stars – a self-begotten music (Cream is/was three stars) whose brilliance seemed born of itself without labour, for everything seemed effortless.[48]

The atmosphere was charged, the audience adoring and the music simply stunning. Cream was showered with confetti and cries for certain songs in one part of the auditorium were answered by shouts from another "play your own choice". And then, three encores later, they were gone. Cream seemed genuinely surprised at the audience reaction, Clapton uttering the immortal words, "I didn't think anybody would remember us", and it momentarily almost changed their minds about breaking up, although it was obviously too late for that to be seriously considered.[49]

That Cream found hidden depths was demonstrated on their last official album as a working outfit, appropriately titled *Goodbye*. A short album, two thirds of it was live, taken from their final US tour. Clapton's playing on the live tracks was nothing short of a revelation, but listening to these tracks is to realise the part played by Jack and Ginger in generating much of that inspiration. It comes over most clearly on live tracks, because there is no cushioning overdubbing. Clapton was on his own and one suspects that he has never worked so hard in performance before or since. On *I'm So Glad*, Ginger was totally relentless. As licks streamed from Clapton's fingers like running water, came punishing cymbal accents, driving snare patterns and bass drums that sounded like twenty-one gun salutes. *Politician* was more subdued but also more menacing and shadowy, relying on heavy bass rather than a studio rhythm sound and on *Sitting On Top Of The World* with Ginger's pressed snare rolls betraying his jazz roots, Eric turned in one of his finest straight blues solos since *Have You Heard?* Of the studio tracks, *Doing That Scrapyard Thing*, was a good Bruce/Brown song, although Jack later implied it was something of a hastily composed filler, while Ginger redeemed all past failings with *What A Bringdown*. But the most significant song on the album was *Badge*, an uncharacteristically short song written by Eric and George Harrison, whose pseudonym of, Angelo Mysterioso was one of rock's worst kept secrets. Beautifully sung by Eric, it contained Harrison's favourite phrase and was supposed to be a nod towards Eric's new found enthusiasm for the Band, although its brevity was the only real manifestation of that.

Eric and George had grown quite close since the acid summer of '67, playing together in a number of diverse situations – on Jackie Lomax's *Is This What You Want* album with Nicky Hopkins, Ringo Starr and Eddie Clayton (aka Eric Clapton) and George's track on the double white album, *While My Guitar Gently Weeps* and the soundtrack of his film *Wonderwall*. It was probably Harrison's sortie into the film world that prompted Eric to make loud pronouncements that he too, would be moving into films as his next project. But neither that, nor any concrete musical involvement with Harrison ever came to fruition.

*Goodbye* was released in March 1969, topping the charts on both sides of the Atlantic, staying in the UK top ten for thirteen weeks, ironically Cream's best chart performance. Another single *White Room/Those Were The Days*, had been released in January, reaching number 6 in America, but *Badge* was a surprising and inexplicable flop. *Crossroads*, too, was released as a single, but only in America. It might have been *Goodbye* as far as Cream were concerned, but the record company had other ideas. The goose that laid so many golden eggs was not to be killed off so easily. By November 1969, there was *Best Of Cream*, to be followed by two live albums in the Seventies and a host of repackages and compilations, plus a boxed set of the whole shooting match. (For further details, see discography).

Cream made a massive contribution to the acceptance of rock as a legitimate musical form, the first band to find major success *because* of their musicianship, rather than in spite of it. Each member of Cream was regarded as the finest exponent of their instrument, Baker and Bruce as important in the history of rock drumming and bass playing as Eric Clapton was to guitar playing. They introduced Miles Davis to the possibilities of utilising rock configurations in a jazz context and numbered Leonard Bernstein and Stravinsky among their admirers. Cream also paved the way for Jimi Hendrix and he paid his own tribute during his appearance on the Lulu Show on 7th January 1969. Halfway through *Hey Joe*, he suddenly announced *Sunshine Of Your Love*, while the studio manager was making frantic throat cutting gestures, because Hendrix was over running and there would be no time for Lulu's closing number. Jimi ignored him.

Cream changed the way rock sounded, influencing the genre up to the mid-Seventies, an influence some critics thought was baleful, but Cream cannot be held responsible for so much of the talentless, dunderhead, stodge-rock that followed in the wake of their success.

Breaking up when they did ensured the band's legendary status. The psychological impact of Cream was possibly even greater than their musical achievement, shaking the Sixties both physically and spiritually and reverberating well into the next decade. If anything was negative about Cream's success, it was the effect it had on the subsequent careers of Eric and Jack, in particular. Both have spent much of their time living down the Cream saga and Eric has been especially vitriolic – denying that Cream ever produced much of value and proclaiming how much of a con the enterprise became, relegating the whole experience to "a few good licks". While there was much truth in this, that Cream did lose its way eventually in a labyrinth of pointless and boring improvisation, Clapton overstated the case in his subsequent revelations to Steve Turner and others. Many fans were upset at Clapton's jibes towards music they remembered as blown from the heart and guts before the terms "heavy" had been coined, striking them from stage and hi-fi in the same places.

Cream could have named their own price to reform and offers have been made to them on many occasions since – to their credit, they have always refused. Blind Faith apart, none of them ever worked together again, meetings have been rare and not always friendly. But they have played together on at least one occasion. At Eric's wedding reception in 1979, a stage was set up in the grounds of Hurtwood Edge and processions of musicians came up to jam together. As midnight approached, just three musicians found themselves together on stage – Eric, Jack and Ginger.

But Alan Aldridge's cover for the *Goodbye* album said it all, from the title to the vaudeville farewell cover shot (choreography courtesy of Lionel Blair) and the track listing engraved on the tombstones inside. And what Shakespeare wrote could have been inscribed on any tombstone by way of epitaph for Cream –

Take pains; be perfit; adieu.

# CHAPTER FIVE
# From Blind Faith
# To Blind Faith

The Cream experience had shown Eric in glorious technicolor, what being a rock star was all about. Here were social battles, arduous touring, business problems, police hassles, fanatical adulation, a probing and fickle press, and in Eric's case, audience expectation of endless soloing night after night, until he didn't really know whether he was coming or going. In less than two years, he had gone from sleeping on people's floors and travelling in freezing bandwagons to being the underground's first superstar. A cult hero even before Cream, Eric was more in the limelight than Jack or Ginger, adored by women for his 'little boy lost' good looks, idolised by legions of males and constantly photographed for serious music magazines and 'teenybopper' pop fanzines alike. The audience projected its own personal fantasies onto him as a figure of power and fascination and he became an urban cowboy with his guitar as his gun or a gladiator in the rock arena.

All this responsibility for somebody who was at heart rather shy and unsure of himself or his talent was rather overwhelming and so, availing himself of his funds, he spent around forty thousand pounds on a hundred-year-old mansion of Moorish design called Hurtwood Edge, set deep in the Surrey stockbroker belt in its own spacious grounds. "It's my security against everything and everyone".[50] With its purchase, Clapton made a conscious decision to distance himself not only from the press and the fans, but also from the voracious 'proto-audience' that populate the rock scene, the often venomous pack of 'liggers' and hangers-on, keen to bathe in the reflected glory of a fashionable personality. They herded round Hendrix and thought they were doing him a big favour by shoving tabs of acid down his throat. But while he wanted to be, Eric was better protected and like George Harrison, managed to secure for himself (apart from a big car) some tangible isolation, a quasi-fortress to keep out undesirables, although you never can be sure in what form they will come.

> "I've changed a lot through living in America. I've tended to withdraw from making contact with people. I'm harder to get to know than I was a few years ago. I don't trust people so readily".[51]

For two short months, from December 1968 to February 1969, Eric kept a low profile. His only semi-public appearance was on 11th December at Intertel Studios, Wembley in North London, for the recording of the Rolling Stones' Rock'n'Roll Circus, meant for television but never shown. Apart from Eric and the rest of Cream, Jagger had brought together the Who, Jethro Tull, Taj Mahal, Mitch Mitchell, Led Zeppelin, Buffalo Springfield and Captain Beefheart. Lennon, Clapton and Richard played together on *Yer Blues*, Eric's characteristic and masterful composure shining through, as he played with clarity and precision. Mick and Eric did *Peggy Sue* and Cream played an instrumental plus a song called *Everybody*, all of which show up on various pirate recordings that have surfaced since. Asked by somebody what he was going to do next, Eric quipped, "I don't know. Probably join John Mayall's band". Neither could he have known that the rock'n'roll circus lurking around the corner would make this one look like a sideshow at a church bazaar.

This omen about a group of star musicians coming together in an artificially created environment to try and make music, was further reinforced in March 1969, when Eric was invited to attend a 'super-session', the brainchild of two film makers, Tom Parkinson and John Crome, involved in the Stones project and the filming of Hendrix at the Albert Hall. They brought together an array of star talent from blues, rock and jazz, including Roland Kirk, Jack Bruce, Buddy Guy, Buddy Miles, Stephen Stills, Jon Hiseman, Dick Heckstall-Smith, the Modern Jazz Quartet and Led Zeppelin, for band and jam sessions filmed over two days at a disused lino factory in Staines, west of London. Jimi Hendrix was invited, but missed the plane. On the second day, around 8.50 p.m. Eric crept in quietly and asked someone rather nervously for a cigarette. At 9.10 Clapton, Kirk, Hiseman, Heckstall-Smith, Jack Bruce, Vernon Martin (string bass) and Ron Burton (organ), took to the stage. Eric began cautiously and was rather thrown by Kirk's intro count of "one, two, one, two, three, four" for a blues number, but that just showed the differences in their musical upbringing. Eric soon settled into a groove of tasteful, understated playing, using a Gibson Firebird. Later on in the evening, he jammed with Buddy Guy and Jack Bruce on organ. Inevitably a bootleg exists, but the film has been rarely seen.

In truth, these sort of sessions which proliferated at the time, were a form of musical nihililism based on a belief that if you put brilliant musicians in the same room together, then brilliant music will emerge. But with no natural growth of ideas, all you got was a scrabbling around for common denominator reference points, invariably the messy 12-bar blues jam which could, in theory, go on for days. The message of the Stones show was its title; the message of the super-session was the idea itself and the degeneration into directionless jamming.

In private, Eric had been working on some ideas with Stevie Winwood, now free of commitments since the break up of Traffic. Winwood stayed with Clapton at Hurtwood Edge over Christmas 1968 and they just played together for hours on end. Only in February, did Eric begin to emerge from his self-imposed exile to hint at possible future developments. Yet there was still no commitment to forming a band, no other musicians were officially involved, nor was it clear from public pronouncements who they might be. "If I do a record with Stevie or form a group with him, I'm kinda stuck for a rhythm section and my immediate reaction would be to call up Ginger and Jack, because they are the only two I'm familiar with (but Steve) might want to call up Jim Capaldi, Chris Woods, etc., so it's a problem".[52] Everything was vague; Eric even suggested that any new band might be shortlived, in order for Cream to reform with Stevie Winwood. But if plans for the future were hazy, coming to terms with success was clearly a continuing problem, not only as a guitarist, but also as a celebrity in whom people were interested. Opposed to the cult of personality that had built up around him, he maintained that just being a good guitarist was not enough to warrant attention. "I expect this year to really drop out of it completely, publicity wise, press wise".[53] Wanting to go out and play without attracting undue attention, Clapton has been accused of being unrealistic and naive – but one earlier incident at least gave a hint of the possible, even though it also demonstrated the problem. At the Kempton Park Festival in the summer of 1968, after Cream had returned from the States, Ginger played with an ailing Phil Seaman, his mentor and inspiration, to try and revive the jazz drummer's flagging career. During their set, Eric appeared at the side of the stage, sidled on, plugged in and started playing. For a good while nobody in the audience recognised him, nor even those on and around the stage, as he leant against the stage rigging, cigarette in mouth. A few comments were passed around about the nice guitar player, then as the realisation dawned, tremendous cheers and mass clapping rent the air – applause for the man, rather than the music.

By April 1969, Ginger Baker had been added to the line-up of the as yet, unnamed band, rehearsing at Winwood's Berkshire cottage, keeping Eric to his promise that he would be included in Eric's future projects. While the rumours and speculations were building up, Eric was trying to keep it all cool, over-compensating through expression of his own self effacement. "I feel as if I've achieved nothing. I've got miles and miles to go . . . I'm very surprised I've got a reputation. You assume people have forgotten you, then you get a supershow and get surprised at how much people expect of you. I do worry a lot about this. I don't know if my playing keeps up with the image. I do my best. I'm happy if I've got a little riff to play. I don't see myself as a great solo guitarist – that's not my bag – that's Jimi's".[54]

In this and other reports about the prospective new collaboration, no clearly defined musical policy was apparent: Eric was listening to Buddy Holly records, two Dylan songs were laid down in the studio (but were never released or performed) and they hadn't even found a bass player. Yet the article concluded "offers for the band are already said to be topping the Cream's financial record". The business machine was already rolling, making the chosen name of Blind Faith, redolent with irony, almost too obvious, and as far as the musicians were concerned, whether they realised it or not, control of the band was out of their hands. America was buying blind, purely on the strength of the individual reputations. The only unknown quantity was the choice of bass player, Ric Grech from Family, who played on their first two (and best) albums. And following on from 'Group's Group' and 'Supersession' came 'Supergroup' for which a contrite Chris Welch was mainly responsible: "I suppose it was my fault really for writing about supergroups and spreading it all over the front pages of *Melody Maker*. But I was just as excited as everyone and I really did think they were a supergroup". On top of all the hype surrounding a manufactured supergroup who nobody had heard or seen, Blind Faith was not a formally constituted group even in the business sense. Separate deals were concluded with the individual members and Blind Faith (like Ginger Baker's Airforce to come) had two managers, Robert Stigwood looking after the interests of Clapton through Atlantic Records, and Chris Blackwell of Island Records, working for Stevie Winwood, "not the best way to form a group. Live and learn", as Stevie said recently.[55] The circumstances of their debut gig too, had all the trappings of a rock'n' roll circus – a free concert in Hyde Park on Saturday 7th June. Put in front of a festival audience after only a few weeks rehearsal except, instead of being at the foot of the bill in front of ten thousand people, they were headlining before anything up to one-hundred-and-fifty thousand. The media build-up was relentless – nearly seven thousand people slept in the park overnight and they were greeted in the morning by bright sunshine – a perfect day for an outdoor concert. There were no crowd problems and the police kept a low profile, despite the unmistakable aromas wafting across on the light breeze. The Third Ear Band came on at 2.30, followed by the Edgar Broughton Band, the *de rigeur* Festival acoutrement, Richie Havens and an unplanned but well received appearance by Donovan, so overwhelmed at seeing this vast army of people peacefully enjoying themselves that he had to get up and sing. Then at 5 p.m. Blind Faith took to the stage, clouds of smoke from nerve calming dope drifting behind them. Clapton, in particular, was very tense and apprehensive; Baker tried to put it all in perspective by announcing at the beginning "this is the first rehearsal" – he could have said "we can't possibly live up to your expectations. We hardly know what we're doing ourselves". They were on stage for about an hour, performing Buddy Holly's *Well Alright*, a blues number *I'd Rather See You Sleeping On The Ground*, Winwood's *Sea Of Joy* and *Means To An End*. *Under My Thumb* may have been done just as an acknowledgement to the presence of Mick Jagger and Marianne Faithful (or a dig at Stig?) while *Do You What You Like* may also have been spontaneously rearranged. Someone yelled at Baker *Toad* and someone else yelled back "It's not Cream, do what you like" and that's how the song, the vehicle for extended individual soloing, was announced.

Their overall performance was not surprisingly reticent and uneasy, born out of their lack of experience as a group and the pressure of public expectation. But on an individual basis, there was much to commend in Eric's performance. He played with grace and elegance, using a Fender on stage for the first time in years, a Telecaster with a Stratocaster neck, standing tight against the amps. No more flamboyant fashion, but simple jeans and T-shirt, a reflection of his new-found rural affections at home and with Winwood at his country cottage. Baker was the only one who really broke sweat, trying to drive the band along as he had done with Cream, but it was not quite appropriate for the mainly very Traffic-oriented material. This was the obvious influence of Stevie Winwood, Blind Faith's lead vocalist and main song writer, although he never performed the leader functions that Eric hoped he would. Neither had Eric nor Ginger developed leader skills and Ric Grech was a new boy, quiet and unassuming, slotting easily into a background role in the midst of such luminaries. This was one Blind Faith's problems and grievances soon surfaced primarily involving Stevie and Ginger, possibly founded in Winwood's desire to have Jim Capaldi as the drummer instead. Rumours along these lines floated around in the weeks ahead, but rarely hit the news.

The Hyde Park gig was pleasant enough, the seeds of a fine band were there, given the opportunity for considered growth. But they were in the invidious position of having started at the top, which meant the only way was down. The press response was muted and journalists were poised to announce the Second Coming, but in the end confined themselves to images of tastefulness and restraint. Fans were less circumspect. "It was very disappointing. It seemed very much like Stevie Winwood plus a backing group. . . . Eric Clapton seemed too content to just ride along and the lack of fire on his part contributed greatly to the group's apparent lack of imagination.[56] Just what Eric was expecting the press reaction to be, was unclear, given his own awareness of the dangers of hype and his consequent apprehension, but he was nevertheless disappointed, confirming his belief since Cream days that English fans didn't really care about what he was doing. "Somehow I never feel necessary or wanted in Britain".[57] Therefore, Eric's first response as far as any British tour was concerned was "stuff that". Neither was it at the forefront of management plans for there were far richer pickings elsewhere. Right after the Hyde Park gig, Stigwood was explicit about the rationale of Blind Faith. "They are going to make a lot of money in appearance and on records and this concert was the best possible beginning they could have got. My own men filmed the whole thing. I am going to make a great deal of money out of it from film and television rights all over the world".[58]

The American tour was due to begin at the Newport Jazz Festival but it was cancelled. Instead, they found themselves in front of twenty-two thousand people at Madison Square Garden, the band coming to the stage like prize fighters. Supported by Free and Delaney and Bonnie, Blind Faith got a fifteen minute standing ovation before they had played a note. It was not a good omen from the musicians' point of view. This concert, like the rest of the tour, was an unmitigated disaster. The contractural commitments regarding the P.A. were not kept, so the sound was woefully inadequate, made worse by the constantly revolving stage which threw the sound out to different sections of the audience at different times. After paying ninety-six thousand dollars for an hour and a half show they could hardly hear, the audience staged their own performance, a riot which went on for forty-five minutes, sparked off by police brutality against those seeking bits of equipment as souvenirs. Feet and fists flew, so did bottles and coins; Stevie Winwood's electric piano was smashed and in an attempt to intervene and cool things down, Ginger got clubbed by the local constabulary. Trouble followed them around. After the Garden concert, they went to the Scene club where two groupies started fighting. Everyone joined in, including members of Sha Na Na and Blind Faith left them to it until the police arrived.

And so it went on – the Blind Faith tour of America was rock exploitation at its most crass – playing to the maximum number of people, in the shortest space of time for excessive amounts of money, in the region of twenty-five thousand dollars a show, against anything up to sixty-five per cent of the gate. This meant appearing at the largest venues in the country. After the Madison gig, Blind Faith took extra amplification with them, but often it wasn't enough. As for the music itself, some nights it was very good, other nights awful, but the band did not stretch themselves overmuch, were uneasy on stage and often strapped for material. Inconsistency of performance was common enough among bands on tour, yet this was supposed to be a SUPERGROUP – that's what the media had been telling the fans and so they expected super music every show – and they expected to be able to hear it. When they couldn't, attention were diverted and there was trouble. Much of it was caused by over enthusiastic police wading into over enthusiastic fans. At the Forum in Los Angeles, the house lights were turned on twice as police dragged fans from the auditorium. The police jumped on to the front of the stage, driving Eric back towards the stacks. Once they decided that Armageddon was not imminent, they vacated the stage leaving Blind Faith and Delaney and Bonnie to encore with a *Sunshine Of Your Love* jam. The applause was ecstatic. It was during a similar jam in Phoenix, Arizona where the worst trouble was, that Bonnie fell ten foot from the stage on to concrete and was rushed to hospital. Stevie Winwood's memories are far from fond. . . . "The show was vulgar, crude, disgusting. It lacked integrity. There were huge crowds everywhere full of mindless adulation, mostly due to Eric and Ginger's success with Cream and to a more modest extent, my own impact. However well or badly they played, it was the same, leading to a situation where we could have gone on and farted and got a response. *That* was one of the times I got so uninspired. The attitude backstage was, these people think we're great, and we'd better damn well give them something great, but it didn't help. And it wasn't the audiences' fault. We did not sound good live, due to the simple lack of experience of being a band. We'd had no natural growth and it was very evident on stage".[59]

Back in England with the tour over, there was much speculation about the future of Blind Faith which, for lack of official statements, rumbled on through the rest of 1969. Rumours of a UK tour, and a second album following the release of the first in August, came to nothing. As the focal point for media attention, Eric became the unofficial band spokesman. The management was obviously hoping for some more scrapings from the pot of gold and Ginger and Rick also wanted to keep it going, but as far as Eric (and Steve) were concerned, Blind Faith was dead. Although denying any definite split, Eric spoke of the band in the past tense, "We were pushed to the forefront without being ready for it. . . . Stevie and I before we went to America thought – we're trapped again . . . we weren't ready to do it, but we had no choice".[60] Yet, even allowing for an unscrupulous industry that can have an artist in a Rolls-Royce with six groupies draped over him one minute, and in court, hospital or the subway busking the next, there had to be a deal of complicity in the marketing of Blind Faith. The musician creates the artistic environment and the business creates the financial one; there is conflict, but also mutual interest. Rock music is a performing art and the performer needs popularity, recognition and of course money. As Stigwood made it plain from the beginning, there was a bundle to be made and the quicker they moved, the bigger the illusion created, the more everyone would make. Take the money and run.

The rush to promote Blind Faith started with the debut album. According to Ahmet Ertegun, it was hustled through because the company did not imagine that the tour would be so successful from a business point of view. If this was true, then it was corporate myopia at its most acute, to believe that American rock fans would not give an arm and a leg to see two thirds of Cream back together again. The precipitate nature of the album mitigated against Blind Faith's attempt to produce it themselves because they hardly knew what they were going to do and it almost defeated Traffic producer Jimmy Miller, drafted in to do the job. But while Blind Faith's erratic live performances and super-hyped existence have faded into dim memory, their one and only official album remains for the judgement of posterity and given such an inauspicious genesis, a totally forgettable album was on the cards. However, against all the odds, the end product did justice in large measure to the assembled talents and showed that locked away from prying notebooks, Blind Faith could deliver music of merit that remains highly listenable.

The combination of Jimmy Miller and Stevie Winwood inevitably meant music with 'Traffic' stamped all over it. Winwood did all the lead vocals, wrote three of the six songs, *Had To Cry Today*, *Can't Find My Way Home* and *Sea Of Joy*, any one of which could have appeared on a Traffic album, except that Baker's heavy rock feel would have been replaced by Capaldi funky shuffle beats. Eric played flowing, relaxed guitar, soloing with economy and understatement. Blind Faith was nowhere near as frantic as Cream and so Clapton had more time to think. "If you can be more economical when you play, you get a chance to be able to see where you can voice things and put things in, rather than just playing full out all the time".[61] He also played across a wide range, a hitherto unrevealed eclecticism: the coda sequence on *Had To Cry Today* stirring memories of Cream's studio work, acoustic guitar on *Can't Find My Way Home*, rocking lead solo on Buddy Holly's *Well Alright* and a latinised Carlos Santana feel on *Do What You Like*, only partially successful as a platform for individual soloing.

But the album's outstanding track was Eric's *Presence Of The Lord*, his first lyric, with an overtly religious theme sung with due reverence by Stevie Winwood. It was probably the nearest Blind Faith ever got to being an English version of the Band, owing something to *I Shall Be Released* on *Music From Big Pink* and a lot to Eric's new found enthusiasm for religion. The song proceeds at a stately pace, then catches its breath, moving into overdrive as Eric cuts in with a wah wah solo of such clarity and beauty, expressing so much in such a short flurry of notes that one has to believe he was inspired by the devotional nature of his lyrics. His finest wah wah solo exposition to rank with Hendrix.

The cover of the album caused more controversy for the band – a pubescent young girl around eleven years old, naked from the waist up, holding a silver aeroplane. Whether it was a crude and obvious way of boosting sales or as Ric Grech explained, "representing a contrast between purity and innocence and the great scientific progress of the day",[62] the American record company Atco vetoed it. By September despite a cool critical response, the album was number one on both sides of the Atlantic.

Perhaps because they are so much in the limelight as lead instrumentalists, vocalists, song writers, band leaders and rock personalities, rock guitarists seem to have needed the solace of religion more than other musicians – John McLaughlin and Carlos Santana (Sri Chinmoy), Pete Townshend (Meher Baba), Jeremy Spencer and Michael Schenker (Children Of God), Peter Green (Christianity/Judaism), Hank Marvin (Jehovah's Witness) and off at a tangent Jimmy Page's infatuation with Aleister Crowley. In a way, Eric's guru was George Harrison who first went to India with his wife Patti late in 1966, just as the Beatles began to disintegrate as a working unit. Ravi Shankar introduced him to his own guru Tat Baba and back in England, Patti joined the Maharishi Mahesh Yogi's Spiritual Regeneration Movement founded on the techniques of Transcendental Meditation. Unlike many of his contemporaries, Eric never involved himself in eastern religions, even to be fashionable, but Harrison went much further and into the early Seventies turned the whole of his career on the fulcrum of Hindu Krishna Enlightenment, which would eventually cost him his marriage.

Clapton has told how his first religious experience occured backstage at a Blind Faith concert, when two Christians got through security and persuaded Eric that a praying session was in order. And lo! a miracle occurred. It came to pass that Eric unrolled a poster of Hendrix in front of these guys and out fell a poster of J.C. himself which hadn't been there before. Apparently this was enough to convince Eric that God had intervened, rather than any thought that two wily Evangelists might have planted it as part of a campaign to recruit to their cause a man who had the ears of millions of young people. He started getting mail from other Christians, at first laudatory and then poisonous when Eric proved himself to be neither the new Messiah nor prepared to preach The Word from the stage. Over the next few years, he came into contact with Christian D.J. Scott Ross, who Clapton later condemned as being no better than any rock star wanting an audience for their show. When all the religious fervour in the world could not prevent Patti Harrison from leaving George for Eric, this finally convinced him of the power of earthly love.

But back in 1969, the banality of his 'conversion' suggested some half-formulated desire for faith, some hook on which to hang a life still full of uncertainty and doubt. Eric was looking for an escape route, a way off the rock merry-go-round. Blind Faith was voted Brightest Hope in the *Melody Maker* poll of Autumn 1969, the album went gold on advanced orders alone, but Eric had already found a trap door in Castle Keep.

On a visit to Los Angeles, George Harrison was invited to Snoopy's, a club in North Hollywood, to hear a band play. He never made it but caught up with them later at a party. He liked what he heard and brought a tape home to play to Eric. What they listened to was a husband and wife white soul team called Delaney and Bonnie. Delaney Bramlett came from Pontotoc County, Mississippi, moving to the West Coast to play in the Shindogs, the house band for Jack Good's TV show, *Shindig*. He met and married Bonnie Lynn from Acton, Illinois and they made their first album for Stax in 1968 called *Home*. Putting together a band of then unknown musicians, Carl Radle, Jim Keltner, Bobby Whitlock, Jerry McGee, Jim Price, Bobby Keys and Rita Coolidge, Delaney and Bonnie and Friends recorded the excellent *Accept No Substitute* for Elektra in 1969. The story goes that when Delaney complained to the label that a relative could not find the album in his local store, Elektra fired them, but they were attracting a lot of attention among West Coast musicians; Hendrix, Dr. John, Stephen Stills, Buddy Miles and Albert Collins all came to clubs where Delaney and Bonnie were appearing for jam sessions. Dave Mason played with them in America, but they did not hit the big time until Eric extended a welcoming hand and invited them on to the Blind Faith tour.

Shortly after the start of the tour, Winwood, Baker and Grech flew back to England, shaken by the New York experience and leaving Eric behind. "I stayed in New York and, as a result, I started hanging around with Delaney because there was no one else there. All our group had gone home. By the time they had come back, I was already one step away from them. And from that point on, I started making very childish comparisons with our group and their group. And there was actually no comparison, but on certain nights, I'd get up there and play tambourine with Delaney's group and enjoy it more than playing with Blind Faith, because (that) was already a thing to worry about. And I was worried about it. And by then, I kind of got this crusade going for Delaney's group. I wanted to bring him over to England".[63] Eric spent increasing amounts of time with them, enjoying their free and easy lifestyle, not pestered by anybody because nobody knew who they were, able to play good music and enjoy themselves. It was everything Blind Faith was not. Eric struck up a special relationship with Delaney Bramlett, which included growing a beard, but more seriously, sharing with him a deep love of southern American music.

"The first time I met Eric was after the first show in New York's Madison Garden. We passed the time of day and then got talking. We realised we both had admired the same people, particularly Robert Johnson and both had an almost identical collection of records. The only difference was that I had been raised on this music, while Eric had raised himself on it".[64]

While he always fulfilled his commitments to Blind Faith and never went AWOL like in Mayall days, the others saw little of him until just before it was time to go on. The entourage spread itself across the Continent and Blind Faith actually broke up on that tour – they just drifted away from one another as the tensions built up.

While plans were being laid for Eric to bring Delaney and Bonnie to Europe, he had another shot of supersessioning. John Lennon was invited to attend a Toronto Rock'n'Roll Revival Festival. He did not just want to appear sitting in the audience for fear of upstaging the event, so the discussion came around to a live performance. Lennon agreed, but had hardly any time to arrange the details. He got hold of ex-Manfred Mann bassist Klaus Voormann and ex-Alan Price drummer Alan White, without too much difficulty – finding Eric was another matter. Lennon's personal assistant, Terry Dolan tried Eric's home and every club he could think of until 5.30 a.m. on the day of the concert, 13th September. The plane was due to leave for Toronto at 10 a.m. Everyone was at Heathrow by 9.15, but Lennon nearly cancelled the whole thing when he was told that Eric could not be found. Meanwhile, in desperation, Terry Dolan sent a telegram to Hurtwood Edge, hoping somebody would know where to locate Eric. As it turned out, Eric had been there all the time asleep, so he hadn't heard the phone. The gardener opened the telegram and told Eric about the concert. It was too late to catch the 10 o'clock flight, so the party left at 3.15 p.m. They had to rehearse acoustically at the back of the Boeing 707, so as not to disturb the other passengers. Working through several numbers, they agreed on a final eight.

The show, with Chuck Berry, Bo Diddley, Gene Vincent and Little Richard (Jerry Lee Lewis pulled out at the last minute), was at the Varsity Stadium, in the middle of the football pitch, the stage set on a 12-foot dais. His first gig since the demise of Blind Faith, Eric was a little nervous, but John Lennon was physically sick with nerves. He had not been on stage since May 1966. At midnight, the Plastic Ono Band took to the stage. Under-rehearsed, even by the standards of Eric's past situations, they played some fine music in keeping with the mood of the occasion, *Blue Suede Shoes*, *Money*, *Dizzy Miss Lizzy* and the *pièce de résistance*, *Yer Blues*, originally recorded by the Beatles as a send up of attempts by white musicians to play the blues but here it was executed with total mastery and vintage blues licks by Eric, with Lennon's powerful vocal; another excellent example of Eric's rapport with a stylish, distinctive vocalist. Lennon's fight with heroin was recalled in *Cold Turkey*, (Eric also playing on the studio version released as a single earlier in the year) and then came *Give Peace A Chance*. For the first part of the concert, Yoko Ono had been cocooned in bag, incomprehensibly wailing some background vocals. Unfortunately, they let her out and she "sang" two songs, interspersed with booing from sections of the audience, *Don't Worry Kyoko (Mummy's Only Looking For A Hand In The Snow)* and *Oh John (Let's Hope For Peace)*. The raucous feedback ending heard on the album *Live Peace In Toronto* was achieved by the simple expedient of leaving the guitars resting against the amplifiers when the band left the stage.

Delaney and Bonnie came to Europe shortly afterwards. Eric's earlier ambition about keeping a low profile in 1969 had obviously failed, but now here was another chance for anonymity, helping a bunch of highly accomplished but unknown musicians gain a wider audience through his patronage. Dave Mason came along and George Harrison who, like Lennon, had not performed live for ages, was swept up by the down-home charm and good time feel of the Delaney and Bonnie caravan. Both he and Eric wanted to play without being the focus of attention.

But Eric more than anyone was setting himself up for a fall. He was still ERIC CLAPTON and unscrupulous tour promoters were not going to let go an opportunity like that. The European tour started in Germany and here the worst problems happened. In Cologne and Hamburg the band was actually billed as Cream, so of course the audiences were none too happy to see Eric standing at the back and Delaney and Bonnie in the spotlight. The Germans were already prejudiced in any case, believing that they were responsible for the break up of Blind Faith – which in part they were. The Cologne concert was abandoned after four songs in a hail of booing, hissing and missiles. Eric was near to tears.

The British tour was more peaceful, opening at the Royal Albert Hall on Monday, 1st December. Chris Welch (*Melody Maker*) and Ray Connolly (*Evening Standard*) went with a photographer to Clapton's Surrey mansion to get the lowdown prior to the tour, but both noted that all was not as it should be. It was one thing for Eric to keep a low profile on stage to allow the limelight to fall on his friends but quite another to do it in his own house where he behaved almost like a hanger-on. Eric's beautiful home was fast taking on a *Fall Of The House Of Usher* air, his priceless blues albums warping against a radiator as shrill cries of "Why haven't the roadies brought the drinks?" tore through the marijuana haze. Chris Welch turned in a straight enough interview, but tinged with some characteristically dry humour hinting at his disquiet. "Bonnie finally woke up and shimmied into the room with her blonde hair in rollers and a croaky voice. She declined to have any photographs taken. . . . Bonnie was full of down home phrases like 'God willing and if the creek don't rise' which roughly corresponds to the well-known English saying, 'May St. George preserve us if the Thames burst its banks above Teddington lock' ".[65] Ray Connolly hit harder. "They say no amount of hype can sell a bad product and in a way they're right. But a certain degree of subtle persuasion from the right quarters never hurt anyone, not least Americans Delaney and Bonnie and Friends, who together with Eric Clapton last night, made their first appearance of their British tour at the Albert Hall. Delaney and Bonnie are currently the most fashionable fad of the rock sophisticates. Mick Jagger, George Harrison and Clapton himself, have all remarked variously, on their being the best band in the world and in this way the whole British popular music industry had come to regard them with some kind of awe".[66]

Duff acoustics apart, the concert itself was exciting enough. Delaney and Bonnie were both fine raunchy singers and, with musicians of the calibre of Jim Gordon, Carl Radle and Bobby Whitlock playing straight ahead soul-based rock'n'roll, they could hardly go wrong. Clapton did exactly what he intended, i.e. very little, apart from some vocals. The Albert Hall management nearly pulled the plugs during the rock'n'roll medley encore, because it had been banned since a mini riot the previous year during a Chuck Berry concert. But they didn't, and everyone had a good time.

Eric revelled in the "back to the roots" simplicity of it all, travelling in the bus, rather than alone in a limousine, motorway service stations, horrible food and lunacy. In Sheffield he planned a water pistol battle, but contented himself with setting off clockwork oranges and lemons across the stage during Ashton, Gardener and Dyke's support set. Billy Preston joined the troupe for the post-British Scandinavian tour and there was much merry prankstering at Christmas when they all joined up with John Lennon and the Plastic Ono Band for the *War Is Over* concert at the Lyceum in London. It took George Harrison most of the tour to summon up the courage to even come out on stage, but by the time they reached Liverpool, Harrison found the self-confidence to play some songs by himself.

The touring over, everyone boarded a plane for Los Angeles to start work on Eric's first solo album to be produced by Delaney. He was a very influential figure in Eric's life at that time, not only because he convinced Eric that he could sing, but also because of his whole attitude to music. "He inspired me a great deal and gave me the confidence that I needed. He told me that anyone could (sing) literally, if they only put their minds to it. . . . I couldn't understand why he was so positive about what he was doing and I wasn't, because we were doing relatively the same thing. And it was just a question of waking up to the fact that whether other people like what you do, as long as you do it and please yourself, then you're bound to please someone else, which is what Delaney instilled in me. Before, I couldn't find other people that would like the same songs as I would like or would really understand why I played the guitar this particular way. And his open enthusiasm for my attempt really put me on the road".[67] Eric had sung in every previous band except Blind Faith but only infrequently; since 1966 he had been in the company of two of rock's more distinctive vocalists, Jack Bruce and Stevie Winwood. Now there were plans to call his first album *Eric Sings*. But the reaction of most Clapton fans to *Eric Clapton* when it was released in August 1970 was one of disappointment. His playing was largely swamped by the burgeoning Shelter Record-style West Coast session sound with Leon Russell on piano, however, the suspicion was that he tried to take over the whole session. Much of the material was a pastel wash of funky white soul lacking in definition or anything readily identifiable as the sound of Eric Clapton. What identity there was belonged to

Delaney Bramlett who dominated the album, contributing heftily to eight of the eleven tracks, playing rhythm guitar, singing, producing and arranging. British fans reacted by making this Eric's first album since leaving the Yardbirds not to reach the Top Ten, while reviewers remarked unfavourably about the blandness of the album and Eric's over-reliance on his friends. In their shortsightedness many British Clapton supporters deserted him, some never to return. Perhaps Eric did feel he was being used, exploited for the self-aggrandisement of others; certainly he looked none too happy on the back cover, sitting to one side, looking away from the bonhomie of the posed entourage shot.

Then again, it can be seen as the price that had to be paid for a complete turn around in Eric's career. Exploited or not, he showed he was still in the business of taking risks, developing his career towards coming trends. Earlier he had left the Yardbirds on the verge of their enormous pop success to stick to the blues, and the success of Cream proved him right. Now he was an established rock guitarist of world stature and heavy rock, the music he helped to pioneer, was riding high with the success of bands like Led Zeppelin, Black Sabbath and Deep Purple. But instead of milking his virtuosity dry, he produced a 'laid back' album as his first album in the first year of the new decade. Again he was proved right – the savage Sixties gave way to the sophisticated (some would say soporific) Seventies and 'laid back' was the pass word. There were certain crucial tracks which signposted the way. *After Midnight* written by one John J. Cale, destined to become something of a cult figure was the epitome of the tenor of American-oriented Seventies sounds, thanks in part to Eric's popularisation of his music. In turn, J.J. Cale was a major influence on Clapton's music in the years to come; the 1977 album *Slowhand* was a virtual anthem to the reticent slowburn maestro from Tulsa. *Let It Rain* was the best Bramlett-Clapton collaboration and a perennial Clapton favourite; *Easy Now*, the first of Eric's many love song ballads and *Blues Power* by Leon Russell, a restatement at this watershed in his career of his devotion to the music that had always sustained him and always would. Incidentally, *Lonesome And A Long Way From Home* was allegedly written for Blind Faith which is curious considering its similarity to the song they already performed, *Can't Find My Way Home*.

His singing had a tremulous, tentative quality about it, not the rock wail of Bruce or Winwood but sweet and lilting. With more confidence, the vocals became less hesitant, more self-assured and even gruff, but still sweet. Eric's vocal strength moved him miles along the road towards the more rounded musician he wanted to be – not just a guitar player but a singer-songwriter as well, where voice, instrument and lyrics could all play their part in opening up the vistas of self expression.

The front cover of the album showed another significant development. Leaning against his leg was a Fender Stratocaster, marking the beginnings of his more away from Gibson to the more delicate tonal colours and range of the Fender, his guitar sound right up to the present day. The amplification was different too, with massive Marshall stacks giving way to much smaller scale Fender equipment.

The album *did* lack a sense of direction but only because it was experimental. Eric was a musician in transition and didn't even know whether he was capable of producing a solo album. The music was embryonic, a sketch plan or blueprint for the future, shortly to have large areas of detail more firmly etched in.

Prior to the release of the solo album, an unremarkable live LP made its appearance – Delaney and Bonnie recorded at the Fairfield Hall, Croydon on 7th December 1969. Clapton's name was plastered all over the front cover as a marketing device but he was virtually inaudible and the album as a whole contained nothing to recommend it. The studio version of *Comin' Home/Groupie (Superstar)*, featuring some very clean, sharp Clapton lines was much better but limited to promotional copies only.

So what is one to make of the Delaney and Bonnie saga? Those who saw anything of the social scene of the time agreed that Eric was being burned for his good intentions. When they got to the States to record the solo album, there were lots of recriminations and arguments about who was going to pay for what and Eric just dug deeper into his pocket to keep the peace. All the media attention just went to their heads and they played the part, particularly Bonnie, at Eric's expense. For a long time afterwards around the Clapton camp, the name of Delaney and Bonnie was about as clean as one of their Mississippi mud holes.

But Delaney did hold up a candle to show Eric the way out of the rock maze and made him think positively about his music. Delaney's message was, quite literally, do what you like. One can only speculate on the paths Eric's career would have taken without the experience of a big, brash flamboyant American from the Southern states convincing him that the most powerful and timeless music is that which is sincere and heartfelt and not the product of mindless crowd pleasing.

If Delaney and Bonnie indirectly caused Blind Faith to split, Eric did the same to their band. He struck up a good relationship with their three key musicians, Jim Gordon (drums), Carl Radle (bass) and Bobby Whitlock (keyboards) and they quit the Friends, enticed away by Leon Russell, Joe Cocker and the Mad Dogs and Englishmen circus. When that scene got too mad they teamed up with Eric, helping him to produce some of the finest music of his career.

# CHAPTER SIX
# Layla-And A Song
# For All Seasons

Thoroughly home sick and eager to shake off the bad memories of his latest American sojourn, Clapton flew back to England with his new musicians to begin rehearsals at Hurtwood Edge, no doubt in that same rehearsal room where so many of those endless promotional photos of Blind Faith were shot.

The debut appearance of the new Clapton band was set for 14th June 1970 at the Lyceum in aid of the Dr. Spock Civil Liberties Defence Fund. Advertised as Eric Clapton and Friends, the band remained unnamed until minutes before they were due to go on stage, when Tony Ashton came up with Del and the Dominoes, Del being his longstanding nickname for Eric (although Eric is 'Ricky' to his close friends). This was modified to Derek and the Dominoes and that's how the band was announced. Clapton later claimed that it was not a conscious quest for anonymity, just a last minute joke which he thought would be an open secret. However, he was anxious that the band should not be promoted on the strength of his name alone, "It was a share and share alike group. Everyone played an equal part and I didn't want any advantage over people who weren't that well known".[68] Dave Mason appeared on stage just for that one concert and would probably have stayed longer but for a successful solo album in America that demanded a promotional tour. The Lyceum gig was Eric's first appearance on stage in England since the Delaney and Bonnie tour. Gone was the beard now he was cleanshaven with a new blow-waved hairstyle and check suit, a Fender Strat round his neck. Reactions to the concert were mixed. One review read "Ordinary – Eric in fairly dull debut".[69] As usual, the more acerbic comments cropped up in the letter pages. Was Eric's crown as the hottest axe in town slipping? One fan left the concert "feeling bored, bewildered and thoroughly sick. Sick of people who cheer the name and not the music".[70] But another review proclaimed "Clapton leads and sings his heart out". The vibrations emanating from the stage were very positive and, backed by a skintight rhythm section, Eric put everything into it, playing material from the solo album and the odd crowd pleaser like *Crossroads*. Above all, Eric looked relaxed and happy, smiling on stage for just about the first time anybody could remember.

The band retired to Clapton's house for more rehearsals, prior to the start of a three week series of low key one-nighters at small clubs and ball-rooms around Britain. Eric insisted as part of the contract that admission charges should be kept to £1 and that his name should not be used as a crowd puller. Although he was right in thinking most fans would know who Derek and the Dominoes were, the stipulation about anonymity did go some way to realising his fantasy of the previous year when he said "If only Blind Faith could go out to a club in Haslemere or somewhere and go on as the Falcons, it would take all the pressure off us".[71] As a playing unit, Derek and the Dominoes made great strides between the Lyceum concert and their opening date at the Dagenham Roundhouse on 1st August. Their Marquee date ten days later was tight, exciting and dynamic – the songs a mixture of old and new including a song dedicated to Hendrix, his own *Little Wing*, an awful prophecy of what lay only weeks away. One of their last gigs before flying to America to record a studio album was at the Birmingham Town Hall. The set was "beautiful, round, balanced and utterly professional, yet still retaining fire and style – the rendering of the programme was a joy to hear."[72] The audience that night may also remember the unplanned ap-pearance of Robert Plant who wandered casually on to the stage expecting to be able to 'sing along with Eric', only to be unceremoniously removed by a road manager.

Much of the material for the album *Layla and Other Assorted Love Songs* had been written during the early months of 1970. However, there were production problems. Phil Spector was Eric's first choice after they had met during sessions for Harrison's *All Things Must Pass*, on which the Dominoes featured heavily. Spare studio time allowed the Dominoes to record a Clapton-Whitlock composition *Tell The Truth* which was scheduled for release as a single. The band was not happy with it and the title was replaced by *After Midnight/Easy Now*. The Phil Spector version appeared later on *History Of Eric Clapton*; the 'official' version surfaced on *Layla*.

Robert Stigwood called up Tom Dowd who had been wanting to work with Eric again since Cream days. Dowd immediately agreed and arranged for the Dominoes to come to the Atlantic-South Criteria Studios in Miami where he was recording the second Allman Brothers album *Idlewild South*. It was a momentous phone call.

The way in which circumstance and coincidence combined to produce such a classic rock album as *Layla* is as elusive as the wind. It happens for some musicians once or twice, for most – never at all. That rare moment when all the elements that go to make up any album come together in a special chemistry. But as with all chemistry, the elements are usually inert unless there is a spark, a force to give meaning and purpose – in this case, one of the most powerful emotional forces known to man – unrequited love.

The public image of Eric in England was one of relaxed poise, but inside there was much anguish. His long standing relationship with George Harrison took a new twist when he became infatuated with Patti, Harrison's

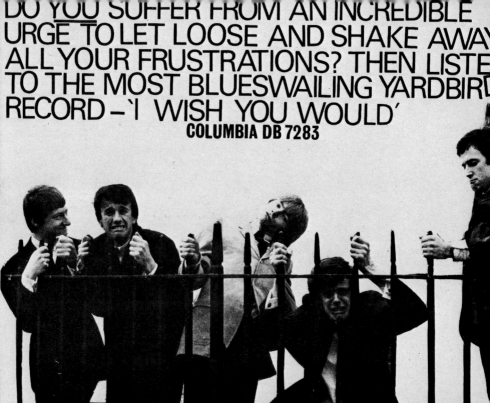

DO YOU SUFFER FROM AN INCREDIBLE
URGE TO LET LOOSE AND SHAKE AWAY
ALL YOUR FRUSTRATIONS? THEN LISTE
TO THE MOST BLUESWAILING YARDBIR
RECORD – 'I WISH YOU WOULD'
COLUMBIA DB 7283

Artists Management: GIORGIO GOMELSKY ASSOCIATES LTD · 18 CARLISLE STREET · LONDON W·1 · GERrard 1232
Press & Public Relations: PRESS PRESENTATIONS LTD · 7 DENMARK STREET · LONDON W·C·2 · TEMple Bar 6304
Published by BURLINGTON MUSIC LTD · 9 ALBERT EMBANKMENT · LONDON S·E·1
E.M.I. RECORDS LTD · E.M.I. HOUSE · 20 MANCHESTER SQUARE · LONDON W·1

Above: A contemporary ad.
for a Yardbird's single with
Eric on the far right
Right: The Yardbirds
Opposite above: Eric in
Cream
Opposite below: Cream:
Eric, Ginger and Jack

Previous page: The
Yardbirds: Eric is second
from left

Above: John Entwhistle and
Keith Moon standing
behind Yoko Ono, Julian &
John Lennon with Brian
Jones on the far right of the
Rolling Stones Rock'n'Roll
Circus, 1969
Above right: Crystal
Palace, July 1976
Right: Eric at the Rainbow,
January 1973 with Pete
Townshend
Left: Eric at the Rainbow,
January 1973 with Ron
Wood and Ric Grech

Above: **Eric and Patti's wedding**
Left: **1976**
Right: **1974**

Next page: **1974**

Left: Eric with Freddie King
and Ron Wood at Crystal
Palace, 1977
Above: With Dylan at
Blackbush
Right: Hammersmith
Odeon, December 1976

Left: **On the Old Grey Whistle Test** in 1977 with Yvonne
Elliman (left) and Marcie Levy (right)

Below: At the LA Forum
for Ronnie Lane benefit,
January 1984

wife. She reciprocated, partly to arouse in George some jealousy in order to wean him away from his other marriage to religion, but changed her mind and went back to him. Eric was shattered. His experience of long standing relationships with women was limited to his engagement in 1969 to Lord Harlech's daughter, Alice Ormsby-Gore, the lady who would be with him through the difficult years ahead. In Cream, only Eric was unmarried. A Sunday Times Magazine profile of Eric back in 1970 spoke to Jo Palmer, Ben Palmer's wife (Ben was at that time Eric's personal confidante) and the only negative word she had to say about Eric was that he wasn't very good at treating women as adults, seeming to benefit most from the fat-bottomed girls who followed the bands about. Eric himself tended to agree with this viewpoint, capable of settling down with any one of them, but also feeling sorry for them. "When I was with the Yardbirds I did (go with women) all the time. It was an obviously novel thing to try and do. You come out of school you know, and you get into a group and you've got thousands of chicks there. I mean you were at school and you were pimply and no one wanted to know you. And then there you are – on stage, with thousands of little girls screaming their heads off. Man, it's power!".[73] But there were groupies and groupies. Most were nondescript camp followers, others were strong personalities in their own right. One to whom Eric was very attracted was Hendrix's sometime lady, Devon, a black vision, a super-sophisticated street-wise groupie queen, first spotted by Quincy Jones, hustling in Las Vegas. When Eric was around New York during Cream days, they met up at the same clubs; Devon played games between Hendrix and Clapton, whose 'English boy long way from home' charm appealed to her. The relationship could not flourish, however, with Eric touring so much and she was only an acquaintance, a face among a sea of faces, yet one that people remembered. All the more tragic therefore, that behind her cool beauty lay a vicious heroin habit and not long after Hendrix died, she fell to her death from an upper storey of New York's infamous Chelsea Hotel in mysterious circumstances.

Eric's relationships with women had all the hallmarks of unsophisticated adolescence, as immature as the very rock music he was playing, an explosive unfocussed musical form, afraid to grow up for fear of dying. His was the anguish of a rejected teenager except that he had the creative talent to give expression to the pain. As the pearl is the much valued, exquisite but morbid secretion of the oyster, the final product of its biological need to rid itself of an irritant, so *Layla* and most particularly the title track, was the pearl of Eric's irritation.

Through playing with the same musicians for over a year, since Delaney and Bonnie first joined the Blind Faith tour, Clapton had been able to build up a working relationship in a slow and natural fashion, something that had never happened before. It was a long while before any official band came into existence and most of the time they hung out together, played on stage and in the studio, jammed unforced and with no media expectations. Eric got to know them all as friends as well as fellow musicians. Clapton wrote much of the album on his own and played the songs to the band in the studio, but the empathy amongst all the musicians outcropped most noticeably in Bobby Whitlock in whom Eric found an accomplished and sympathetic song writing partner and back-up vocalist. Together they wrote many of the best songs.

When Tom Dowd got the call from Stigwood about the new album, he mentioned the up and coming session to Duane Allman, already there with the rest of the Allman Brothers band. Tom asked Duane whether he wanted to get in on the session but Duane declined, saying he'd just slip quietly into the studio and listen. He had long been a fan of Eric's, travelling all over California to see him play at various times. The admiration was reciprocated. Like many people, Eric was very impressed by Allman's session work with Atlantic artists Wilson Pickett and Aretha Franklin, and the story goes that they first met at a Delaney and Bonnie session. On arriving in Miami, Eric heard that the Allmans were playing an open air concert and he and Tom Dowd went off to see them. On stage the Allmans were an impressive sight, identical wafer-thin bodies, long hair blowing in the breeze, guitars in the attack position. Eric and Tom arrived and sat down on the grass close to the stage. Duane was soloing, eyes closed and head up to the sky, a perfect picture of the inspired guitarist letting the music flow through him in endless waves and out into the warm air. When he looked down, Eric Clapton was staring him full in the face. Duane Allman stared back in disbelief and later berated Tom for bringing Eric along, complaining that he hadn't played well that night, even though all through the concert, Eric was saying "how did he do *that*?". When Duane eventually walked into the studio, Eric greeted him like a long lost friend, part of that special bond that ties musicians at levels deeper than simple friendship. They sat together in the studio, swapping licks, trading ideas and working through the songs, both embellishing and honing the music as *Layla* began to take shape, not as a deliberate and artificially conceived 'concept' album, but as the full title suggested, an aggregation of Eric's feelings at the time. If Patti Harrison was the spark, then Duane Allman was the catalyst. Eric has admitted at times to being a lazy musician, particularly in the studio, needing the drive of others to propel him along and make him work. Spurred on by the genius of Duane Allman, the music gushed out, much of it recorded live in less than a month. There was too much material for a single album so extra tracks were recorded for a double. As one reviewer put it, "The most valid double since *Blonde On Blonde*," and there have been few better ones since.

The original love songs penned for sides one and two, ooze references to Eric's personal situation, the first two tracks are at once heartfelt, intensely painful and very beautiful. *I Looked Away* with lines about loving another man's woman and *Bell Bottom Blues* with its characteristic Harrison style guitar break. *I Am Yours* is steeped in Eastern flavours, driven along by a tabla drum accompaniment. Clapton included three long blues tracks, Jimmie Cox's *Nobody Knows You When You're Down And Out*, Bill Broonzy's *Key To The Highway* and Billy Myles' *Have You Ever Loved A Woman* plus a gloriously majestic tribute to Jimi Hendrix *Little Wing*, another sort of love song. Delaney and Bonnie days were evoked with *Anyday* and *Keep On Growing*, and the whole recording was blues music at its most rich, lush and textured. Clapton's singing and playing scaled new heights; the tentative quality of the first album had been replaced by a strident self assurance, born of a hunger to play and a realisation that pseudonyms notwithstanding, he could assume the responsibilities of his own band and for the writing and presentation of the material.

But there was no question that the title track of the album was one of Eric's finest moments. The interplay between Clapton and Allman was fluid and dynamic throughout the album, especially on *Why Has Love Got To Be So Bad*, but on *Layla* it was nothing short of historic. The title derived from a Persian love story called Layla and Mashoun, whose tale bore little resemblance to Eric's, he just liked the title. From such a casual encounter came a piece of rock music that deserves its latter day status as a classic. Duane Allman's dramatic riff opened the song like a fanfare after which the band ripped through the song with a life or death urgency. Allman tended to run his phrases into one another at the top end of the guitar on the high strings, while Clapton's were more defined and using a Fender coaxed a thinner brighter sound than Allman, whose Gibson screeched when played as a slide guitar. Allman's solo flight at the end, just lifted the whole song, signing off an astonishing performance by a remarkable guitarist. Drummer Jim Gordon's magisterial piano concerto was added some while afterwards during a play back session and Tom Dowd was more than happy to remix the track in order to incorporate the end section. Dave Marsh of Rolling Stone, listed certain songs that he felt were performed as if life depended on it, including *Like A Rolling Stone*, *Reach Out And I'll Be There* and *Love Child* by the Supremes. Who could argue with his judgement that *Layla* is the greatest of them all?[74]

The ghost of Robert Johnson haunted the album. Eric was standing at the crossroads, having come down a long and tricky road. The spectre was waiting for him when he got there, but with *Layla* Eric succeeded in exorcising his personal blues. He had tapped into that same essence that set a young black Mississippi blues player off on his travels anything up to forty years earlier, just by living and experiencing – now there were decisions to be made. Which road to take? Where would it lead? By the time *Layla* was finished, Eric had already began travelling along one road which would turn out to be a dangerous trail and a dead end. It took him over three years to find his way back again.

With *Layla* completed, the Dominoes were sent out on tour and that's when things started going sour. This personal exorcism of *Layla*, while liberating Eric to a certain extent, also drained him and he began to lose his hunger for being a musician. Heroin first came into the picture for Eric back in England, during the sessions for *All Things Must Pass* carrying over to the recording of *Layla*, where everything you could think of in the way of drugs seemed to be readily available. Drugs, particularly those arbitrarily labelled as 'hard', set up extra lines of communication between musicians that underline the essentially tribal nature of the community, creating unspoken inner sanctums of understanding. Musicians get into drugs for a variety of reasons, not least of which is the idea that they are the passports to the upper echelons of the rock fraternity where the wasted musician becomes a symbol of artistic suffering and the cut and thrust of the rock life. Strong too, is the belief in drugs as liberators of the creative imagination; certainly in the *Layla* studio, while not being the 'cause' of the good music that emerged, drugs did help to perpetuate a sense of shared experience between the musicians in such a confined environment and this undoubtedly influenced what happened. But in the end, any over indulgence is debilitating and counter-productive. Apart from his premier production work, Tom Dowd had to dish out some fatherly advice about the dangers of a free and easy studio atmosphere, getting just a bit too loose and out of hand. Eric called the Criteria studio "a womb"; the album was recorded in an aura of physical and spiritual closeness and security. Out on the road it was a different ball game.

In England, Eric had been able to exercise some control over the conduct of the tour. The venues were small and there was sufficient publicity in the music press for promoters not to have any worries about the public knowing who Derek and the Dominoes were. In America, it was very different. *Layla* had not been released, the Dominoes had hardly been in America at all and of course the Stigwood Organisation wanted the band to play the big, lucrative theatres and arenas. The company swamped the nation with DEREK IS ERIC badges, just to be sure.

Derek and the Dominoes opened at the Fillmore East to an ecstatic welcome but the press response was almost uniformly negative. "Clapton is doing a disservice to his audience when he allows them to accept the kind of music Derek and the Dominoes played – a surfeit of tail end blues licks, mainly undigested, realizing little connection with any coherent style or with the source of its inspiration. And Clapton's fans do him a disservice when they cheer at any high pitched technical display or some irrelevant and at best decorative bottleneck exercise".[75] And as if to prove the point about image adulation rather than musical appreciation, the following note arrived in the Rolling Stones offices a few days after the concert. "Wow, Eric Clapton is really far out. The Derek and the Dominoes concert at the Fillmore was unreal. When Eric first appeared on stage, he walked over to the microphone and in his beautiful voice said 'Hello, hello'. Man, just the way he said it, really turned me on". Press vitriol continued unabated, reaching the nadir towards the end of the tour in Los Angeles. A report filed from America headlined "Is God Dead?" waded in with the apocalyptic statement "It's time for Eric Clapton to re-evaluate his position in rock and roll. Two double concerts . . . left more to be desired than any concert in recent memory. Possibly the problem was aggravated by the fact that the musicianship is so fine; what else would anyone expect? Yet the evenings were boring, plagued by loud sound and muddled singing. The audience was absolutely no help either. Many walked out during the performances and those that stayed seemed bent upon calling out Clapton's name during his solos. The sold out houses that were hoped for during this Eric Clapton tour never materialized; in fact many shows were less than half filled. It's time the Robert Stigwood Organisation stopped shoving Clapton into positions that he cannot and possibly does not want to fill".[76]

Undoubtedly there were problems with the Dominoes as a live band, which were exposed in 1973 on a double album (the first release by the newly formed Stigwood label RSO to cash in on Eric's absence from the music scene), *Derek And The Dominoes In Concert*. Eric was back to being the sole lead instrumentalist. There was no Duane Allman to trade licks with nor even any other musician in Jack Bruce or Stevie Winwood's mould to play against, organist Bobby Whitlock being too understated a player. Coupled with a rather limited blues-oriented repertoire, it meant that the ideas began to wear thin when the band launched into over-long jams. Often the band tended to wander aimlessly through a song, stretching it well beyond its limits like *Let It Rain* and Clapton would try and compensate for the lack of another guitarist and overplay on *Tell The Truth*.

But what the critics failed to take into account was that all the problems of the Dominoes were a corollary of the type of guitarist Clapton was – an instinctive player, and that has a very positive side to it as well. Clapton plays from the heart; it's written all over his face as he plays, and it is almost physically impossible for him to cover up his mood amidst a flurry of gross and excessive soloing. By his own admission he is not the world's greatest technician, but there isn't a guitarist around who can wring such emotion from a lump of wood with metal strings. On top of that, he is a blues player, which means passion or nothing at all, playing as good or as bad as he feels. And naturally his mood will effect the rest of the band, particularly in the Dominoes where not only was he the lead instrumentalist but the band leader as well, a totally new situation for him. Some nights the Dominoes were sluggish and uninspired, other nights they were electric and, when Eric decided to get all his chops together, the playing was staggering. The stand out track on the live album was *Have You Ever Loved A Woman* – Eric just spat fire from the guitar, detonating runs and figures that exploded from his fingers. Yet he was on a hiding to nowhere. Criticised for the obscurity of his guitar playing on the solo album, he was now being attacked for gratuitous pyrotechnics.

Eric fared no better with the record company. According to Giorgio Gomelsky, the cover painting for the album was discovered by Eric in Giorgio's house in the South of France. The Dominoes debut gig was supposed to be at a Nice rock festival that was cancelled by the police and Eric and the band used the house while they were over in France. Eric wanted the cover painting and nothing else, no names or logos. The Americans said yes but Polydor UK refused. When it was released in December 1970, *Layla* was a critical and commercial flop. Lack of critical acclaim was always on the cards and, amazing as it may seem, Eric had hardly a good notice in Britain since Cream broke up – no wonder he felt unwanted in his own country. But the album did not make the Top Ten in America either and its commercial failure was almost suspicious. Polydor did not exactly break sweat in promoting the album, was it malice? Could they have decided to show Eric that without proper and explicit promotion no musician could succeed? Or was it that Eric's popularity *was* on the wane and that insufficient people on both sides of the Atlantic knew who Derek and the Dominoes really were? All the more ironic then, that when *Layla* was released as a single in July 1972, it was a smash hit in Britain and America. By then Eric had dropped out entirely and it was virtually posthumous acclaim, the success of a musician who had died. Re-released a second time in 1982, it was a hit all over again, both strange and gratifying that Eric's greatest triumph should have come in a form he had often desired – anonymously.

But when in 1970 *Layla* died, a little bit of Eric died with it. In February 1971, Eric announced that he was retiring temporarily from live performance in order to take stock. Shortly after the Dominoes went into the studio to record a second album, but the attempt to re-create the *Layla* atmosphere failed, there were fights and the band broke up.

Eric made only two more public appearances that year. On 1st August at George Harrison's invitation, he played both shows for the Bangladesh Benefit Concert. On the album he played only *While My Guitar Gently Weeps* with Harrison himself but at the end he took part in an all-star jam, using a Fender Stratocaster for the afternoon show and a Gibson Byrdland in the evening. But he was not at all well, only managing to make it to the stage at all because he had acquired some methadone linctus, a heroin substitute. New York heroin was (and still is) usually adulterated with anything from harmless milk sugar to deadly strychnine but in any event there wasn't much heroin in the preferred powders even for a rock star and he obviously couldn't risk bringing his own, as musicians are always prime targets for Customs searches.

His only other appearance was at the Leon Russell/Shelter concert at the Rainbow Theatre, London, in December. He arrived unannounced on to the stage. Nobody was expecting him and he just stood behind an amp and played out the set. In between times and for the next two years, Eric took to his own shelter, behind the ornate and secure splendour of Hurtwood Edge, cocooned in the blanket of heroin invulnerability. A constellation of forces had driven him there. Patti Harrison had rejected him. (When Lennon broke up with Yoko Ono for a year and a half, he spent most of the time in an alcohol/heroin haze. Love was Lennon's drug substitute – when they re-united, he switched his dependence from heroin to Yoko, almost literally *never* letting her out of his sight, so deep was his insecurity.) For a time, Eric moved the other way from love to drug. The rejection by the woman was followed by the rejection of the music he wrote for her and his other mistress, the fickle and unreliable rock business turned its back on him. Sandwiched between rejection, was death. On 18th September 1970, Jimi Hendrix died – Eric went out and cried for the man and for himself, because he had been left behind. A few weeks later, halfway through the Dominoes tour Eric had to fly home because his adopted father John Clapp was taken seriously ill. He never recovered and tragically died. A further blow on 29th October 1971, was the death of Duane Allman, killed in a motorbike accident in Macon, Georgia, when he smashed into a truck. In the winter of 1959, Gregg Allman got a guitar for Christmas, while his brother got a Harley 165. He smashed that up too, except that time he survived and traded in the bits for his first guitar.

Successful people in all walks of life can be suddenly beset by waves of anxiety, irrational fears about failure, scared they might be uncovered as frauds. Eric had always been a reticent guitar hero, overly modest about his abilities, taking any opportunity to stay out of the limelight. More was involved than merely living up to the expectations of others which was a big enough problem in itself, stretching back to his days in Cream; but worse, Eric's sternest critic, his most vitriolic admonisher, was himself. However thick the walls, however high the gates, he was the only person from whom he could not run away, except by resort to the temporary expedient of a powerful specific. In physiological terms, heroin remains the world's most potent painkiller and what it can do for the body, it can also do for the mind. The junkie slips away in his reverie to an alternative reality, crossing the divide only when it is time to consider where the next fix is coming from. And in Eric's position he didn't even have to worry about that. Yet he was in a transitional state, carrying with it certain dangers which had already claimed the lives of four famous rock personalities – Brian Jones, Jimi Hendrix, Janis Joplin and Jim Morrison. The actual circumstances of each death are at once different and irrelevant. They all died directly or indirectly through drug use and each was racked by personal anxieties about the future of their careers, which were all in a state of flux or decline at the time. Thus, in theory, the danger for Eric was clear. However, he was on safer ground for a number of reasons. He was better protected with members of the entourage close at hand. Unlike Keith Richard and Brian Jones, Eric's home remained a sanctuary from police intrusion, probably due to the presence of his current lady, Alice Ormsby-Gore. She too was a heroin user, but as Lord Harlech's daughter, moved in rarified atmospheres where the police have always been loath to intervene. This meant that obtaining the drug was a safer operation than it otherwise might have been. In addition, heroin would have been available from reputable Harley Street sources, affording extra security and ensuring absolute purity. By snorting rather than injecting, Eric and Alice both avoided any repercussions from dirty needles and damaged veins. This method was more expensive, however, as more of the drug is required for the same effect and Eric was quite literally paying through the nose for his indulgence. Not having immediate access to the money he earned, the habit did cost him the odd car and some of his very rare guitars, but at least he survived.

In truth, Eric was never the raddled junkie the press portrayed when they later documented his 'miraculous' recovery. In fact the "raddled junkie" is something of a myth in itself – the image of the cheap novel and sensational film. Many regular heroin users are also regular 'nine to five' employees and many others use the drug recreationally at weekends, for example, without ever becoming addicted. Part of the addict mythology, in fact a central part, is the "horror" of withdrawal. The psychological fear this generates is enough for many addicts to rationalise away the need to kick the habit. However, withdrawing somebody from heroin, is far safer than barbiturates or alcohol and is, in purely physiological terms, generally no worse than a bad bout of 'flu lasting a few days. With somebody to care and watch over them, anyone can be safely withdrawn from heroin. From this point of view, Eric could have stopped whenever he wanted to. The point was, he *didn't* want to, and the question to ask, is not so much why did Eric start using heroin in the first place but why did he absent himself from the public arena for so long?

This was not the first time he had gone into self-imposed exile. There was the Greek episode and the period immediately after Cream when he bought Hurtwood Edge. Like anyone else, he needed time away from people but unlike most people, he was a public figure, a world famous musician and a hard working one at that and had spent eight solid years on the road with hardly a break. "Bearing in mind how many changes he'd been through and the amount of time he'd spent on the road and in the studio, there's no doubt he became sick to the teeth with it all and needed an equal amount of time to recover".[77] "When you work, you work so fucking hard. It's physical and mental. It's so hard. It's not like a job where you can just stand there all day and stick bricks on top of one another and think about something else while you're doing it. It's concentration and mental fatigue and if you do it long enough, you just run yourself into the fucking ground. You've got to have a break and that break can last forever sometimes".[78]

Speculation was rife about Eric, but the silence was shattering. Unless you knew the special code for the number of rings, the telephone at Clapton Towers remained unanswered. There was genuine concern about Eric's health among some rock journalists, particularly when rumours about drug problems began to surface. But until Eric's 'confessional' interview with Steve Turner for Rolling Stones in 1974, Clapton's absence was put down to 'tiredness'; no mention was made of drugs, always a sensitive subject and one liable to generate a flurry of litigation. Instead, as antidotes to the vindictive murmurs about "Eric Claptout" circulated by the rock reptiles, retrospectives of Eric were published with titles like "Come Home Clapton", "Eric; Silent God of Rock and Roll" and "Clapton's Layla; tragedy of the historic album that was ignored by the fickle world".[79] Even if tinged with a sense of epitaph, these articles were sincere and heartfelt, restating Eric's contribution to rock history, lamenting the failure of *Layla* (surmising how much that must have effected him) and pointing out the inherent dangers of setting up rock musicians as living legends and gods, putting them on narrow-based pedestals from which it is so easy to topple. They were expressing the feelings of many rock fans -- without Eric around there was a void, a sense of loss; people wanted him back doing what he did best. The record company did *its* best to fill the void – no less than seven albums with strong Clapton affiliations were released during the 1972–73 period (see discography), the most important being *Layla*. When he was around, the reviews of his work on stage and on record were as unpredictable and contradictory as the man himself. *Layla* just got lost in the unrelenting and monotonous Press litany of a post-Cream withdrawal syndrome. However, amidst a sea of dark silence, *Layla* stood out like a beacon to which grateful fans flocked. When it was re-released in July 1972, *Layla* shot up the charts – the lost masterpiece had come in from the cold.

Clapton made few journeys away from Hurtwood Edge. He was rumoured to be topping the bill at the Lincoln Festival in August with none other than Stevie Wonder. Robert Stigwood even went so far as to announce that a live album would be recorded. None of this took place but Eric did play on the sessions of Air Studios in London during October for an unreleased Stevie Wonder album called *I'm Free*. He also showed up at the Olympia Stadium in Paris for a Who concert. He was coaxed there by Pete Townshend who, more than anybody, was responsible for rekindling Eric's interest in his career.[80]

In August, Eric had invited Pete over to the studio he'd built at Hurtwood Edge to help get together an album he had half finished. Some of it was his own material, the rest was the unfinished second album by Derek and the Dominoes with a number of tracks that had been laid down in Eric's own studio, left after the bust up. At about the same time, Lord Harlech was trying to organise an event as part of the Fanfare For Youth to mark Britain's entry into the Common Market on 1st January 1973. The idea of a concert was mooted, Eric was asked and after much persuasion by Townshend and Alice, he agreed.

Pete began to gather some musicians together – Stevie Winwood on keyboards, Ron Wood on bass and drummer Jim Keltner, although this soon changed. Ron Wood switched to second lead guitar, in came Ric Grech on bass, Keltner was replaced by J.J. Cale and Taj Mahal drummer Jimmy Karstein and Jim Capaldi was added as a second drummer. The rehearsals were fairly shambolic and disorganised and Grech christened the band the Palpitations. Everyone was nervous and apart from Townshend, seemed easily distracted. But by the day of the concert, Saturday 13th June 1973, the show had come together.

Two shows were planned with the Average White Band playing support for both, an inspired choice as warm up. It was a testament to their ability that an unknown band could have drawn such a warm response from a crowd eagerly awaiting the return of their hero. The first show from Clapton and the band was rather hesitant but the appreciation of the audience was total. After the encore, there was pandemonium as numerous people without tickets tried to stay behind for the second show. Outside, the second house were freezing to death while the bouncers ejected those who had outstayed their welcome and the police were checking a forged ticket scare.

AWB played for three quarters of an hour. At 10.30 John Martin, presenting the concert for Great Western (the company headed by Harlech and actor Stanley Baker), came on to the stage to announce that "the first house got carried away understandably, on such a unique occasion. Ladies and gentlemen, I have only two words to say – Eric Clapton". And there he stood, hair long and lank, full beard, resplendent in a tailored white suit and white boots, clutching a red Gibson Les Paul tightly to his chest, cigarette dangling characteristically from his lips, his first scheduled UK stage appearance in three years. The running order of the songs was *Layla, Badge, Blues Power, Nobody Knows You When You're Down And Out, Why Has Love Got To Be So Bad, Little Wing, Roll It Over, In The Presence Of The Lord, Tell The Truth, Pearly Queen, Key To The Highway, Let It Rain, Crossroads* and finally *Layla* again as an encore. No surprises but a complete triumph. The whole band was magnificent with Ron Wood taking lead on *Little Wing*, Jim Capaldi taking over centre stage from Jimmy Kurstein and Stevie Winwood too, worthy of a special mention. The other musicians, all superstars in their own right, were keenly aware that it was Eric's show and the problems he had in just being there at all. Their playing was supportive, even protective, complementing each other as well as Eric. The feeling of brotherhood that emanated from the stage added extra heart and poignancy to the resonant, deep and measured delivery of the songs, most marked on *Presence Of The Lord, Badge* and a half-paced version of *After Midnight* (not in the second show, along with *Bell Bottom Blues*). Rhythms were laid easily on each other, a multi-textured groundswell beneath the guitars, as each song unfurled in front of the audience.

Surprisingly small in stature and almost dwarfed by Pete Townshend, Eric made his guitar soar above the large ensemble on stage, one keyboard player, two drummers, a conga player, a bass player and two other guitarists. As if in rememberance of days gone by, Eric broke a string just as he swooped into the solo of *Let It Rain*. He played the solo and moved backwards to get his guitar restrung; unhappy with the result, he took up a Fender Stratocaster instead. Meanwhile the whole band was building up a rhythmic storm on percussion and when Eric was ready, they cracked straight back into the song where they had left off. Earlier, Eric's punishing wah-wah solo on *Presence Of The Lord* ruined the pedal for the rest of the concert. He remained unruffled and when it was over, he went and hugged Pete Townshend, the man who made it all possible. "Thank these", Eric said to the audience, pointing to the band. And then he was gone. 'Nice One, Eric', was the headline of one concert review and there was general press agreement that from an emotional and musical point of view, it had been a great night.

A pity therefore, that so much of this subtle and dynamic instrumentation was totally lost in the production of the concert album that appeared in September 1973.

Glyn Johns was originally assigned to handle the album but pressure of work forced him off the project. Instead, using Ronnie Lane's mobile studio, the Who's soundman, Bob Pridden, recorded the concert, but his lack of experience was evident. Through inadequate miking, many of the instruments were just not there – eight tracks were needed for the two drum kits alone. Johns was called in at the eleventh hour to try and rescue the tapes but eventually he wanted nothing to do with it – even though his name was on the cover. The result was a single album of muddy, indifferent sound, which by no stretch of the imagination did justice to such a historic concert.

What on stage was vigorous and elevating sounded merely ponderous. Those who bought the album who didn't see the concert must have wondered what all the fuss was about. Obviously, no album could really have caught the true magic of the evening, but there was absolutely no excuse for such a shameful travesty of what actually took place. The occasion demanded an album of impeccable pedigree – all we got was a dog.

The concert itself was touted as Eric's comeback but it was to be a further two years before Eric would be back on a British stage. Eric went back into hiding and was still using heroin with no particular inclination to give it up. However, immediate cash was running low and he was being pressured by Lord Harlech, now very concerned about the welfare of his own daughter, to try a revolutionary new treatment for heroin addiction, colloquially known as 'the black box'.

The treatment was discovered by chance in 1972 when a Scottish doctor, Meg Patterson, was working in the Tung Wah Hospital, Hong Kong with a Dr. Wen. He was experimenting with electro-acupuncture, the modern form of an older oriental medical technique. Dr. Wen was sending an electric current through acupuncture needles as a form of anaesthesia during surgery. On an island with a substantial addict population, several of his patients were addicts and in hospital they were naturally deprived of supplies. To their surprise, doctors Wen and Patterson were getting reports from addict patients that electro-acupuncture as well as deadening the pain of surgery, was also relieving withdrawal symptoms on a scale which ruled out coincidence. Back in England, the technique was translated into a small box which generated an electric current, not through needles, but through electrodes attached to the ears. Eric spent two weeks in Meg Patterson's clinic then was given a box, a set of instructions and told to get on with it for an hour per session, three times a day. He was pretty sceptical about the whole thing but it did alleviate withdrawal symptoms. Why it worked, nobody really knew . . . and they still don't. One theory postulated in 1975 was that the current stimulated the recently discovered natural opiates of the brain known as endorphins. The brain has its own drug receptors, including one for opiates. During heroin addiction, the artificial opiate replaces the natural drug in the brain, so that when heroin is stopped, there is a space in the receptor where an opiate should be – hence withdrawal. Or so the theory goes. Eric's name along with Pete Townshend, Jack Bruce, Cliff Richard, Jimmy Page and George Harrison became associated as sponsors with the charity set up to fund a clinic at Broadhurst Manor in Sussex, launched in 1976. Other contributors included RSO, a rare example of a record company showing interest in the well-being of its artists. There was a lot of ballyhoo about neuro-electric therapy (NET) as it was called and the work of the newly opened Pharmakon Clinic. Nobody really had a clue as to what was happening clinically, what brain chemicals were being stimulated, if correct voltages were being applied and so on. The established medical profession showed a typically Calvinistic attitude to this new development and was reluctant to give it much in the way of credibility. On the other hand, there were some unscrupulous and misleading attempts by some associated with the charity to market 'the black box' as a miracle cure for heroin addiction. Black boxes are now commercially available although some very recent research, not as yet published questions the whole basis of NET as a method of detoxification. In 1981, the funds ran out for the Clinic, and unable to attract Government funding, Meg Patterson and her husband George, moved to California, where ironically they were sought out by Pete Townshend, by then himself a victim of drink and drug indulgence.

Whether scientifically sound or an elaborate act of faith on the part of patient and doctor alike, NET did give Eric the breathing space he needed to make some very necessary decisions but it did not 'cure' him of heroin addiction. A famous musician once asked a doctor to cure him of his drink problem. "I can cure your drinking", said the doctor, "but I'll also 'cure' your talent". Eric clung on to his 'desire' and 'craving' for life and music, until the need to get back to work became stronger than the need for heroin. After the Clinic, he went to a farm in North Wales owned by Frank Gore, Alice's younger brother. She herself had by now had been whisked away, back to cloistered calm.

"I still wasn't really sure, you know, that if I'd walked out of the Clinic I could have actually, you know, gone and scored again. So what I did, was to get on a train, went straight to Wales and worked on the farm for a month. That was it. I got up at six in the morning, drove a tractor and baled hay and had no chance to think of anything else. Frank, he just took me on as a hired hand and worked me like a dog. That was actually the best part of the cure".[81] In between mucking out, he started working on some songs, finally heeding the advice of his own words written six years ago – "And you'd better pick yourself up from the ground/Before they bring the curtain down".

At the beginning of April 1974, Eric decided he was fit enough to come back to London and look certain temptations in the face. His discussion with Robert Stigwood went something along the lines of "I want to work, get me some studio time, get me Tom Dowd and we'll see what happens". Stigwood replied with a promise that Eric will work harder than he has ever done, but before the graft, the celebrations – Stigwood heralded the return of Eric Clapton with a party at Soho's China Garden restaurant. Eric arrived smiling in a white Rolls-Royce wearing a Scandinavian style sweater and the beginning of a beard beneath a shorn crop of hair. He was greeted by old friends like Pete Townshend, Ric Grech, Ron Wood, John Baldry and Elton John. Looking happier than he had done for many a moon, Eric led the entourage to Robert Stigwood's north London home in Stanmore, where the festivities continued. A few days later Eric flew to Miami, to record a new album. E.C. was back.

# CHAPTER SEVEN
# A Working Class Guitar
# Hero Is Something To Be

When Clapton flew out to the Criteria Studios in Miami during May 1974 to start work again, there were no clues as to what was going to happen – he didn't even have a band. Carl Radle was cabled from England and he turned up with two other Tulsa-based musicians, organist Dick Sims and drummer Jamie Oldaker. These two had played together on numerous sessions, with J.J. Cale and in Bob Seger's excellent band that cut the album *Back In '72*, while Oldaker and Radle formed the rhythm section of the Shelter Records' house band and toured with Leon Russell. Since Delaney and Bonnie days, Carl Radle and Eric kept vaguely in touch and in mid-73 Radle had sent over some tapes of what he was doing. Clapton did nothing about it then, but knew when the time was right, he could probably call upon the services of some first rate musicians.

When Eric got to the studio, however, the others had not arrived, so he jammed with whoever happened to be around at the time: drummers Jim Fox (ex-James Gang) and Al Jackson (Booker T. Jones), bassists Howard Cowart and Chuck Rainey and George Terry, a young session guitarist who had backed Neil Diamond and Sonny & Cher. Eric had first met George on the *Layla* session, and the young guitarist happened to be working next door when Eric turned up again. "I asked him if he'd like to jam whenever he got bored with his other stuff. He had all these tunes he'd written in England and it started to fall together, so that he wanted to make an album – he likes spur-of-the-moment stuff".[82] Eric got George Terry involved primarily because he did not want to be the only guitarist around. Terry had brought some of his own players along but after about a week the Tulsa boys showed up and they replaced everyone in Eric's studio apart from Terry. This caused some initial friction, but, from this group of musicians gathered together in such a casual fashion, would emerge Eric's band of the next four years, the longest time he has ever been associated with one outfit. Two singers were also in the line-up; former *Jesus Christ Superstar* vocalist, Yvonne Elliman (married to RSO President Bill Oakes) and another Oklahoma Kid, Marcy Levy, an ex-Bob Seger band member who joined a couple of months later. The line-up then was Radle (bass), Oldaker (drums),

Sims (keyboards), Terry (guitar), Yvonne Elliman and later Marcy Levy (vocals).

The material too, was acquired in a similarly *ad hoc* manner. Nobody wanted to rush Eric. For about three weeks, the studio was booked for twenty-four hours a day, so that ideas could be worked out when the feeling was right. Producer Tom Dowd was playing it cool so soon after Eric's return; "We were just trying to occupy his mind creatively, getting a flow going so that he would say he wanted to do this or that. In the meantime, we were funnelling songs into him, trying to prompt him".[83] There were a number of songs laying at the back of Eric's mind that he wanted to do and material was coming in from a wide range of sources. In the end thirty tracks were laid down and the result was Eric's most eclectic work so far; blues, soul/funk, gospel, country and reggae. It was obviously a very important album for Eric, marking his return to the recording scene and, for someone who never believed he could sing, the vocals were surprisingly confident. The album was positive but also painful, as if the music was very gradually coaxed into existence. "I suppose I was excited, keyed up, frightened and very pent up. There was a lot of energy there waiting to burst out".[84]

One reviewer accused Eric of taking too literally the adage that the greatest art is that which conceals itself and certainly Eric kept the light of his solo guitar work well and truly hidden under a bushel, the exception being the rich eroticism of his licks on Elmore James' *I Can't Hold Out*, the only track where he plays the solo. In the main, he restricted himself to occasional embellishments, twin leading behind George Terry on *Mainline Florida* or short, quicksilver slide breaks on *Motherless Children* and some tasteful dobro work. (The dobro is an acoustic guitar with a vibrating metal plate over the soundbox to enhance the volume and tonal qualities.) Dobro was featured on the albums two most emotive songs, *Let It Grow* and *Give Me Strength*. *Let It Grow* was probably the stronger of the two, with a haunting, repetitive guitar figure echoing the days of *Badge*, *Presence Of The Lord* and the contemplative influence of George Harrison. Much was made of *Give Me Strength* as a song written by Eric at the bottom of the heroin abyss, proving his strong religious convictions. In fact, Eric himself was quite dismissive of any heavy spiritual connotations to the lyric, implying that even the most godless among us come out with phrases like 'Jesus Christ' and 'God, give me strength' in moments of exasperation and despair. More to the point, Eric did not even write *Give Me Strength* but had heard the song on a friend's tape recorder long ago, during his days of sleeping on other people's floors. He did not know who wrote it, credited himself, but was later sued by the real composer.

Yet *Give Me Strength* was the key song on a record which held up a mirror to various aspects of Clapton's past; the overtly titled *Motherless Children*, a much re-arranged version of Robert Johnson's *Steady Rollin' Man* and *Please Be With Me*. Written by Charles Scott Boyer of the country band, Cowboy, Eric dedicated it to Duane Allman who played dobro on the original version on the Cowboy's album *5'll Get You Ten* and Eric's dobro was a sweet and fitting tribute to his departed friend. Few songs from the album were regularly featured in concert, but one was a slow paced arrangement of Johnny Otis' *Willie And The Hand Jive*, a dirge on bad nights but uplifting when the mood was right. The Sly Stone/Stevie Wonder funky sleaze beats of *Get Ready* written by Eric and Yvonne Elliman led down easily to the album's most famous track *I Shot The Sheriff* which Eric first heard when George Terry played him the Bob Marley album *Burnin'*. Lacking the edge of Marley's version, nonetheless the song went to number one in the US singles charts after its release in July, a first for Eric, and it made the UK top ten as well. Eric's cover of the song also played some part in introducing reggae to white audiences, popularising the music of Bob Marley and all this from a song that Eric didn't even want on the album in the first place, because he did not feel that he did the song justice.

*Feed The Cook* and *When Pinky Gets The Blues* were two of the many names thought up for Clapton's comeback release, but eventually they hit on the inspired title of *461 Ocean Boulevard*, simply the address of the studio. Starved of new Clapton material, American fans bought the album by the box load when it was released in August, making it another No. 1 for Eric, while in Britain *461* went to No. 3, an astonishing achievement after such a long lay off. It was an album to luxuriate in; warm, soulful washes of sound which helped to gel together musicians from so many backgrounds in a kind of musical communism where each was playing for the band rather than themselves. It was a style which lent itself to integration in contrast to rock or electric blues which relies heavily on solo instrumentation. Clapton has always had the knack of making musicians *want* to work for him and he managed to capture a 'family feel' on this and all subsequent albums whether good, bad or indifferent and irrespective of the particular groove of the moment. For Eric it was an experimental approach, and although not fully developed as yet, worked very well.

Not so the stage performances however, and a satisfactory cohesion here took longer to achieve. Clapton was put straight back into the big time of arena rock when he probably would have preferred an easier baptism. A twenty-three-date tour of America was announced for the summer of 1974, his first tour of America in three years, but they kicked off with some warm up gigs in Scandinavia where a welcoming hand was always extended to any venture involving Eric. Concerts at the Tivoli Gardens and a fairground in Stockholm were followed by two dates at the three-thousand-seater K.B. Hallen Sports Dome in Copenhagen. Clapton's anxieties about recording paled into insignificance against those attached to performing and the whole trip was a diet of diversionary lunacy to combat nerves, washed down with liberal amounts of alcohol (heavy drinking also a commonly-reported consequence of coming off heroin). The entourage went along with the game for the band was new and full of unknown musicians. Eric was the star and called the tune, not liking anyone around who was not willing to join in the spirit of looning about. Killjoys were *personae non gratae*. Master of ceremonial lunacy 'Legs' Larry Smith, formerly of the Bonzos, played the tour's official court jester, concocting some kind of manic support act prior to announcing the band. With a wicked sense of the down-market, Eric stumbled on to the stage wearing an old torn jacket and outsize dungarees, a perverse antithesis of rock glamour. The set they played on the second night was fairly untogether, loose starts and ragged finishes and some rambling, aimless jamming in the middle, as Eric's concentration wandered. *Willie And The Hand Jive* was the only song from the as yet unreleased album and, for the most part, it was old favourites executed in a lacklustre, laborious manner.

After the concert, and two clubs later, the entourage was ensconsed in a Danish sex club awaiting their own private show. The source of unrelenting duck calls, verbal abuse and other even less savoury antics, Clapton took over as King Clown, egged on by cries of "Good ol' Eric" from the roadies, in a grim determination to get wasted and have a good time. Finally, he had to be carried out. Forbidden any interviews, the attendant journalists could only stand and observe; Steve Clark of NME was so appalled at his hero's off stage performance that his report was headlined "Question; how does the world's greatest guitarist spend his spare time? Answer; gets drunk as a skunk and piddles on Persian carpets".[85]

Eric's rather slapdash and uninvolved attitude carried over into the first part of the American tour and the audiences at those early concerts got a fairly raw deal. George Terry was largely responsible for holding everything together on stage. However, by the time the tour reached the showcase date at Madison Square Garden, Eric had begun to conquer his nerves. There was more commitment to arranging the vocal harmonies with Yvonne Elliman which resulted in one concert surprise, the inclusion of Charlie Chaplin's one hit record *Smile* (*Modern Times* was often quoted as Eric's favourite film). The atmosphere of the Garden was highly charged and expectant. Mick Jagger, Gregg Allman and Dicky Betts of the Allman Brothers were there and hope of an all-star jam was in the air. In the event, Todd Rundgren came on for the encore, *Little Queenie*, the first of several guest appearances by famous musicians during Clapton gigs since then. That night, Eric tamed the frenetic excitement of New York with a liberal dousing of good natured warm funk music.

So enthusiastic was America about the return of Eric Clapton, a whole string of extra dates were added after a few weeks rest at the end of July. At this point, Marcy Levy joined the band, initially to Yvonne Elliman's chagrin, who thought she was poaching, but the effect was to enable Eric to concentrate more on his playing.

From America, Eric went to Japan. "Japan was amazing", Yvonne Elliman told Barbara Charone, "they'd sit quietly through each song and at the end of every tune they'd shout out 'Rayra, Rayra, Rayra, Rayra, Elic Crapton, Elic Crapton, Rayra . . .' and as soon as we'd start *Layla*, they'd charge the stage. Boys would run up to kiss Eric. They were so passionate. It was like Beatlemania! And the Japanese don't show their feelings, but *Layla* breaks everyone up, something about that song is magic. It frightens Eric when he sees how people act when they hear it".[86] She was speaking after the band's European tour and their two rather cheeseparing nights at

Hammersmith Odeon in December, the only British dates on the tour. It's a fact that Clapton concerts in his native land are never quite as relaxed as those abroad and the problem of acceptance in Britain went back to the earliest days of Cream and since his comeback he has been virtually ignored at home. Living here is one thing, playing here another. "You can be rejected so many times and London really is the place for it. Every time I walk on a stage in London I'm looking for it, waiting for it. And if, after three or four numbers, there's nothing coming back, I say to myself 'Okay sods, I'll just play for myself and the band and it doesn't matter if you like it nor not'." Even so, the hesitant raggedness of the early concerts was replaced by an effortless professionalism. There was no need to search around for a jokey or pseudonymous name for the band – in all senses of the word it *was* the Eric Clapton Band and he had enough confidence now not to hide the fact. "At last Eric seems to have found a satisfactory halfway point between the flashy frontman pyrotechnics of *Crossroads* days and his introverted shadowy presence as the Delaney and Bonnie sideman. At present he is firmly stage centre, happy to be the centrepiece when the music calls for a solo, able to lie back and rely on the band to keep things choogling along in that distinctly easy way that Clapton music has".[87] Eric's much sought after niche had been located, it was a comfortable groove and one he has been in ever since. The same applies to the music. It would not be fanciful to say that Eric is wedded to his music and, over the last nine years he has often invoked the traditional ritual of something old, something new, something borrowed, something blue. This is not to say that it is always the same; the songs have changed, several performed on stage have never been recorded (see discography), the arrangement of each set is different and of course, no band plays exactly the same way twice, particularly where a sensitive musician like Clapton is involved. At the risk of stating the obvious, playing a concert *is* work for a musician and like most people, some days a musician feels great, other days lousy, so he might play with commitment or dispassionately, with aggression or gently, thus it is unfair to judge a musician on the strength of one concert. Yet Clapton's remembrance of British audiences did colour his attitude towards the gigs in Britain and it was a fitful return to the home arena, tight but cool.

During August 1974, in between the two American tours, the band went to the Dynamic Sound Studios in Kingston, Jamaica on Tom Dowd's suggestion, to record their second album in two months. Eric wanted to call it *The Best Guitarist In The World – There's One In Every Crowd*, but on the company's insistence the prefix was dropped. The mix of blues, reggae and gospel was much as before, except with the experience of playing together, they managed to capture a more uniform sound overall, less of a patchwork than *461* and in the process more convincing. This was certainly true of the two reggae tracks, *Swing Low Sweet Chariot* (with an authentic rhythm backing by Byron Lee's Ironmen) and a Clapton/Terry sequel to *I Shot The Sheriff* called *Don't Blame Me*. Eric's other four songs were bunched together on side two, while Shelter artists Jim Byfield and Mary McCreary contributed *Little Rachel* and *Singing The Blues* respectively.

The blues song was Elmore James' *The Sky Is Crying*, the spiritual uplift provided by Willie Johnson's *We've Been Told (Jesus Comin' Soon)*.

Although the band achieved a strong cohesiveness, bolted together by the exemplary open-spaced drumming of Jamie Oldaker, there was little sense of challenge or bite about the music, demonstrated by the lackadaisical ending of the Willie Johnson song which set the tone for the rest. The emotional commitment was there but the groove was *too* easy and comfortable, sundrenched well-being with more than a hint of complacency generated by the resounding success of *461*. Having said that, it was an underrated album, rounding off Eric's Jamaican experiment and improving with repeated listenings. You hear things you missed before, like the Auld Lang Syne phrase at the end of *Opposites*, included during the remixing of the track over New Year 1974/5.

Eric's guitar playing was marginally more to the fore, although still very understated – an obvious vehicle like *The Sky Is Growing*, a slow blues, was vocally rather guitar focussed. Both came together on Eric's *Better Make It Through The Day*, the quiet intimacy of the vocals combining with a peach of a solo to make it the best track on the album. Eric's vocal strengths were more clearly defined now, the earthy booze-blasted sound of *Little Rachel* rather than the strained, contrived, high register sweetness of *Pretty Blue Eyes*.

When it was released in April 1975, the critics were cautious and the fans kept their money in their pockets; neither the album nor *Swing Low Sweet Chariot* (UK single only) made much impact on the charts, although the single received a surprising amount of airplay. Eric was down, but not out. "I wasn't surprised the album didn't do too well. I like the studio, but I just don't play the same way as I would on stage".[88]

For tax reasons, Eric could spend no more than sixty days in the UK during the financial year 1975/6 and when he was here, he could neither write, play a gig or even get up on a stage and jam as he wanted to with Santana later in the year. Instead he toured Australia/New Zealand and Hawaii in April and the American mainland again in June, July and August. The sell-out tours of America were a great success with Eric playing at his most relaxed and dignified since the alcoholic ignominies of the summer of '74. Now able to abandon its previous caution, the band was much more confident and in turn, pushed Eric harder, a situation in which he has always thrived. The main thrust came from George Terry, once an acolyte at the master's feet and then a crutch, now a perfect foil for Eric. For the first time Clapton had another guitarist to play against as part of a touring band. Of Terry, Eric said "He's very good for me that way, 'cos I'm lazy. I need the help. Given the choice between accomplishing something or just lying around, I'd rather lie around. No contest".[89]

Although he has always insisted that he enjoys going out on the road and is lazy in the studio, the schizophrenic nature of his music on record and on stage suggests that concerts are for the fans and the records are for Eric. The commercial failure of *Every Crowd* aside, this would help to explain the absence of songs from the new album in the concert repertoire which was full of old favourites like *Badge, Bell Bottom Blues* and even *Sunshine Of Your Love* and *Crossroads*. Less bothered about reliving the past on stage, Eric now blasted off each concert with the ultimate crowd pleaser *Layla*, instead of saving it as a reluctant encore. The laborious plodding through standards of a year earlier had been replaced by a new injection of energy and vitality, refinement rather than repetition, with George Terry pushing Clapton to the peak of performance.

Eric's split motivations between recording and touring also help to explain his resistance to RSO's plan to release a live album. The company had been worried by the poor sales of *There's One In Every Crowd* and was eager to take advantage of the successful American tour. Eric instead, offered a single *Knockin' On Heaven's Door*, but Eric playing more reggae was something RSO definitely did not want. (For the story of this single, see discography). "There was a long battle about this album and I refused to let it go out until I heard *Have You Ever Loved A Woman* which was played to me by Tom Dowd in the studio in Criteria, just saying 'Listen to this' and the rest of it was built round that for me. He convinced me with that one track that it was worth doing a live album and he had complete control over what went on there".[90] Tom Dowd pieced together live cuts from Clapton gigs at Hammersmith Odeon in December 1974 and Long Beach, California 1975 and so the final result was without real structure or coherence. Eric's basic objection was that the material did not properly represent the band on stage, but then neither did his studio output. It obviously was a mixture of the two, with greater or lesser emphasis on soloing, depending on the night. Eric did not have to 'prove' anything to anybody, but RSO did want to show that contrary to popular belief, Eric was playing some mean guitar – a point worth making to concert-starved audiences outside America. The tracks selected were *Have You Ever Loved A Woman, Presence Of The Lord, Driftin' Blues, Can't Find My Home, Ramblin' On My Mind* and *Farther On Up The Road*. *Have You Ever Loved A Woman* was the key track, but it meant some judicious editing of *Ramblin' On My Mind* recorded at Hammersmith, because the band moved from one song to the other half way through. Dowd presented the other numbers straight and they were uniformly excellent. The opening track of the album *E.C. Was Here* saw Eric take the edges off a song thick with emotion when performed during the Domino days, by slipping in *Did I Mention Any Names?* after singing the lines . . . "And all the time you know she belongs to your very best friend . . ." but the playing was as hard and powerful as ever. Memories of John Mayall and the heyday of Eric's blues playing were reinforced by his use of a Gibson Explorer instead of the usual Stratocaster, which Terry used to masterful effect, matching Eric note for note. Acoustic guitar was also featured most notably on *Driftin' Blues*, virtually *Ramblin' On My Mind*, with different lyrics, but an honest reworking of the Delta blues guitar/vocal sound, shamefully faded out just when things began to get going. Yvonne Elliman showed her worth with two excellent vocal performances on *Presence Of The Lord* and *Can't Find My Home*, guiding him through odd areas of uncertainty, while Jamie

Oldaker powered the band through *Farther On Up The Road* with some sparkling shuffle rhythms.

But the stand out track was *Ramblin' On My Mind*, sung and played with the self assurance of a mature blues player, light years away from his solo vocal debut on the Bluesbreakers album. Clapton was in complete control, calling out an authoritative "F Sharp" to start off a sequence of announced key changes that took the song to a scintillating climax. This was not pointless pyrotechnics but careful and measured electric blues guitar playing. Clapton clearly demonstrated that he was still in the business of serious guitar work but either the fans didn't believe it, or else the record company didn't tell them loud enough because, released in August 1975 as the American tour reached its climax, it only did one chart place better in the States than *There's One In Every Crowd*. It didn't even make the top thirty in Britain. 1975–1976 were spent in much informal jamming and sessions, both in concert and in the studio, as Eric fully immersed himself in the business of being a working musician once more. Santana backed the Clapton band on the '75 tour of America and Carlos Santana and John McLaughlin appeared on stage with Eric at Nassau Coliseum, Long Island, New York in June. The same month Eric did some studio work with the Rolling Stones who were also touring at the time. Over the years, Jagger had dropped the odd hint about Eric joining his band but had never come out with it as a positive proposal. "Ron Wood, Keith and I, all played lead . . . the best takes were very early on, when nobody knew what they were doing. Later on, when everyone worked out what part to play, it got too sophisticated". In late July, Bob Dylan gathered together a whole crowd of people at the Columbia Studios in New York to do sessions for *Desire*, among them was Eric.

"That was amazing. He was trying to find a situation, you see, where he could make music with new people. He was just driving around picking musicians up and bringing them back to the sessions. It ended up with like twenty-four musicians in the studio all playing these incredibly incongruous instruments, accordion, violin – and it didn't really work. He was after a large sound, but the songs were so personal that he wasn't comfortable with all the people around. But anyway, we did take on about twelve songs. He even wrote one on the spot all in one night. It was very hard to keep up with him. . . . I had to get out in the fresh air, 'cos it was madness in there . . . it was very difficult to play and not listen to what he was saying at the same time".[91] Most of the ensemble playing was wiped and the tracks re-recorded, using a smaller group of musicians. Eric played on *Romance In Durango* on 28th July 1975, released on *Desire* the following January.

It was almost inevitable that at some point in his career, Eric would get to record with the Band, whose *Music From Big Pink* had made such an impact on him back in 1968. In March 1976, he appeared with Rick Danko, Elton John and Stevie Wonder as part of an all-star jam with the Crusaders at the Roxy in Los Angeles, while working on his next album at the Band's Shangri-La Studios overlooking the Pacific, north of Malibu. The world and his wife turned up for this one, not only the Band and Bob Dylan, but also Jesse Ed Davis, George Harrison, Chris Jagger, Ron Wood, Billy Preston, Georgie Fame and a new addition to the Clapton band itself, percussionist Sergio Pastora Rodriguez. Tom Dowd was unable to produce this album because of a dispute between RSO and Warners (who had Atlantic, Dowd's employers, under contract), so Eric and Carl Radle took on the job, assisted by Ed Anderson, the Band's soundman and later Rob Fraboni who mixed the album. Between them all, they did a first rate job on what was in many respects, a strange album.

No Reason To Cry (a title taken from Marcy Levy's Innocent Times) marked another transition for Eric, away from soul/funk and reggae feels, towards American rural roots music, on the borderline of country and heavily influenced by the presence of the Band. Where Dylan was eventually uncomfortable surrounded by a posse of musicians, trimming it down to a basic line-up, Eric revelled in it. In consequence, No Reason To Cry was probably Eric's most anonymous performance since the first solo album back in 1970, swallowed up by the relaxed West Coast ambiance. Obviously, the circumstances were very different but the effect was the same and from the 'total experience' point of view, the album was a success. Clapton was one of four lead guitarists and with (deliberately?) uninformative sleeve notes, it was often difficult to sort out who was doing what which, presumably, was the whole point of the exercise. Clapton himself stuck to a string of rather uninspired and repetitive slide guitar solos, pushing himself out front instrumentally only on Otis Rush's Double Trouble, where he proved once again what a matchless slow blues guitarist/vocalist he was. That side, most of the songs were a mix of contributions from the Band and Clapton camps with none of them being particularly memorable – Beautiful Thing (Manuel/Danko), All Our Past Times (Danko), Hello Old Friend (Clapton), Innocent Times (Clapton/Levy) and Black Rain (Clapton) – all medium-to-slow paced country-oriented melodies. Only Carnival (Clapton) and Hungry (Sims/Levy) made any attempt to get the adrenalin going. Part of the problem was Eric's desire to transfer the emotion of the songs he was writing from the guitar to the lyrics and the vocals, and he had yet to get the balance right.

On Dylan's Sign Language, the man himself (almost) sang in unison with Eric. "He played me a song in New York called Sign Language. He said he'd woken up that day and just written down the whole thing. And he didn't understand why or what it meant. And as I listened to it, I realised it didn't have any kind of story line to it, it was just a series of images and powerful vocals put together. It was very stirring".[92] It was also a mess, for instance, trying to rhyme "sandwich" with "language", perhaps Zim should have gone back to bed and forgotten the whole thing! The major plus points on the album were the vocal performances. Eric had never sung better, trading verses with Rick Danko on All Our Past Times, rumbling in a gorgeous low register growl through County Jail Blues and characteristically anguished on Black Rain. Marcy Levy's solo spot on Innocent Times and the back-up vocals on Beautiful Thing and Hello Old Friend were both excellent.

Eric obviously enjoyed recording this album immensely, naming it since as his favourite album, but probably more for the complete memory of the Shangri-La Studio and the musicians than just the album material itself. What appeared on *No Reason To Cry* was only a small part of the recorded material, it might have been a classic album.

> "We cut something like twenty-five tracks in three weeks out of nowhere, out of the blue, it was just like falling rain and the out-takes – whoever's got them, is sitting on a mint because they're beautiful. Some of the best stuff didn't get on the album, like instrumentals".[93]

Released in August 1976, *No Reason To Cry* put a smile back on the face of RSO. It reached number fifteen in the US album charts and broke into the UK top ten just as Eric was about to tour Britain, his only tour of 1976 and the first at home since the Derek and Dominoes tour of 1970. There was a sense of *déjà vu* about the unprestigious venues like Torquay Town Hall and Pontin's Camber Sands. Eric dubbed his tour "Eric's Summer Paddle" and wanted to play at only typical British seaside resorts, but had to compromise with a few conventional venues like the Glasgow Apollo and Manchester Belle Vue.

His first UK tour in years marked another shift in Clapton's public persona – not in appearance this time but more in demeanour. Probably buried through a long association with America and Americans, it is best conceptualised as a 'cor blimey' approach to music and life. Having delved into the roots of black working class music, the blues and more superficially, reggae, Eric seemed to be looking back to his own roots as a labourer's son. Eric increasingly immersed himself over the next few years in the British working class beer culture, drinking pints and being 'one of the lads'. The intro to *Carnival* on *No Reason To Cry* was a resounding 'Oi' from Eric. Cockney interjections in his speech were often matched by jibes at anyone with the sort of modulated accent that Eric himself used to have (check out the interview in Tony Palmer's 1968 Cream film) and of course, playing the 'jellied eel and winkle' holiday resorts of England was a kind of homage to the carnival of working class leisure. Later he tagged himself "a labourer guitarist", bringing in the bar room duo of Chas and Dave on his 1980 tour by which time the band itself was made up entirely of British musicians. Unfortunately on the 1976 tour, he also gave expression to less savoury aspects of British society – institutionalised racism.

The tour started on 29th July with a virtually unannounced warm up gig at the Pavilion, Hemel Hempstead, north of London. The band arrived on stage around nine o'clock to face a packed audience. The long gaps between songs suggested no pre-arranged running order, but they played well enough, Eric chain smoking his way through *Hello Old Friend* and *All My Past Times*, opting for a low key, acoustic start, moving on to *Blues Power, Layla, I Shot The Sheriff, Knockin' On Heaven's Door*, plus two slow blues, *Goin' Down Slow* and *Double Trouble*, leaving *Key To The*

*Highway* as an encore. Cries for *Crossroads* were drowned in the tumultuous applause; he hadn't been seen for a long time outside London and the audience was pleased, even honoured, to see him so, even as a joke, Eric's "I don't know about you, but I'm borin' myself silly" was uncalled for. "Finally, he picked up his by now near empty packet of cigarettes and clutching his beer can in his other hand, made for the exit. It is as if he had suddenly decided to end a game of darts at the local".[94] The second gig, two days later was in London, at the Crystal Palace Bowl. The water surrounding the stage proved no obstacle to those who wanted to see not only Eric and his band at close range, but also the guests who had joined them on stage – Freddie King, Larry Coryell and Ron Wood.

Even more unfortunate than his *faux pas* at Hemel Hempstead, was his drunken outburst about how Enoch Powell was right and so on in front of a concert audience on 5th August at Birmingham Odeon, smack in the middle of a racially sensitive area of the Midlands.[95] He might have got away with it in private, but as it transpired, he had a hard job living it down because it happened to coincide with statements by rock's other chameleon, David Bowie during his Berlin days, to the effect that what Britain needed was a good dose of fascism. Alarmed at such rantings from influential public figures, a left-wing group called Rock Against Racism was formed which held concerts and rallies throughout the Seventies. In an interview given around 1978, Eric said "It's terrible . . . I've been rehearsing at Island a little bit recently with Ginger because he wants to get an album out and I said I'd give him a hand. All the time down at Island's Hammersmith complex, there's lots of Rasta men about, just hanging around, playing pool, having a smoke. One of them came up to me the other day and said 'Is it true you really don't like black people?' I went, oh, no and it all came back to me about the night in Birmingham, when I said something about Enoch Powell. I must've rabbitted on about nothing . . . foreigners and actually I remember the other day what started it, was the upsurge in London of Arab money-spending and their lack of respect for other people's property. 'How much is Hyde Park?' and all that, and for some reason it all came pouring out of me that night and Enoch Powell was involved in it".[96] There was a story that one particular Arab had made a grab for Patti, not guaranteed to endear them to Eric at all.

The publicity surrounding the controversy tended to overshadow what was a fine tour. Audiences were genuinely pleased to see him back and for those who took themselves to the Hammersmith Odeon in October, there was the chance to see more of Eric, playing elegant dobro accompaniment for the country artist whose music now filled the Clapton residence, Don Williams.

"When audiences react like they've been reacting, it makes you feel good, because its very much a compliment, but I don't know what to do with it. Compliments and recognition and such as that, is just kinda embarrassing . . . really I don't know if I'll ever learn to deal with it. If I'm around and somebody starts bragging about me, then I'm ready to leave the room".[97] Another slice of self-effacement from Eric? No, this time it was

Don Williams in whom Eric found a soul mate, both quiet, sensitive artists where music is concerned who like to do the business, please the people, and slip away. Eric turned up at the opening concert of the Don Williams tour at the Fairfield Halls, Croydon and invited him back to Hurtwood Edge for a jam session. The following night, Eric stood unobtrusively towards the back of the stage at the Hammersmith Odeon, Don Williams' dobro player for the evening. "He's an incredible picker. . . . Eric plays a lot of rhythms and stuff that are very close to the way I feel and some of the songs that he's written are just really fine. He's phenomenal".[98] During the '78 tour of America, Williams reciprocated by opening for Eric in Nashville, winning over ten thousand ardent rock fans to his music, but for the rest of 1976 and the first half of 1977, Eric stayed at home.

1977 was to prove an eventful and unpredictable year, heralded by an unpublicised show, a St. Valentine's Day dance at Cranleigh Village Hall, near Eric's mansion. The invitation was the brainchild of the local Round Table, a body of businessmen who organise local events for worthy causes – in this case, the proceeds were to go to a local hospital. They wrote to him and he called back. "That dance of yours. I'll do it". In accepting the invitation, he may have had in mind an interview with Barbara Charone the previous October. "I'm actually going to form a group called the Hypocrites with Ronnie Lane . . . we'll record on our own label called Get Away With Murder Records. This first gig is at the Cranleigh Village Hall".[99] Alternatively, they may have already invited him but either way the chance to play incognito and have a laugh and a drink has always had its appeal for Eric and they went out as Eddie Earthquake and the Tremors. Essentially it was Eric plus Ronnie Lane's Slim Chance – Bruce Rowlands, Brian Belshaw and Charlie Hart. They played Slim Chance numbers plus *Willie And The Hand Jive*. Mrs. Clapton and Mrs. Lane did a can-can during *Ooo La La Alberta, Alberta* and one wag was heard to comment "Do *Layla* or we won't ask you again".

The UK tour started in April, supported by Slim Chance. By way of unhappy irony, the reporter sent by NME to review the Hammersmith Odeon concert in May, said he'd heard tell that Eric was drinking so much he was surprised to see him upright. Catching the end of the Slim Chance set "rumour had it that Ron (Lane) himself, was not averse to draining a fair few bevvies of an evening, so it came as some surprise to see his slight frame perfectly co-ordinating itself".[100] Wonder how that reporter felt when it became known that Ronnie Lane had been stricken with the crippling disease multiple sclerosis?

Extra dates were added to the itinerary and Eric's only free time was spent travelling between gigs and finally it all became too much. Roger Forrester, Clapton's manager, decided to put on another London date at the Rainbow but towards the end of the set Eric began to feel very ill. "It got worse and worse and as I got to the end of a number I thought if I don't get off, I'm going to fall over . . . I walked off stage and he (Roger Forrester) took me outside to get some fresh air and he was saying, you don't have to go back on boy – you don't have to go back on. So I'm sitting down in the dressing room and Townshend comes in and he comes up to me and says 'YOU CALL THIS SHOWBUSINESS!'[101] And he was right". Townshend hauled him back on stage and he stayed there for *Crossroads* and *Layla* which Eric virtually mimed behind Pete. Interviewed by the Sun newspaper in August, Eric had thankfully changed his mind about "a few good years then go". "Some people have short, frantic careers during which they reach incredible heights and do amazing things. But I don't want that. I want to be a rock and roll marathon runner, not a sprinter". And without doubt, he was due for some kind of endurance prize to go with the musician poll awards he continued to collect by the armful. Barely recovered from the UK tour, he was in the studio in June to record his next album *Slowhand*, followed by tours to Europe, Japan and Hawaii, all before mid-October.

Meeting up with Don Williams and playing his music put into sharper focus the embryonic country style of *No Reason To Cry*, Eric's main groove over the next two albums. The first of these was *Slowhand*, recorded at Olympic Studios, London, the first album since *Fresh Cream* that he had recorded on home territory. Still unable to call upon the services of Tom Dowd, Eric's choice of Glyn Johns as producer had its difficulties. Johns pushed harder than Dowd and there was a certain resentment on Eric's part of enforced studio discipline. Apparently, Patti would send notes to the studio explaining why Eric was going to be late just as though he was still at school. Eric works when he wants to, and if you miss it, tough luck. Glyn Johns worked hard to get the album done but it was well worth it. It was Eric's best since *Layla*, containing his best song since then, in *Wonderful Tonight*.

J.J. Cale's *Cocaine* opened the album and it became an instant concert favourite. Clapton admired Cale a lot and during the recording of *Slowhand*, Eric and the band went to see him play. They stood marvelling at the man and his music, playing an acoustic guitar with no back and eight pick ups, an ability to get a wah-wah sound without using a pedal and the sheer intensity of his technique. Later, after Cale had heard Clapton's version of the song, he asked him to join him on stage to play it again. Although Eric obviously asked permission to use *Cocaine*, he light-heartedly maintained that the riff was stolen from *Sunshine Of Your Love* and admittedly, it *was* pretty similar.

It has so often been the way that the best tracks on Clapton's albums have been self penned and *Wonderful Tonight* was no exception. A simple love song, with a haunting guitar refrain, it speaks volumes to anyone who has loved and shows how far along the road he had come since the days of *Layla*, although paradoxically for anyone who has loved and lost, it is harder to listen to than *Layla*. With this song, Eric found a whole new audience.

"Every now and then you fall in love again, albeit with the same woman, just one night for some reason – something she's said or the way she's approached the situation and bang! you're in love again and it's such a strong feeling you can't do anything else but write it down".[102]

*Cocaine* was not actually recorded as a tribute to J.J. Cale, that was Clapton and Levy's *Lay Down Sally*, a very 'English' country song, under-laid with Chuck Berry rock'n'roll phrases and a lightweight solo from Eric in homage to Cale's sparing style.

Eric is a master of the intimate vocal which make lines like "If you see her again/I will surely kill you" delivered with quiet venom on Don Williams' *Next Time You See Her* even more menacing. *We're All The Way* was probably a bit too feather light but the band bounced back with a gutsy song, *The Core*. Containing a strong riff, excellent vocal harmonies and some powerful keyboard, guitar and horn interplay (courtesy of Mel Collins, the first Clapton album since 1970 to feature a horn), which was mercifully not faded out.

Two non-originals followed, John Martyn's *May You Never* where Eric nicely captures Martyn's slurred intonation and Arthur Crudup's *Mean Old 'Frisco Blues*, slide guitar and vocal working in tight unison. *Peaches And Diesel*, the final track, was an instrumental very similar in feel to *Wonderful Night* and they were put on a single together, providing a perfect emotional resolution to the whole album, which deservedly got to No. 2 in the American album charts with the single *Lay Down Sally/Cocaine* reaching No. 3.

After the album was finished, the band suffered its first personnel change when Yvonne Elliman left to pursue a solo career. The percussionist, Sergio Rodriguez also departed back to South America.

For the European tour of Summer '77, it was decided to dispense with planes and limousines and travel by train instead. A set of private coaches including sleepers and a dining car from the Orient Express were hitched up to scheduled European services and went all over Europe, from Copenhagen to Germany, Holland, Belgium, France, Switzerland and back to Germany for a final concert in Munich. It was an eventful trip; Ronnie Lane collected £4 by busking on the ferry from Copenhagen to Bremen and Patti was beseiged by newshounds *wherever* they stopped, because news of her divorce from George Harrison had come through en route. With the disgruntled Americans sloping off to find hotels because they didn't want to sleep on the train, the Brits in the camp turned the tour into a works outing, Cockney carousing and four part harmonies on *Maybe It's Because I'm A Londoner* and *My Old Man Said Follow The Van*.

The repertoire was different every night and so was the atmosphere. In Paris, they played a converted abattoir called the Pavilion, in front of eight thousand screaming French. The gig in Brussels was a good example of what could happen when everything was going well and the audience was responsive. The whole band were very relaxed on a hot, sultry night and Eric turned a seven thousand seater stadium into a small club much as Bruce Springsteen did at Wembley in 1981. Wearing a light kaftan shirt, Eric was playing loose and easy. During *Stormy Monday* he strolled over to Jamie Oldaker's kit, sat down and reeled off the most stunning blues licks you've ever heard.

Tacked on to the end of the '77 Grand Tour were two Spanish gigs.

On 5th August, they were playing the Bullring in Ibiza. "When you walked into the dressing room, there was the operating table with blood gutters down the side of it for the matadors, when they get patched up. It was all a bit grim. I thought it was going to be a lovely old building like a rodeo place and it turned out to be a concrete monstrosity in the middle of nowhere. Terrible sound. Horrible people".[103] The yacht *Welsh Liberty* took Eric to Barcelona for the final gig at the Nuevo Pabellon Club on 11th August, then a six week gap before Japan (26th September–6th October) and Hawaii (7th–9th October.[104]

The band went into 1978 with a two-month American tour supported by Muddy Waters. Eric played brilliantly, he had to! But as for the rest of the band, there were the beginnings of problems. George Terry for one was losing interest after being on the road virtually non-stop since 1974.

Bob Dylan was touring Europe during the summer of 1978 and Eric appeared with him at Rotterdam (23rd June), at the Zeppelinfield, Nuremburg where Hitler held his rallies (1st July), and finally at Blackbushe Aerodrome in Surrey (15th July), where he played on *Forever Young*.

A much travelled musician, Eric had never played in Ireland, and this was rectified by two dates at the Dublin Stadium on 7th and 8th July. Whether the reporter sent to review the concert by an Irish paper was so overwhelmed at seeing Eric that he couldn't write straight or the sub-editor was a dyslexic Martian, the following is so full of howlers, it is worth reprinting in full. How many goofs can you spot?

"Clapton made his entrance to resounding cheers and tremendous applause. The storm broke with his first number *The Cave*. Along with him on vocals and tambourine, was Marcie Levy, who has an incredible voice, both powerful and musical. Marcie backed Clapton on a few numbers and did a fabulous rock number of her own with *Fools' Paradise*. The second lead guitarist was George Terry, and although a great guitarist, was overshadowed by Clapton's tremendous guitar work. I never knew a guitar, without gimmicks of any kind could do so many things. James O'Decher was on drums, with Carl Rodel on bass and Dick Simms on the keyboards. Rodel and Simms were with Derek and the Dominoes, when Clapton used to play with them. The second number was a blues number, sounding the way that only Clapton can sound on blues. It was stamped with Clapton's rock blues style. To calm the crowd, the next number was a slow blues number, *Wonderful Tinight*. But it didn't work, the cheering was phenomenal and after *Way Down Sally*, the storm was in full swing, with a standing ovation! All the favourite Clapton numbers were played, along with a superb version of Dylan's *Knocking On Heaven's Door*, played Clapton style and the rock-country number *Rodeo Man* and Marcie's solo version of *Nobody Knows You When You're Down*, with the famous *Cocaine* nearly bringing the house down. Clapton was again accompanied by Marcie on the harmonica with *Badge, Double Trouble, Precedence Of The Land* and *Back To The Border*, all showed Clapton's amazing handling of a guitar and built the crowd up to a climax which reached its height with the final number *Lola*.

The storm was ranging, and Clapton had to come back to do a wonderful blues encore and the crowd wouldn't let him go with their continuous applause and standing ovation that nearly drowned the encore.

Clapton had certainly stirred up a storm that a lot of people will find hard to forget. . . ."

The band came off the road during August and September, returning to Olympic Studios to record *Backless*. The title derived from Clapton's blow with Dylan at Blackbush and Dylan's habit of turning to face the band when he thought things were going wrong. So if you played to his back, you knew everything was okay.

The studio atmosphere was apathetic, and it showed. *Backless* could equally have been entitled *Spineless* or *Gutless*. Eric was still into writing "ditties and pleasant melodies" as he later called them and there is no better vehicle for that than bad country music. Of Clapton's four songs, the only one delivered with any conviction was *Golden Ring*, largely because Eric was determined that the song should be on the album. The other two reasonable tracks were both non-originals, *I'll Make Love To You Anytime* by J.J. Cale, Eric doing another spot-on guitar/vocal interpretation and *Tulsa Time* written by Don Williams' guitarist Danny Flowers which was regularly featured on stage. The album sold well enough but the writing was on the wall. As soon as the album was finished, George Terry left and went back to session work, followed by Marcy Levy who went solo.

The band carried on as a four piece until January 1979 when guitarist Albert Lee was brought in to replace George Terry, the first British musician to play in a band with Eric for ten years. Lee was a very accomplished country-style guitarist who had his first break back in 1964 with Chris Farlowe and the Thunderbirds. He had worked on numerous sessions and gigs with country bands, building his reputation all the while, until he landed a plum job in Emmylou Harris' Hot Band, replacing the legendary James Burton. Lee made his debut appearance during the band's eight-date tour of Ireland from 8th–17th March 1979, shortly before commencing a forty-seven city tour of America at the end of the month.

But the biggest event of 1979 as far as Eric was concerned, was his marriage to Patti Boyd at a secret ceremony in Tucson, Arizona. The outfits were tuxedos and tennis shoes, both the groom and the bride wore white and the service was conducted in Spanish. Having gone through hell to get her, Eric kept Patti waiting at the Marriage License Bureau – but *Layla* had come home.

Supported again by Muddy Waters, the American tour following the wedding was another triumph; the pairing of the master and one of his most successful heirs, moved even the most hardened and cynical of rock critics "... called back for an encore, Waters introduced his 'son' Eric Clapton (for) *Got My Mojo Working* . . . and when Willie Dixon came out to sing a verse, the emotion couldn't be denied. One tear into the show, I felt as if it were already over". Clapton was clearly inspired and challenged by the aura of electric blues guitar history hanging in the air. . . . "He barked out vicious and convoluted runs that had no beginning and no end, with melodies that came from nowhere and pointed everywhere. In the middle of the storm, I thought I heard Jimi Hendrix, smiled and felt the second tear".[105]

As John Mayall had done for him, Eric gave George Terry his wings and he flew, while the arrival of Albert Lee marked a turning point in Eric's attitude to having an American band – at least for the time being. In the end, the Americans in the Clapton camp became unwilling to participate in Eric's "family approach" to being a band leader. Lee's presence "showed me that although American musicians may be closer to some of the music, they are not necessarily the right kind of people to play in a rock band and keep company with".[106] The camp often split in two during the '77 train tour of Europe, apathy ruled while *Backless* was in production and finally at the end of the '79 American tour, Eric dispensed with their services.

The break up of the band must have hit Carl Radle the hardest; associated with Eric for ten years and regarded in the past by his boss as something of a father figure. "Carl is mostly our leader. He's The Rock. He's The Elder. If I'm ever in doubt about anything, he'll put me straight . . . he can be a philosophical guide towards what is happening in your life. He's got all the answers you need".[107] But the man with all the answers died in June 1980 of a kidney infection brought on by heroin addiction, which Ron Wood inferred was Eric's fault for splitting up the band. "Carl was a lovely guy. He had nothing left after the Ric thing".[108]

Asked in 1978, when Eric was still completely enthusiastic about playing with American musicians, he said "Well, they're the best. I think they play better than most British musicians. The only two I've met who can come anywhere near Jamie and Carl are Henry Spinetti (drums) and Dave Markee (bass). I think they're fine. But they're session musicians, studio men".[109] And it was in the studio that they first met up with them, in 1977 during the recording of the Pete Townshend/Ronnie Lane album *Rough Mix*. A second meeting took place the following year, while Eric was doing sessions for an American Civil War concept album *White Mansions*. Spinetti and Markee had a long track record of sessions, together as the rhythm section for Joan Armatrading, Leo Sayer and a band called Lazy Racer and separately for artists such as Michael Chapman, Alan Price, Roger Daltrey and Roger Chapman. So Eric built up his new band from the rhythm section, brought in ex-Joe Cocker/Grease Band keyboard man Chris Stainton and together with Albert Lee, took the all-British troupe for his first visit behind the Iron Curtain in October 1979. Eric hoped for a challenge, the chance to play to new audiences – what he got was one of his worst experiences as a working musician.

The trouble happened in Poland where Clapton albums were as rare as oranges and his name was uttered only in hushed whispers, so intense was the power of the legend among those who had never seen him. The Warsaw concerts were not much different from "business nights" back home – rather stiff and formal with civic dignitaries replacing record company executives in the front rows. The effect on the band, albeit different musicians was the same – bad. The young audience in Katowice were far more responsive, reacting like any Western rock audience. But the police responded to this natural exuberance with blatant thuggery, reminiscent of the worst excesses of the American police during some of the Blind Faith concerts. The PA system was wrecked, the police storm-trooped all over the stage, using face freezing Mace against young kids. The band were powerless to intervene with either the audience or the heavies, because of the language barrier and Eric just refused to play the second show. The Poles blamed the management for everything and Roger Forrester was forced to forfeit the fee in order to escape the country which they did at the first opportunity.

December saw the band in much friendlier surroundings on tour in Japan. Inevitably they played the famous Budokan Theatre in Tokyo and there was an equal inevitability about the recording of a live album there, a two-record set, *Just One Night*. As the title suggested, the album was a recording of a whole concert on one night, in just about the best environment for making a live album anywhere in the world. The technical back-up, acoustics and facilities were fautless; albums recorded there normally do very well and this one was no exception. Eric laid out a tried and tested catalogue of exemplary performances executed with easy finesse and heard by audience and record buyer with bell-like clarity.

There were no surprises, but the mix of old favourites and slow blues numbers neatly summarised the point which Eric has reached in his career – playing the first, to earn himself the right to play the second.

Against a backdrop of press criticism, accusing Eric of being "a poetic talent turned prosaic" and churning out music that "was once revivalist and is now structured and formalised", the album was a top five seller in America and in Britain, where its release in May 1980 coincided with Eric's first UK tour in eighteen months.

If the music on *Just One Night* sounded a shade tired, it was perhaps less to do with Eric becoming jaded and more the result of the personnel change. In concert, the British musicians who were as Eric himself said basically session guys, did not push Eric as hard as their predecessors. Albert Lee and George Terry were very different players – Terry's hard edged rock/blues style gave way to Lee's highly talented but essentially unobtrusive country playing. The rhythm section of Dave Markee and Henry Spinetti while airtight, tended to restrict Eric somewhat, if he wanted to get into a loose jam at which the Americans were more adept and there were occasional problems in deviating from the regular charts.

The addition of Gary Brooker did nothing to alter the situation on stage, but it did add a distinctive and powerful vocal sound and a chance to extend the repertoire, by taking advantage of Brooker's writing skills. However, there were no solo Brooker songs on the band's first studio album *Another Ticket* released in 1981.

Produced once again by Tom Dowd, the album broke no new ground, but did show Eric in a mood to play with more verve and attack than of late and here the disciplined session experience of the rest of the band came into its own, on songs like *Something Special, I Can't Stand It* and *Rita Mae*, all Clapton originals.

Since his comeback in 1974, Eric has not progressed in his music, apart from demonstrating a growing confidence as a singer. This seems to be deliberate on his part; far from being a musician who develops through experimentation, Eric has meandered through the lexicon of popular music, finding a particular groove that suits the mood for an album or two and then moving on. This is a process fraught with danger. He has not always managed to avoid sounding run of the mill on record and at his worst Clapton is representative of the bland and slick face of corporate (American) rock and a servant of the legions of Hip Easy Listeners. On the other hand, certain elements of surprise are retained in the music; there is no guarantee that the fan of one album will be equally enthusiastic about the next as Eric moves through reggae, country and rock while retaining his hold on the blues. At the end of the day it is a formula that works; whatever the groove, each phase has a distinctive Clapton gloss, making it instantly recognisable and perennially marketable.

The success of *Another Ticket* in 1981 continued to prove the point, but it was one of the few bright spots in a year of disaster. Eight dates into a fifty-seven date tour of America, his biggest ever, Clapton was rushed to hospital after collapsing at the Dano County Expo Centre, Madison, Wisconsin. Perforated ulcers were diagnosed, the result of years of drinking and rich food and he was very seriously warned about his future alcohol intake. He spent four weeks and his 36th birthday in St. Paul's United Hospital, Philadelphia. Four days after his discharge, the car he was travelling in, shot a red light in downtown Seattle, hit another car and smashed into a telegraph pole. Eric was sidelined again, the rest of the U.S. tour was cancelled along with projected tours to Japan and South America. Amazingly due to this rest period, not only did bogus Clapton managers crawl out of the woodwork, but so did a Clapton clone who went round America clocking up bills in Eric's name, almost persuading Fender to hand over some expensive guitars.

To his eternal credit, Clapton has always been keen to do benefit gigs. He only made two more stage appearances during 1981 both in England. One was at the Wolverhampton Civic Hall in November for John Wile, captain of West Bromwich Albion football team and the other was alongside Jeff Beck at the Amnesty International Show in London. They played *Farther On Up The Road, Crossroads, 'Cos We've Been Lovers* and the finale, *I Shall Be Released* with Sting and Phil Collins, the first time Beck and Clapton had been recorded together.

Beck and Clapton are peas from the same pod, constantly changing tack over the years and often hypercritical of past achievements. The main difference is their approach to playing. At the Amnesty Show, Eric played well within himself, relying on a stock of licks built up over the years, but as ever, capable of making the plainest phrases sing. Beck on the other hand, played with far more aggression, finding new expression even within the well worn idiomatic phrasing of standards like *Crossroads*.

Events off stage rather than on, were the focus of interest for Clapton watchers during 1982. Apart from a short Spring tour to America to fulfill previous commitments, Eric stayed off the road and no new records were released. However, 1982 did mark the end of his sixteen year association with Robert Stigwood. Clapton had steadily built up closer links with Roger Forrester his manager, who wanted to branch out on his own, form a new label and take Eric with him. What probably brought matters to a head was RSO's ruthless pruning of its UK operation at this time. Eric too, was tired of being an anonymous number in a large corporation and so Great Records was created, (later renamed Duck Records). Not that the shadow of corporate rock was exactly shaken off; the label's product is distributed by Warner Brothers.

For a musician of his status and wealth, Clapton has shown remarkably little interest in his business affairs, for instance, he knew nothing of the plans for the Polish trip until a week before. Roger Forrester takes care of everything and has cocooned 'his boy' from financial concerns and undue media pressure for quite some time.

Eric has been encouraged to diversify his business interests with assets in racehorses and Barberstown Castle a hotel in Ireland. But although a fully paid up member of the rock elite, he continues to sing for his supper. Clapton might not always extend himself as a player and his studio discipline is a bit wayward, but he remains a serious and dedicated musician. His touring schedules, too, have been awesome since his comeback. How much he runs and how much he is pushed is difficult to determine, but he has gone on record as saying that he finds it a problem being off the road for too long. Yet recently he has announced in private that he reckons he is too old to tour and wants to give it up. If that happens (which is doubtful), he may find that for a "labourer guitarist", it is not so easy, for while his money might be diversified, his own activities are not.

During the latter part of 1982, Eric broke up his all British band, retaining Albert Lee and Chris Stainton. In drummer Henry Spinetti's case, the new persona of a Born Again Christian proved too much for the others to take and contributed to his departure. Dave Markee went with him, the pair of them being replaced by a 22 carat American rhythm section, the legendary bassist Duck Dann and Roger Hawkins, lynchpin of the Muscle Shoals Studio.

Eric's appearances on television have been few and far between, so for him to make two appearances on British T.V. within months of one another was something of a landmark, although the events themselves were less than memorable. In December 1982, he guested on Chas and Dave's Xmas Show. Given Eric's cockney proclivities, the spectre of Eric coming on to do a *Knees Up Mother Brown* finale number loomed large. Thankfully, we were spared that degrading spectacle and instead, Eric along with Albert Lee, played some tasteful country rock material. He followed this up with a farcical "interview" on breakfast television. All the way through the programme, the presenters were building up the atmosphere, along the lines of "Eric Clapton's first T.V. interview since The Flood", etc. The grand finale was a five minute interview of moronic (presumably vetted) questioning intercut with clips from Cream's farewell Albert Hall concert, captioned 18th May 1973!

1983 – Eric Clapton celebrated twenty years as a professional musician in the only way he knew how, another album and another tour. The new band went to Compass Point to record Eric's latest album to date, *Money and Cigarettes* released in February. (At the time of writing, Eric is back there with Phil Collins as producer doing the album for '84). Inspired perhaps by Salvador Dali's soft watches, the cover featured a soft guitar draped over an ironing board. Critics of Clapton would say a limp guitar sums up Eric's approach to music these days, while his supporters could equally charge that a melted guitar is the perfect symbol for the blistering blue guitarist Clapton still is. *Money and Cigarettes* did not change the mind of either camp, but even so made a very respectable chart showing on both sides of the Atlantic. An interesting marketing ploy to promote the cassette version was to launch it as a double play, with the music on one side and an interview with Eric on the other explaining the genesis of each track. The guest musician was another great guitarist Ry Cooder and what comes across in the interview is Clapton's sincere respect for his fellow musicians, how much they play a part in the creation of his music and what inspiration he draws from them, particularly other guitarists. Clapton and Cooder traded some nice licks on *The Shape You're In* and *Pretty Girl*. Also clear is the ad hoc manner in which a Clapton album is cobbled together, with little pre-planning and no idea of the end result.

The presence of Dunn and Hawkins gave the music a harder and funkier edge than most of Clapton's post *Layla* output, Sleepy John Estes' *Everybody Oughta Make A Change* and Albert King's *Crosscut Saw* were two good examples. Probably more than most, Albert King has been Clapton's stylistic mentor and it was a nice gesture to Eric's blues fans to include that song. Eric said the track came about because Dunn and Hawkins started playing it and he wanted to prove to them that he could still bend those strings like in the old days, but the studio is not Clapton's best environment and there was nowhere near enough bite on this track or the others that went up to make the album. One is forced to conclude that Clapton has done it all before and done it better. On stage, Eric still has much to offer, but his recorded output continues to frustrate. It was significant that his sell out tours of America, Britain and Europe during the months following the release of *Money and Cigarettes* featured few songs from the new album.

Eric has lived with hit records and sell out concerts for the past twenty years, so he had to do something a bit special to mark this anniversary year and in the best traditions of the camaraderie that exists between some of Britain's troubadour musicians of the Sixties, it happened at the Albert Hall on 20th September.

Ronnie Lane's long, heroic fight against multiple sclerosis is now well known. A fellow MS sufferer, DJ Stuart Henry was branded an alcoholic because his movements became progressively uncoordinated and Lane too, was subject to similar thoughtless diagnosis by the unenlightened during the early manifestations of the disease. Personal acceptance was very difficult and Ronnie Lane was often deep in despair about his crippling condition. A special kind of oxygen treatment gave him relief and hope, but as is so often the case, further research was itself crippled by lack of funds. Ronnie's wife Boo, contacted Pete Townshend with a view to staging a benefit concert for Action Research into MS (ARMS). Not only did this come off, but it brought together on stage for the first time, the most glittering array of British rock talent ever assembled. Standing side by side were Eric Clapton, Jeff Beck, Jimmy Page together with Charlie Watts, Bill Wyman, Andy Fairweather Low, Kenney Jones and Stevie Winwood.

The background to the staging of the concerts was quite complex. Originally the ARMS benefit was due to be held at Hammersmith. Unknown to the organisers, Eric arranged to do a concert at the Albert Hall in aid of the Prince Charles Trust Charity. Eventually, the ARMS date switched to the Albert Hall so that the first night would be for ARMS, the second night for the Charity, using the same set of musicians. There developed some animosity between the Clapton management and the Royal Palace officials who not only viewed the ARMS concert as a "warm up" for Charles and Di, but actually expected the Royals to get paid. Further aggravation flared up later; the concerts were so successful that the whole entourage went to America for an 8 date, 4 city tour to which Paul Rodgers and Joe Cocker were added. Rod Stewart wanted to get in on the act, but Eric was so disgusted at Stewart's previous lack of support for his one time Faces cohort that he threatened to walk off the stage if Stewart walked on.

None of this however detracted from the marvellous spirit that bound the musicians together on stage, generating a true sense of occasion. Eric opened the Albert Hall concert with Watts, Jones and Ray Cooper on percussion, Chris Stainton and Stevie Winwood on keyboards, Bill Wyman and Andy Fairweather Low belting out a clutch of Clapton favourites. On the opening notes of *Cocaine*, the audience rose as one. Stevie Winwood in particularly fine voice and Andy Fairweather Low took turns at the mike doing standards followed by a blistering set from Jeff Beck, using his American band plus ace English drummer Simon Phillips. Beck delighted the audience with *Hi Ho Silver Lining*, a clear indication how good everyone was feeling that night. In the dressing room later, a smiling Eric was heard to comment on how he thought Jeff really was the best guitarist in England. Certainly Beck has lost nothing of his astonishing skill. Jimmy Page's contribution was curious. He played well enough but spent most of the time moving in backward circles. He offered an instrumental version of *Stairway To Heaven* among other numbers then it happened; Beck, Page and Clapton came on to the stage together – *Tulsa Time, Louise* and a hilarious version of *Layla*. Andy Fairweather Low's rhythm guitar suddenly came up very loud and he was playing too fast. He drowned out the triple lead opening which the three guitarists started at fractionally different times anyway. But nobody really cared; the audience witnessed a historic good time shambles and justifiably loved every minute of it. Not surprisingly, the biggest cheer of the evening was reserved for Ronnie Lane, helped on to the stage for a poignant rendition of *Bombers Moon* – scarcely a dry eye in the house.

Throughout the whole occasion, Eric was as self-effacing as ever. He is probably the only musician of world stature who does not consider himself a frontman. No billing hassles about Eric going on first at the ARMS concert! Later when Beck and Page were strutting their stuff at the front of the stage, Eric was standing near the back among the other musicians, happy to be just one of the crowd. Yet however much he may try and disown the past, it was during the Sixties and early Seventies that Eric made his finest statements; it is for John Mayall, Cream and *Layla* that Clapton will be *most* remembered so the last word in this look at Eric's distinguished career is going to another master of the blues guitar, Mike Bloomfield, now sadly no longer with us. He is talking about Eric back in 1968, during the period when Clapton and Hendrix were spoken of in the same breath. Bloomfield's words still strike resonant chords when Eric Clapton is up there on stage, doing what he does better than anyone else – the blues pure and simple.

"His attack is flawless, that's one of the things. A perfect musician is dedicated. He has ideas, attack, touch. His ability to transmit his ideas and his emotion logically is kineticism; he can build. Eric does all of these about as well as you can do them. It shows in the area that he plays that his attack is perfect. His tone is vocal; his ideas are superb; he plays almost exclusively blues – all the lines he plays in the Cream are blues lines. He plays nothing but blues; he's a blues guitarist and he's taken blues guitar to its ultimate thing. In that field he's B.B. King cum the Freddie King and Ernie Cahill style of guitar playing. Eric is the master in the world. That is why he is a perfect guitarist. Eric plays in bad taste when he wants to. He can play crappy. But, like Eric plays almost exclusively perfect".

# DISCOGRAPHY

**THE YARDBIRDS**

Singles:

| | |
|---|---|
| *I Wish You Would/A Certain Girl* | Columbia DB7283 (1964) |
| *Good Morning Little Schoolgirl/I Ain't Got You* | Columbia DB7391 (1964) |
| *For Your Love/Got To Hurry* | Columbia DB7499 (1965) |
| *Boom Boom/Honey In Your Hips* | Buzz 101 |

Bootleg single – released in Holland and withdrawn.

EPs:
Contrary to popular opinion, Eric did not play on *Five Yardbirds* Columbia 8421 (1965), although he is on the front cover. The guitarist is Jeff Beck.

Albums:
**Five Live Yardbirds**                    Columbia 33SX1677 (1964)
*Too Much Monkey Business/I Got Love If You Want It/Smokestack Lightnin'/
Good Mornin' Little Schoolgirl/Respectable/Five Long Years/Pretty Girl/Louise/
I'm A Man/Here 'Tis.*
Re-released on Charly CR30173 (1979).
**Sonny Boy Williamson And The Yardbirds**        Fontana TL5277 (1966)
*Bye Bye Bird/Mister Downchild/23 Hours Too Long/Out On The Waterfront/
Baby Don't Worry/Pontiac Blues/Take It Easy Baby/ I Don't Care No More/
Do The Weston*
Re-released on Fontana 1966, 1967, Mercury 1966 (US), and Philips 1975.
In 1980, the German label L&R released an album called *Live In London With
Sonny Boy Williamson* (L&R 42020). Bye Bye Bird/Mr Downchild/The River Rhine/
23 Hours Too Long/Lost Care/Pontiac Blues/Take It Easy Baby/On The Waterfront/
I Don't Care No More/Honey In Your Hips/Western Arizona.
These tracks are mostly different takes from the ones on the original Fontana album.
*Honey In Your Hips* is a different studio take and *Western Arizona* is *Do The
Weston* renamed.

**Having A Rave Up With The Yardbirds**        EPIC 26177 (1965) (US)
                                                    CBS GCX28 (1965) (Ger)
Some tracks from **Five Live Yardbirds** – the rest is studio material with Jeff Beck.
**Remember The Yardbirds**                EMI Starline SRS 5069 (1971)
*Heart Full Of Soul/Smokestack Lightnin'/I Wish You Would*/Good Morning
Little Schoolgirl/Evil Hearted You/For Your Love/Shapes Of Things/Still I'm Sad/
My Girl Sloopy/A Certain Girl/I Ain't Done Wrong/I'm A Man*
\* Different version from the single taken from US Album.
*For Your Love*                            Epic 26167 (1965).
**The Yardbirds: Rock Generation No. 1**      BYG 529701 (1972) (Fr)
*Too Much Monkey Business/Got Love If You Want It/Smokestack Lightnin'/Good
Morning Little Schoolgirl/She's So Respectable*
**Rock Generation No. 2**                BYG 529702 (1972) (Fr)
*Five Long Years/Pretty Girl/Louise/I'm A Man/Here 'Tis*
**Rock Generation No. 5**                BYG 522705 (1972) (Fr)
*Slow Walk/Yardbirds Beat/My Little Cabin*
Tracks released in France only taken from two sessions – Crawdaddy December
1968 and Birmingham Town Hall 1964.
**The Yardbirds: London 1963. The First
Recordings**                             L&R 44001 (1981)
*Smokestack Lightnin'/You Can't Judge A Book By Looking At The Cover/Take It
Easy Baby/Talkin' About You/Let It Rock/I Wish You Would/Boom Boom/Honey
In Your Hips/Who Do You Love*
Tracks 1–6 recorded live at The Crawdaddy December 7th and 8th 1963. Tracks
7 and 8 released as a single then withdrawn. Track 9 recorded at the same session.

*Selected other Yardbirds material with Eric Clapton*
**The Yardbirds Story** (double)          Riviera 521.177/78 (Spa)
Includes *Got To Hurry* with a different guitar solo.
**Jeff Beck And The Yardbirds**            BYG 200.139 (Ger)
                                                  CHARLY CR30013 (1975)
Contains one Clapton track *For RSG* (Ready, Steady Go) which is really a studio
version of *Here 'Tis*.
**Performances By Clapton, Beck And Page**    EPIC 30135 (1970) (US)
**Eric Clapton And The Yardbirds**        Springboard 4036 (197 ) (US)
**The Yardbirds With Eric Clapton**       Charly CR 30012 (1977)
**Shapes Of Things** (double)             Charly CDXI (1977)

Bootlegs:
**More Golden Eggs**                        TMOQ 61003
Two versions of *I Wish You Would* – both Clapton. The rest is Beck.
It is very likely that other material featuring Eric with the Yardbirds is still buried in
vaults and basements most probably in Europe.

# ERIC CLAPTON AND THE POWERHOUSE

Albums:
**What's Shakin'**                                    Elektra EKL 4002 (1966)
Three tracks only: *I Want To Know/Crossroads/Steppin' Out*

# JOHN MAYALL'S BLUESBREAKERS

Singles:
*I'm Your Witchdoctor/Telephone Blues*        Immediate IMO12 (1965)
*On Top Of The World* was recorded at the same session and appeared on a British
Blues sampler.
*Lonely Years/Bernard Jenkins*                Purdah 3502 (1966)
Both tracks appeared on *Raw Blues*           Ace Of Clubs ACL1220 (1967)
*Key To Love/Parchman Farm*                   Decca F12490 (1966)

Albums:
**John Mayall's Bluesbreakers featuring
Eric Clapton**                                Decca SKL 4804 (1966)
*All Your Love/Hideaway/Little Girl/Another Man/Double Crossing Time/What'd I
Say/Key To Love/Parchman Farm/Have You Heard/Ramblin' On My Mind/
Steppin' Out/It Ain't Right*
**Looking Back**                              Decca SKL 5010 (1970)
Live cut of *Stormy Monday*
**Primal Solos**                              London LC50003 (1977)
                                              Decca Tab 66 1983
Side One with the Mayall/Clapton/Flint/McVie lineup recorded live at the
Flamingo in April 1966.
*Maudie/It Hurts To Be In Love/Have You Ever Loved A Woman/Bye Bye Bird/
I'm Your Hoochie Coochie Man*
Numerous re-packagings over the years, but one album of interest was:
**Back To The Roots**                         Polydor 2483 016 (1971)
Mayall actually got his old sidemen together to record tracks for a double album –
glaring omissions were Peter Green, Aynsley Dunbar and Jack Bruce (who refused
to do it). Eric played on *Prisons On The Road* with Mayall (piano/vocals),
Sugarcane Harris (violin), Larry Taylor (bass), Paul Lagos (drums) – *Accidental
Suicide* with Mick Taylor and Harvey Mandel (guitars), Sugarcane Harris, Larry
Taylor. Tasty wah-wah solo on this ironically anti-drug song with references to
Hendrix in it.
Also plays on *Home Again, Looking At Tomorrow, Force Of Nature* and *Goodbye
December*.

# CREAM

Singles:
*Wrapping Paper/Cat Squirrel*                 Reaction 591007 (1966)
*I Feel Free/NSU*                             Reaction 591011 (1966)

| | |
|---|---|
| *Strange Brew/Tales Of Brave Ulysses* | Reaction 591015 (1967) |
| *Anyone For Tennis/Pressed Rat And Warthog* | Polydor 56358 (1968) |
| *Sunshine Of Your Love/SWLABR* | Polydor 56286 (1968) |
| *White Room/Those Were The Days* | Polydor 56300 (1969) |
| *Badge/What A Bringdown* | Polydor 56315 (1969) |
| *Crossroads/Passing The Time* | Atco 14293 (1969) (US only) |
| *Badge/Tales Of Brave Ulysses* | 7 inch RSO (1982) |
| *Badge/Tales Of Brave Ulysses/White Room* | 12 inch RSO (1982) |

EPs:

**Top Of The Milk**                       MTGL 332788
*Steppin' Out/Big Black Woman Blues/Lawdy Mama/Crossroads*
Bootleg


Albums:

**Fresh Cream**                           Reaction 593001 (1966)
*NSU/Sleepy Time Time/Dreaming/Sweet Wine/Spoonful/Cat Squirrel/Four Until Late/Rollin' And Tumblin'/I'm So Glad/Toad*
**Full Cream**                            Polydor 2447010 (1966)
Same as *Fresh Cream* with a shortened version of *Spoonful*.
**I Feel Free**                           Triumph 2496007 (1971) (Fr)
Same as *Fresh Cream*, minus *Cat's Squirrel* and *Sweet Wine* but with *I Feel Free, Wrapping Paper, The Coffee Song* and *Sunshine Of Your Love*.
**Disraeli Gears**                        Reaction 594003 (1967)
*Strange Brew/Sunshine Of Your Love/World Of Pain/Dance The Night Away/ Blue Condition/Tales Of Brave Ulysses/SWLABR/We're Going Wrong/Outside Woman Blues/Take It Back/Mother's Lament*
**Wheels Of Fire** (double)               Polydor 583 031/2 (1968)
*White Room/Sitting On Top Of The World/Passing The Time/As You Said/ Pressed Rat And Warthog/Politician/Those Were The Days/Born Under A Bad Sign/ Deserted Cities Of The Heart* (Studio Album)/*Crossroads/Spoonful/Train Time/ Toad* (Live at the Fillmore)
*Wheels Of Fire* also released as two LPs.
**Wheels Of Fire** (Studio Album)         Polydor 583 033 (1968)
**Wheels Of Fire** (Live at Fillmore album)   Polydor 583 040 (1968)
**Goodbye**                               Polydor 583 053 (1969)
*I'm So Glad/Politician/Sitting On Top Of The World/Badge/Doing That Scrapyard Thing/What A Bringdown*
**Best Of Cream**                         Polydor 583060 (1969)*
*Sunshine Of Your Love/Badge/Crossroads/White Room*/SWLABR/Born Under A Bad Sign/Spoonful/Tales Of Brave Ulysses/Strange Brew/I Feel Free*
* Shorter version than on *Wheels Of Fire* with one verse missing.
**Live Cream**                            Polydor 2383016 (1970)
*NSU/Sleepy Time Time/Lawdy Mama* (Studio)/*Sweet Wine/Rollin' Tumblin'*
**Live Cream Vol. II**                    Polydor 2383119 (1972)
*Deserted Cities Of The Heart/White Room/Politician/Tales Of Brave Ulysses/ Sunshine Of Your Love/Steppin' Out*

Numerous re-packagings including:

| | |
|---|---|
| **Heavy Cream** | RSO 2659 022 (1973) |
| **Cream** | Polydor Standard 2384 067 (1975) |
| **Portrait Of Cream** | Polydor 2482 142 (1975) |
| **The Best Of Cream Vol. II** | Polydor 2675 087 (1975) |
| **Pop Giants** | Brunswick 2911 528 (1976) |
| **Best Of Cream Live** | Polydor 2674 018 (1976) |
| **Pop History** | Polydor 2675 014 (1977) |
| **Cream Vol. II** | RSO 2479 701 (1978) |
| **Early Cream** | Springboard 4037 (1977) (US) |
| *Once Upon A Time* – Cream (double) | RSO 2658 139 (1981) |

A boxed set of albums was also issued recently in Germany.


Bootlegs:

**Hello Again On Tour**                                 ZAP 7865
*Steppin' Out/Sweet Wine/Lost Love/NSU/Big Mama Blues/Sleepy Time Time/
Crossroads*
**Royal Albert Hall 1968**                              WRMB 366
*Cat Squirrel/Hey Lawdy Mama/Spoonful/Crossroads/NSU/White Room/Sunshine
Of Your Love*
**'67–'68**                                             CBM 47-106
*Steppin' Out/Sweet Wine/Lost Love/NSU/Big Black Woman Blues/Sleepy Time
Time/Crossroads* (All from Amsterdam 1967)
*White Room/Politician/Crossroads/Sitting On Top Of The World/I'm So Glad/
Sunshine Of Your Love* (All from Albert Hall 1968)
**BBC '66 (9.12.66)**
*Cat Squirrel/Traintime/Lawdy Mama/I'm So Glad/NSU/Steppin' Out/Big Mama
Blues/Sleepy Time Time/Crossroads*
There are at least two more Cream Bootleg albums – one was called *Steppin' Out*
which included *White Room* and *Sunshine Of Your Love* from the Albert Hall and
*SWLABR, Steppin' Out* and *We're Going Wrong* from the BBC radio show Top
Gear recorded in 1967. The other album was recorded live in Rotterdam.


## BLIND FAITH

Singles:
Instrumental jam (repeated on both sides) Mono.  Island Promo (1969)
Island sent out records instead of cards to announce their change of address from
23rd June 1969. Very rare.

Albums:
**Blind Faith**                                         Polydor 583 059 (1969)
*Had To Cry Today/Can't Find My Way Home/Well All Right/Presence Of The
Lord/Sea Of Joy/Do What You Like*

Bootlegs:
**US Tour**                                             TAKRL 1902

*Crossroads/Presence Of The Lord/Means To An End/Well All Right/Can't Find My Way Home/Had To Cry Today*
Recorded at the Winterland, San Francisco.

## DELANEY AND BONNIE AND FRIENDS

Single:
*Comin' Home/Groupie (Superstar)*          Atlantic (1970)

Albums:
**Delaney And Bonnie On Tour With Eric Clapton** Atlantic K30030 (1970)
*Things Get Better/Poor Elijah/Tribute To Robert Johnson/Only You Know And I Know/I Don't Want To Discuss It/That's What My Man Is For/Where There's A Will There's A Way/Comin' Home/Long Tall Sally/Jenny Jenny/The Girl Can't Help It/Tutti Frutti*
**Delaney And Bonnie Together**          CBS 64959 (1972)
*Only You Know And I Know/Wade In The River Jordan/Sound Of The City/ Well Well/I Know How It Feels To Be Lonely/Comin' Home/Move 'Em Out/Big Change Comin'/A Good Thing (I'm On Fire)/Groupie (Superstar)/I Know Something/Good About You/Country Life*

## DEREK AND THE DOMINOES

Singles:
*Tell The Truth/Roll It Over*    N.B. Withdrawn    Polydor 2058057 (1970)
*Layla/Bell Bottom Blues*                   Polydor 2058130 (1970)
Re-released in 1972.

Albums:
**Layla** (double)               Polydor 2625005 (1970)
*I Looked Away/Bell Bottom Blues/Keep On Growing/Nobody Knows You (When You're Down And Out)/I Am Yours/Anyday/Key To The Highway/Tell The Truth/ Why Does Love Got To Be So Sad/Have You Ever Loved A Woman/Little Wing/ It's Too Late/Layla/Thorn Tree In The Garden*
**In Concert** (double)            RSO 2659 020 (1973)
*Why Does Love Got To Be So Sad/Got To Get Better In A Little While/Let It Rain/ Presence Of The Lord/Tell The Truth/Bottle Of Red Wine/Roll It Over/Blues Power/Have You Ever Loved A Woman*

Bootlegs:
**Stormy Monday** (Live Santa Monica Civic
20.11.70)                     TMOQ 71082
*Derek's Boogie/Blues Power/Stormy Monday/Let It Rain*

## ERIC CLAPTON

Single:
*After Midnight/Easy Now*             Polydor 2001 096 (1970)

Albums:
**Eric Clapton**                                   Polydor 2323021 (1970)
*Slunky/Bad Boy/Lonesome And A Long Way From Home/After Midnight/Easy*
*Now/Blues Power/Bottle Of Red Wine/Lovin' You Lovin' Me/I've Told You For*
*The Last Time/I Don't Know Why/Let It Rain*
**History Of Eric Clapton**                        Polydor 2659012 (1972)
*I Ain't Got You/Hideaway/Tales Of Brave Ulysses/I Want To Know/Sunshine Of*
*Your Love/Crossroads/Sea Of Joy/Only You Know And I Know/I Don't Want To*
*Discuss It/Teasin'/Blues Power/Spoonful/Badge/Tell The Truth/Tell The Truth*
*(Jam)/Layla*
Definitely not yer average compilation album, including such gems as *I Ain't Got*
*You* by the Yardbirds and *Teasin'* recorded for King Curtis cited by Eric in one
interview as his favourite recording of his own music. Good sleeve notes by Jean-
Charles Costa.
**Rainbow Concert**                                RSO 2394116 (1973)
*Badge/Roll It Over/Presence Of The Lord/Pearly Queen/After Midnight/Little Wing*


## ERIC CLAPTON AND HIS BAND 1974


Singles:
| | |
|---|---|
| *I Shot The Sheriff/Give Me Strength* | RSO 2090 132 (1974) |
| *Willie And The Hand Jive/Mainline Florida* | RSO 2090 139 (1974) |
| *Swing Low Sweet Chariot/Pretty Blue Eyes* | RSO 2090 158 (1975) |
| *Knockin' On Heaven's Door/Someone Like You* | RSO 2090 166 (1975) |
| *Hello Old Friend/All Our Past Times* | RSO 2090 208 (1976) |
| *Carnival/Hungry* | RSO 2090 222 (1977) |
| *Lay Down Sally/Cocaine* | RSO 2090 264 (1977) |
| *Wonderful Tonight/Peaches And Diesel* | RSO 2090 275 (1978) |
| *Promises/Watch Out For Lucy* | RSO 21 (1978) |
| *If I Don't Be There By Morning/Tulsa Time* | RSO 24 (1979) |
| *I Can't Stand It/Black Rose* | RSO 74 (1980) |
| *Another Ticket/Rita Mae* | RSO 75 (1981) |
| *Layla/Wonderful Tonight* (Live) | RSO 87 (1982) |
| *Layla/Wonderful Tonight* (Live) 12 inch | RSOX 87 (1982) |
| *I Shot The Sheriff/Cocaine* | RSO 88 (1982) |
| *I Shot The Sheriff/Cocaine/* | |
| *Knockin' On Heaven's Door* (Live) 12 inch | RSOX 88 (1982) |
| *I've Got A Rock'n'Roll Heart/Man In Love/* | |
|    *Everybody Oughta Make A Change* 12 inch | WB W9780T (1983) |
| *I've Got A Rock'n'Roll Heart/Man In Love* | WB W9780 (1983) |
| *The Shape You're In/Crosscut Saw/Pretty Girl* | |
|    12 inch | WB W9701T (1983) |
| *The Shape You're In/Crosscut Saw* | WB W9801 (1983) |
| *The Shape You're In/Crosscut Saw* | WB W9701P (1983) |
| | (Picture Disc) |
| *Slow Down Linda/Crazy Country Hop* | WB W9851 (1983) |

This was due to come out as a 12 inch with a live version of *The Shape You're In*,
but was never released.

EPs:
10 inch EP
*Prime Cuts*                                    RSO Single (1974)
*Smile* (Live)

Albums:
**461 Ocean Boulevard**                         RSO 2479 118 (1974)
*Motherless Children/Give Me Strength/Willie And The Hand Jive/Get Ready/*
*I Shot The Sheriff/I Can't Hold Out/Please Be With Me/Let It Grow/Steady*
*Rollin' Man/Mainline Florida*
**There's One In Every Crowd**                  RSO 2479 132 (1975)
*We've Been Told (Jesus Coming Soon)/Swing Low Sweet Chariot/Little Rachel/*
*Don't Blame Me/The Sky Is Crying/Singin' The Blues/Better Make It Through*
*Today/Pretty Blue Eyes/High/Opposites*
**E.C. Was Here**                               RSO 2394 160 (1975)
*Have You Ever Loved A Woman/Presence Of The Lord/Drifting Blues/Can't Find*
*My Way Home/Ramblin' On My Mind/Further On Up The Road*
**No Reason To Cry**                            RSO 2479 179 (1976)
*Beautiful Thing/Carnival/Sign Language/County Jail Blues/All Our Past Times/*
*Hello Old Friend/Double Trouble/Innocent Times/Hungry/Black Summer Rain*
**Slowhand**                                    RSO 2479 201 (1977)
*Cocaine/Wonderful Tonight/Lay Down Sally/Next Time You See Her/We're All*
*The Way/The Core/May You Never/Mean Old Frisco/Peaches And Diesel*
**Backless**                                    RSO 5001 (1978)
*Walk Out In The Rain/Watch Out For Lucy/I'll Make Love To You Anytime/*
*Roll It/Tell Me That You Love Me/If I Don't Be There By Morning/Early In The*
*Morning/Promises/Golden Ring/Tulsa Time*
**Just One Night** (double)                     RSDX 2 (1980)
*Tulsa Time/Early In The Morning/Lay Down Sally/Wonderful Tonight/If I Don't*
*Be There By Morning/Worried Life Blues/All Our Past Times/After Midnight/*
*Double Trouble/Setting Me Up/Blues Power/Ramblin' On My Mind/Cocaine/*
*Further On Up The Road*
**Another Ticket**                              RSD 5008 (1981)
*Something Special/Black Rose/Blow Wind Blow/Another Ticket/ I Can't Stand It/*
*Hold Me Lord/Floating Bridge/Catch Me If You Can/Rita Mae*
**Money And Cigarettes**                        WB W3773 (1983)
*Everybody Oughta Make A Change/The Shape You're In/Ain't Going Down/I've*
*Got A Rock'n'Roll Heart/Man Overboard/Pretty Girl/Man In Love/Crosscut Saw/*
*Slow Down Linda/Crazy Country Hop*
**Money And Cigarettes**                        WB W3773-4 (1983)
Limited edition cassette version has an interview with Eric on side two conducted by
Ray Coleman for American Radio. Recorded in January 1983, Eric tells how the
album came together. It is likely that the contractual obligations associated with this
interview precluded Eric talking to John Tobler and Stuart Grundy for their
excellent "Guitar Greats" radio series. Shame.

Compilations:
Not surprisingly there are many Clapton compilation albums including albums in

the Pop Giants and Pop History series, *Eric Clapton At His Best* (double and the most recent called *Timepiece – The Best Of Eric Clapton* issued (like the Cream singles) in 1982 by RSO as a passing shot when Eric left the label. One of the more palatable compilation albums of late is Decca's *Blues World Of Eric Clapton* (SPA 387) whose track listing is *Steppin' Out/Calcutta Blues/Lonely Years/ Stormy Monday/Shimmy Sham Shimmy/Ramblin' On My Mind/Pretty Girls Everywhere/ Hideaway/Key To Love/Bernard Jenkins/Third Degree/Have You Heard*.
Deutsche Grammophon has issued a thirteen-album box set to complement other German boxed issues of Yardbirds, Mayall and Cream albums. Also available is a three album box-set comprising *Slowhand, Backless* and *Ocean Boulevard*

**Promo Discs** (not for sale to the public)　　　RSO 2658 152 (1982)
**Eric Clapton On White**　　　　　　　　　　RSO PRO 035
*Cocaine/The Core/Lay Down Sally/Wonderful Tonight/*12 inch white vinyl
**Eric Clapton Special 12 inch AOR Disc**　　　RSO PRO 1005
*Promises/Watch Out For Lucy*
12 inch black vinyl
**Eric Clapton Limited Backless**　　　　　　　RSO PRO 1009
*Watch Out For Lucy/I'll Make Love To You Anytime/Roll It/Promises/If I Don't Be There By Morning/Tell Me That You Love Me*
12 inch white vinyl with picture label of Eric playing his Fender.
**Eric Clapton**　　　　　　　　　　　　　　　No Code
*Wonderful Tonight/Further On Up The Road*
12 inch black vinyl, both tracks live from *Just One Night* released in numbered edition of 1000.


Bootlegs:
**Georgia Peach** (Live Dallas Nov. '76)　　　　FLAT 8223
*Hello Old Friend/Badge/Knocking On Heaven's Door/One Night With You/Tell The Truth/Can't Find My Way Home/Blues Power*
**An Electic Collection 1974 Tour Vol. 1**　　　ZAP 7851
*Easy Now/Let It Grow/I Shot The Sheriff/Layla/Smile/Little Wing/Willie And The Hand Jive/Get Ready*
**An Electic Collection 1974 Tour Vol. 2**　　　ZAP 7852
*Badge/Can't Find My Way Home/Driftin' And Driftin'/Let It Rain/Presence Of The Lord/Crossroads/Steady Rollin' Man/Little Queenie*
Both the above LP's were recorded at the Long Beach Arena 20.7.74.
**Hand Jive** (Live Boston 12.7.74 and Providence
10.7.74)　　　　　　　　　　　　　　　　　　ZAP 7884
*Willie And The Hand Jive/Get Ready/Untitled/Layla/Little Queenie/Badge*
**Slowhand In Boston 12.7.74**　　　　　　　　ZAP 7880
*Smile/Have You Ever Been Lonely/Have You Ever Loved A Woman/Blues Power/ Can't Find My Way Home/Presence Of The Lord/Bright Lights Big City*
**Smile** (Live in Providence 10.7.74)　　　　　ZAP 7881
*Smile/Let It Grow/Willie And The Hand Jive/Layla/Blues Power/Little Queenie*
**74** (Live at Madison Square Garden 13.7.74)　BERKELEY RECORDS
*Can't Find My Way Home/Willie And The Hand Jive/Layla/Presence Of The Lord/ Blues Power/Badge*

**Live In London** (In fact Germany 1974)   CAUTION MUSIC
*I Shot The Sheriff/Little Rachel/Let It Grow/Get Ready/Badge/Layla/Dream Dream
Dream*
**Snowhead** (Live Santa Monica Feb. '78
and Dallas '76)   EC (1978)
*Knocking On Heaven's Door/Lay Down Sally/Next Time You See Her/Cocaine/
Badge/Sign Language/Layla*

Other Bootlegs where E.C. can be found:
1. Rolling Stones single: *Brown Sugar*   Hard On Records
2. **Bonzo Dog Band** LP *Loose Caboose*   TAKRL (1922)
   Eric only plays on *Paper Round.*
3. **Rock and Roll Circus** LP only on one track   PHONYGRAF
   *Yer Blues* with John Lennon, Mitch Mitchell, Keith Richards.
4. **Bangla Desh Concerts.**
   Various LP's came out from the two concerts Afternoon and Evening.
5. **Delaney And Bonnie With Eric Clapton
   And George Harrison**   CBM 4450
   Tracks: *Oh Lord/I Don't Know Why/Those Who Will/Special Life/You're My
   Girl/Someone/Coming Home/Tutti Frutti.*
   Recorded live at the Falkover in Copenhagen 1969. It is worth noting that E.C.
   live is very different than in the studio, in that he plays more guitar, more blues
   and a large number of songs that have never found their way on to (legitimate)
   vinyl such as *Alberta, Little Queenie, Matchbox, Stay Away From Me Baby,
   Loving You, Going Down Slow* and many more.

SESSION WORK
Unless particular sessions form part of the wider chronology of the Clapton story,
Eric's session work has not been included in the main body of the text, but is set out
below. As far as the author is aware, this is the most comprehensive session listing
on Eric Clapton ever to appear. For somebody who is so reluctant to do session
work, Eric has done a lot over the years. Eric is particularly reluctant if he doesn't
know the musicians involved too well. He gets invited along in a friendly manner
only to be put on the spot when he gets there. He becomes the centre of attention,
feels pressured and inevitably somebody goes away from the session bragging how
he burned Clapton up and how Clapton can't play any more.
Singles:

| | | |
|---|---|---|
| Otis Spann | *Stirs It Up* | Decca F 11972 (1964) |
| The Who | *Substitute/Waltz For A Pig* | Reaction 591001 (1966) |

Waltz For A Pig was written by Ginger Baker and the track personnel was not the
Who, but the Graham Bond Organisation with Eric Clapton. According to Pete
Townshend "the Pig" was Shel Talmy for screwing the band on percentages.

| | | |
|---|---|---|
| Plastic Ono Band | *Cold Turkey/Don't Worry Kyoko* | Apple 3392 (1969) |
| King Curtis | *Teasin'/Soulin'* | Atco 2091 012 (1969) |

| | | |
|---|---|---|
| Billy Preston | *That's The Way God Planned It* | Apple 12 (1969) |
| Jackie Lomax | *Sour Milk Sea/The Eagle Laughs At You* | Apple 3 (1969) |
| Jackie Lomax | *New Day/I Fall Inside Your Eyes* | Apple 11 (1969) |
| Doris Troy | *Ain't That Cute/Vaya Con Dios* | Apple 24 (1970) |
| Doris Troy | *Jacob's Ladder/Get Back* | Apple 28 (1970) |

Other musicians on these sessions included George Harrison, Steve Stills, Billy Preston, Ringo Starr and Peter Frampton.

| | | |
|---|---|---|
| Vivian Stanshall | *Labio-Dental Fricative/ Paper Round* | Liberty 15309 (1970) |
| Jonathan Kelly | *Don't You Believe It/ Billy* | Parlophone R5851 (1970) |
| Leon Russell | *Roll Away The Stone/ The Hummingbird* | AMS 788 (1970) |
| Plastic Ono Band | *Instant Karma/Who Has Seen The Wind* | Apple 1003 (1970) |
| George Harrison | *Bangla Desh/Deep Blue* | Apple 1836 (1971) |
| Arthur Louis | *Knockin' On Heaven's Door/Plum* | Plum 001 (1975) |
| Arthur Louis | *Knockin' On Heaven's Door/The Dealer* | Island WIP 6448 (1975) |

Interesting story about Clapton's involvement with reggae star Arthur Louis. Ten days after Clapton played on Louis' version of "Knockin' On Heaven's Door", Eric's own version came out just as Louis' song was about to become Johnny Walker's record of the week on Radio One. Louis had been told that in the U.K. the Dylan song would be on the B side, while the A side was supposed to be Louis' own "Someone Like You". As it was, the record company reversed it.

| | | |
|---|---|---|
| George Harrison | *Love Comes To Everyone/ Soft Hearted Hana* | 1979 |
| Gary Brooker | *Leave The Candle/ Chasing The Chop* | Chrysalis CHS 2396 (1980) |
| Gary Brooker | *Home Lovin'/Chasing The Chop* | Mercury MER 70 (1981) |
| Phil Collins | *If Leaving Me Is Easy/ Drawing Board* | Virgin VS 423 (1981) |
| Arthur Louis | *Still, It Feels Good/Come On And Love Me* | Mainstreet MS 104 (1981) |
| Colonel Doug Bogie Champion Jack Dupree | *Cokey Cokey/Away In A Manger* | ABC 12148 (no date) |

Nobody I know has ever seen this single, so it may well be a hoax.

Albums:

| | | |
|---|---|---|
| Otis Spann | **The Blues Of Otis Spann** | Decca LK 4615 (1964) |
| | **From New Orleans To Chicago** | Decca LK 4747 (1966) |

| | | |
|---|---|---|
| Blues Anytime Vol. 1 | | Immediate IMLP 014 (1967) |
| Blues Anytime Vol. 2 | | Immediate IMCP 015 (1967) |
| Blues Anytime Vol. 3 | | Immediate IMLP 019 (1968) |
| Anthology Of British Blues Vol. 1 | | Immediate IMALO 314 (1969) |
| Anthology Of British Blues Vol. 2 | | Immediate IMALO 516 (1969) |

Happy To Be Part Of The Industry Of Human
  Happiness                              Immediate IMLYIN 2 (1969)

**Immediate Let's You In**          Immediate IMLYIN 1 (1968)

Spread across these Sixties albums are blues jams involving Clapton, Jimmy Page, Mick Jagger, Ian Stewart and Bill Wyman in various combinations: *Dragging My Tail*, *Choker*, *Snakedrive*, *Tribute To Elmore*, *Miles Road* and *West Coast Idea*.

**Raw Blues**                 Ace of Clubs 12ZO (1967) '

Clapton tracks are *Lonely Years* and *Bernard Jenkins* (also released as a single on Purdah records) together with the Otis Spann track *Pretty Girls Everywhere* and Champion Jack Dupree's *Calcutta Blues*.

Mothers Of Invention   **We're Only In It For The**
                           **Money**       Verve VLP 9199 (1967)

Zappa invited Eric to a recording session while Eric was on tour with Cream. Zappa then edited some of Eric's conversation on to two tracks, *Are You Hung Up?* and *Nasal Retentive Caliope Music*. Eric was also rumoured to be on *Lumpy Gravy* singing in the chorus. However, this is impossible to confirm just by listening to the album.

| | | |
|---|---|---|
| Aretha Franklin | **Lady Soul** | Atlantic 588099 (1968) |
| The Beatles | **White Album** | Parlophone PC57067/68 (1968) |

Eric played on *While My Guitar Gently Weeps*. *Savoy Truffle* was inspired by Eric's sweet tooth. Eric is rumoured to be on *Abbey Road*, but this author remains unconvinced. The only Clapton connection is that Harrison wrote *Here Comes The Sun* in Clapton's garden.

George Harrison      **Wonderwall**       Apple SAPCOR 1 (1968)

Eric appears as "Eddie Clayton".

King Curtis           **Get Ready**         Atco 33338 (1969)
                                     (US only)

Billy Preston        **That's The Way God**
                        **Planned It**      Apple SAPCOR 9 (1969)

| | | |
|---|---|---|
| Billy Preston | **Encouraging Words** | Apple SAPCOR 14 (1969) |
| Martha Velez | **Fiends And Angels** | London SHK 8395 (1969) |

When this album was first released, contractual problems prevented a listing of the musicians involved. A subsequent release revealed all: Eric Clapton, Jack Bruce, Paul Kossoff, Mitch Mitchell, Duster Bennett, all of Chicken Shack including Christine Perfect, Chris Wood, Brian Auger and Jim Capaldi being the most notable names.

| | | |
|---|---|---|
| Plastic Ono Band | **Live Peace In Toronto** | Apple Core 2001 (1969) |
| Jackie Lomax | **Is This What You Want** | Apple SAPCOR 6 (1969) |
| Joe Cocker | **Joe Cocker** | Regal Zonophone SLRZ 1011 |
| | | (1970) |
| Doris Troy | **Doris Troy** | Apple SAPCOR 13 (1970) |
| Leon Russell | **Leon Russell** | Island ISA 500 5 (1970) |

Russell's debut album, recorded in London. Another all-star get together including
George Harrison, Ringo Starr, Joe Cocker, Charlie Watts and Bill Wyman.

| | | |
|---|---|---|
| Stephen Stills | **Stephen Stills** | Atlantic 2401 004 (1970) |
| Shawn Phillips | **Contribution** | AMLS 978 (1970) |
| The Crickets | **Rockin' 50's Rock And Roll** | CBS 64301 (1971) |
| Ashton Gardner and Dyke | **The Worst Of** | EMI E-ST 563 (1971) |
| Leon Russell | **And The Shelter People** | Island ISA 500 6 (1971) |
| Yoko Ono | **Fly** | Apple SAPTU 101/102 (1971) |
| George Harrison | **All Things Must Pass** | Apple ST CH (1971) |
| Dr. John | **Sun, Moon And Herbs** | Atlantic 2400 161 (1971) |

Recorded in London with a large cast including Eric, Mick Jagger and Graham
Bond. The personnel listing on any individual track is actually unreliable because
the album was supposed to be a triple as reflected in the three-part title.
Unfortunately, after the sessions, the tapes suddenly vanished and Mac Rebennack
"discovered" he had recorded a single album instead.

| | | |
|---|---|---|
| Howlin Wolf | **London Sessions** | COC 49101 (1971) |

A first-rate album, particularly when Howlin Wolf and Eric go two-handed on
"Do The Do".

| | | |
|---|---|---|
| Jesse Ed Davis | **Jesse Ed Davis** | Atlantic 2400 106 (1971) |
| Lord Sutch and Heavy Friends | **Hand Of Jack The Ripper** | Atlantic K40313 (1972) |

(Only a possible).

| | | |
|---|---|---|
| Stephen Stills | **Stephen Stills 2** | Atlantic K40249 (1972) |
| Duane Allman | **An Anthology** | Capricorn 67502 (1972) |

Clapton duets with Allman on *Mean Old World*. *Layla* is also included.

| | | |
|---|---|---|
| George Harrison | **Concert For Bangla Desh** | Apple STOX 3385 (1972) |
| James Luther Dickinson | **Dixie Fried** | Atlantic SD8299 (1972) |
| Bobby Whitlock | **Bobby Whitlock** | CBS 65109 (1972) |
| Bobby Keys | **Bobby Keys** | Warner K46141 (1972) |
| Bobby Whitlock | **Raw Velvet** | CBS 65301 (1972) |
| Buddy Guy and Junior Wells | **Play The Blues** | Atlantic K40240 (1972) |
| John Lennon | **Sometime In New York City** | Apple PCSP 7161 (1972) |
| Rick Grech | **The Last Five Years** | RSO 2394111 (1973) |
| Various | **Music From Free Creek** | CA DS 101 (1973) |

A messy jam session, involving The World and his Wife, not forgetting Eric, Keith
Emerson, Mitch Mitchell and Linda Ronstadt somewhere in there.

| | | |
|---|---|---|
| Ron Wood | **I've Got My Own Album To Do** | Warners K56065 (1974) |

(Only a possible).

| | | |
|---|---|---|
| Freddie King | **Burglar** | RSO 4803 (1974) |
| George Harrison | **Dark Horse** | EMI PAS (1974) |

In which Eric played guitar and Patti sang backing vocals.

| | | |
|---|---|---|
| Bonzo Dog Band | **History Of The Bonzos** | VAD 60071/72 (1974) |

| Howlin Wolf and Muddy | | |
|---|---|---|
| Waters | **London Revisited** | Chess 60028 (1974) |
| Arthur Louis | **First Album** | Polydor MP2 547 (1975) |
| Dr. John | **Hollywood Be Thy Name** | VALA 552 (1975) |
| Tommy Soundtrack | **Tommy** | Polydor PD29502 (1975) |

Eric played The Preacher and sang the Sonny Boy Williamson song *Eyesight To The Blind*.

| Joe Cocker | **Stingray** | A&M AMLH 64574 (1976) |
|---|---|---|

An early meeting for Eric and Albert Lee at Dynamic Studios, Jamaica, where this album was recorded.

| Bob Dylan | **Desire** | CBS 86003 (1976) |
|---|---|---|
| Ringo Starr | **Rotogravure** | Polydor 2302040 (1976) |

Of The Beatles, only Paul McCartney has not used Eric on a solo album. Eric laid down some good country guitar here, but also contributed a song, *This Be Called A Song*, which was not so good.

| Kinky Friedman | **Lasso From El Passo** | EPIC 81640 (1976) |
|---|---|---|

Dobro from Eric on *Kinky* and *Ol Ben Lucas* for Friedman's second album—**Mel Brooks Meets Hank Williams**.

| Stephen Bishop | **Careless** | ABC ABCL 5201 (1976) |
|---|---|---|
| Corky Laing | **Makin' It On The Street** | Elektra 7E 1097 (1977) |
| Roger Daltrey | **One Of The Boys** | Polydor 2441146 (1977) |

Clapton is listed on the album but doesn't actually play. The story goes that Roger Daltrey's gift of beer to Eric for doing the session was 'paid' in advance and Eric didn't make the session.

| Delaney Bramlett | **Class Reunion** | Prodigal P7 10017 (1977) |
|---|---|---|
| Freddie King | **1934–1976** | RSO 2494192 (1977) |

Said Eric, "He taught me just about everything I needed to know . . . when and when not to make a stand . . . when and when not to show your hand . . . and most important of all . . . how to make love to a guitar." On this memorial album for Freddie King, Eric Clapton and the band play through side two featuring tracks recorded for the *Burglar* session; *Sugar Sweet*, *T.V. Mama* and *Gambling Woman Blues* plus a live version of *Farther On Up The Road*.

| Pete Townsend/Ronnie | | |
|---|---|---|
| Lane | **Rough Mix** | Polydor 2442147 (1977) |

This album has been thoughtfully re-released to coincide with Ronnie Lane's MS tour of America. As good now as it was then.

| The Band | **The Last Waltz** | Warners K66076 (1978) |
|---|---|---|

A meeting of two master guitarists Robbie Robertson and Eric Clapton who gave us *Farther On Up The Road* and nearly dropped his guitar in all the excitement of the Band's farewell concert at the Winterland Ballroom.

| Rick Danko | **Rick Danko** | Arista 1037 (1978) |
|---|---|---|
| Various | **White Mansions** | A&M AMLX64691 (1978) |

An unsuccessful attempt to conceptualise the American Civil War in music, but it did help cement the relationship between Eric and his rhythm section-to be, Dave Markee and Henry Spinetti.

| Marc Benno | **Lost In Austin** | A&M AMLH64767 (1979) |
|---|---|---|
| Danny Douma | **Night Eyes** | Warner BSN 3306 (1979) |

| Alexis Korner | **The Party Album** | Intercord 170 000 (1979) |
| Chas and Dave | **Don't Give A Monkeys** | EMI EMC 3303 (1979) |

Eric is rumoured to be on this live album, but although he was in the audience, there is nothing to suggest he is actually playing.

| George Harrison | **George Harrison** | Dark Horse 56562 (1979) |
| Ronnie Lane | **See Me** | RCA GEMLP 107 (1979) |
| Phil Collins | **Face Value** | Virgin V2185 (1980) |

The musical relationship between Phil Collins and Eric Clapton has blossomed to the point where Phil is producing Eric's new album at Compass Point.

| Stephen Bishop | **Red Cab To Manhattan** | Warner K56863 (1980) |
| John Martyn | **Glorious Fool** | WEA K 99178 (1981) |
| Various | **Secret Policeman's Other Ball** | Springtime Haha 6004 (1982) |
| Gary Brooker | **Lead Me To The Water** | Mercury 6359098 (1982) |
| Ringo Starr | **Old Wave** | Boardwalk 26016029 (1983) (Germany) |
| Christine McVie | **Christine McVie** | WB 925059-1 (1984) |
| Roger Waters (solo) | No further information at time of writing. | |

According to Pete Frame's Clapton "Tree", Eric played on an album by Duckweed Fish called *Ham Strangled Bastard*. Well, I'm going to blow the gaff and reveal this as one of Pete's little traps for the journalists who rip his work off without giving him the credit for it.

## KNOWN STUDIO SESSIONS NOT RELEASED (WHY NOT?)

1969 Recorded with George Harrison, Ric Grech, Denny Laine, Trevor Burton at Olympic Studios, London.

1970 Recorded with Jimi Hendrix, Steve Stills, Calvin Samuels, Conrad Isidore at Island Studios, London.

1971 Recorded a side's worth of material as Derek and the Dominoes.

1972 Recorded with Stevie Wonder at Air Studios, London.

1976 Recorded with Van Morrison and various Crusaders in Los Angeles.

c. 1978 Recorded with Ginger Baker, Island Studios, London.

1979 Recorded with Steve Cropper in Los Angeles.

There were also a lot of concerts that were recorded along the 1975 U.S.A. tour as well as a concert with Muddy Waters at Dingwalls in London in 1978.

## TAPES

These are tapes known to be in the possession of private collectors, but obviously it is possible that every show Clapton has ever done has been recorded by somebody.

## CREAM

Klooks Kleek 11/66, Stockholm 7/3/67, Backbay Theatre, Boston 5/4/68, San Jose Civic Auditorium 25/5/68, Oakdale Theatre, Wallingford 15/6/68, Albuquerque 5/10/68, Newhaven Arena 11/10/68, Memorial Auditorium, Dallas 25/10/68, Madison Square Garden 2/11/68, Royal Albert Hall, London 26/11/68.

## BLIND FAITH
Madison Square Garden 69, Milwaukee 8/69, Santa Barbara 8/69, Hyde Park,
London 69. Greek Theatre L.A. 8/69.

## DEREK AND THE DOMINOES
Marquee, London 11/9/70, Lyceum, London 11/10/70, Fillmore East 24/10/70,
Ludlow's Garage, Cincinnatti 10/70, McFarlin Auditorium, Dallas 6/11/70, Painter's
Mill, Baltimore 14/11/70, Memorial Auditorium, Sacramento 17/11/70, Curtis
Hickson Hall, Tampa (with Duane Allman) 1/12/70, Capitol Theatre, Portchester
5/12/70, Suffolk College, New York 6/12/70. Of special interest is a jam tape from
the Layla Sessions at Criteria Studios with Eric and Duane trading licks, 9/70.

## ERIC CLAPTON BAND
Rainbow, London (5.30 p.m. show) and (8.30 p.m. show).

| | | |
|---|---|---|
| | 13/1/73 | |
| Nassau Coliseum, New York | 2/7/74 | |
| Roosevelt Stadium, New Jersey | 7/7/74 | (with Freddie King) |
| War Memorial, Buffalo | 6/7/74 | (with Freddie King) |
| Civic Centre, Providence | 10/7/74 | |
| Boston Garden, Boston | 12/7/74 | |
| Cow Palace, San Francisco | 21/7/74 | |
| Omni, Atlanta | 1/8/74 | |
| Budokan, Tokyo | 2/11/74 | |
| Tampa Stadium, Florida | 14/6/75 | |
| Convention Centre, Niagara Falls | 23/6/75 | |
| Providence Civic Centre, Providence | 25/6/75 | |
| Stanford University, California | 9/8/75 | (with Carlos Santana) |
| L.A. Forum, Los Angeles | 14/8/75 | (with Keith Moon, Carlos Santana, Joe Cocker) |
| Convention Center, Dallas | 15/11/76 | (with Freddie King) |
| Crystal Palace, London | 31/7/76 | (with Ronnie Wood, Freddie King, Larry Coryell) |
| Forest National, Brussels | 13/6/77 | |
| The Old Grey Whistle Test BBC TV | 26/4/77 | |
| Hammersmith Odeon, London | 27/4/77 | |
| Hammersmith Odeon, London | 28/4/77 | |
| Rainbow, London | 29/4/77 | (with Pete Townshend) |
| Koseinkein Hall, Osaka | 1/10/77 | |
| Santa Monica Civic Centre, Santa Monica | 11/2/78 | |
| Nuremberg, Germany | 1/7/78 | |
| Blackbushe Festival, Surrey | 15/7/78 | |
| Club Juventud, Barcelona | 6/11/78 | |
| Palais des Sports, Lyon | 8/11/78 | |
| Festhalle, Frankfurt | 11/11/78 | |
| Phillipshalle, Dusseldorf | 14/11/78 | (with Muddy Waters) |
| Le Pavillion, Paris | 18/11/78 | |
| Forest National, Brussels | 19/11/78 | |

| | |
|---|---|
| Apollo, Glasgow | 24/11/78 |
| City Hall, Newcastle | 25/11/78 (with Muddy Waters) |
| Hammersmith Odeon, London | 5/12/78 (with Muddy Waters) |
| Hammersmith Odeon, London | 6/12/78 |
| Civic Hall, Guildford | 7/12/78 (with George Harrison, Elton John) |
| | |
| Richfield Coliseum, Cleveland | 2/6/79 |
| Stadhalle Vienna, Austria | 6/10/79 |
| Newcastle City Hall | 7/5/80 |
| Hammersmith Odeon, London | 17/5/80 |
| Civic Hall, Guildford | 18/5/80 (with Jeff Beck) |
| Rainbow, London | 5/2/81 |
| Portland, Maine | 17/6/82 |
| Long Beach Arena, L.A. | 19/2/83 |
| Convention Centre, Sacramento | 6/2/83 |
| Philadelphia | 7/7/83 |
| Edinburgh Playhouse | 8/4/83 and 9/4/83 |
| Newcastle City Hall | 11/4/83 |
| Liverpool Empire | 12/4/83 |
| Dublin Stadium | 14–16/4/83 |
| Paris | 24/4/83 |
| Rotterdam | 23/4/83 |
| Essen | 21/4/83 |
| Sportshallen, Cologne | 26/4/83 |
| Jakobsttalle, Basle | 30/4/83 |
| St. Austell Coliseum, Cornwall | 13/5/83 |
| Poole Arts Centre | 14/5/83 |
| Hammersmith Odeon | 16–19/5/83 |
| Manchester Apollo | 21/5/83 |
| De Montfort Hall, Leicester | 22/5/83 |
| Guildford Civic Hall | 24/5/83 (with Jimmy Page and Phil Collins) |

# GROUPOGRAPHY

**THE ROOSTERS** (sometimes called Rhode Island Red and the Roosters)
January–August 1963
Terry Brennan (vocals), Robin Mason (drums), Ben Palmer (piano), Tom
McGuinness (guitar), E.C. (guitar).
The Roosters never found a bass player.

**CASEY JONES AND THE ENGINEERS**
September 1963
Tom McGuinness (guitar), Ray Stock (drums), Casey Jones (vocals), E.C. (guitar),
Dave McCumisky (bass).

**THE YARDBIRDS**
October 1963–March 1965
Keith Relf (vocals/harp), Paul Samwell-Smith (bass), Jim McCarty (drums), Chris
Dreja (guitar/vocals), E.C. (guitar – replaced Tony Topham).

**JOHN MAYALL'S BLUESBREAKERS**
April 1965–August 1965
John Mayall (vocals/keyboards/guitar/harp), Hughie Flint (drums), John McVie
(bass), E.C. (guitar – replaced Roger Dean).

**JOHN MAYALL'S BLUESBREAKERS**
November 1965–June 1966
*Line up as above*, but Jack Bruce was in the band during November/December 1965
and played gigs with Eric.

**THE GLANDS** (Greek Band)
August 1965–October 1965
Bernie Greenwood (sax), Jake Milton (drums), John Baily (vocals), Ben Palmer
(piano), Bob Ray (bass), E.C. (guitar).

## ERIC CLAPTON AND THE POWERHOUSE
*c.* April 1966
E.C. (guitar), Pete York (drums), Jack Bruce (bass), Stevie Winwood (vocals/organ),
Paul Jones (harp), Ben Palmer (piano).
Formed for one studio session only.


## CREAM
June 1966–November 1968
Jack Bruce (bass/harp/vocals), Ginger Baker (drums), E.C. (guitar/vocals).

## BLIND FAITH
February 1969–January 1970
Stevie Winwood (keyboards/vocals), Ginger Baker (drums), Ric Grech (bass),
E.C. (guitar/vocals).
This band were effectively finished by September 1969, but nobody was saying so in
public, hence the overlap with Delaney and Bonnie and Friends.

## PLASTIC ONO BAND
13th September 1969
John Lennon (guitar/vocals), Klaus Vormann (bass), Alan White (drums), Yoko Ono
(vocals), E.C. (guitar).
One-off band – Toronto Rock'n'Roll Festival.

## DELANEY AND BONNIE AND FRIENDS
November 1969–January 1970
Delaney Bramlett (guitar/vocals), Bonnie Bramlett (vocals), Jim Price (trumpet),
Rita Coolidge (vocals), Bobby Keys (sax), Carl Radle (bass), Bobby Whitlock
(keyboards), Jim Gordon (drums), E.C. (guitar).
Other friends were George Harrison and Dave Mason.

## DEREK AND THE DOMINOES
May 1970–April 1971
E.C. (guitar/vocals), Carl Radle (bass), Bobby Whitlock (keyboards/vocals), Jim
Gordon (drums).
Dave Mason played one gig – Lyceum 14th June 1970.

## GEORGE HARRISON'S BANGLA DESH CONCERT BAND
1st August 1971
George Harrison (guitar/vocals), E.C. (guitar), Ringo Starr (drums), Klaus Vormann
(bass), Leon Russell (piano), Jim Keltner (drums), Billy Preston (organ), Jesse Ed
Davis (guitar), Carl Radle (bass), Memphis Horns; back-up vocalists.

## THE PALPITATIONS – E.C. RAINBOW CONCERT BAND
13th January 1973
E.C. (guitar/vocals), Pete Townshend (guitar), Ron Wood (guitar), Stevie Winwood
(keyboards/vocals), Jim Capaldi (drums), Jimmy Karstein (drums), Ric Grech

E.C. (guitar/vocals), Albert Lee (guitar), Donald 'Duck' Dunn (bass, Roger Hawkins (drums), Chris Stainton (keyboards).

## ERIC CLAPTON BAND 1
April 1974–June 1977
E.C. (guitar/vocals), Carl Radle (bass), Jamie Oldaker (drums), George Terry (guitar), Dick Sims (keyboards), Marcy Levy, Yvonne Elliman (vocals).
Sergio Pastora Rodriguez (percussion) was in the band from 1976–June 1977.

## EDDIE EARTHQUAKE AND THE TREMORS
15th February 1977
E.C. (guitar/vocals), Ronnie Lane (guitar/vocals), Bruce Rowland (drums), Charlie Hart (keyboards/violin), Brian Belshaw (bass).
One off St. Valentine's Day charity gig at Cranleigh Village Hall. Eric plus Ronnie Lane's Slim Chance.

## ERIC CLAPTON BAND 2
June 1977–August 1978
As 1 without Yvonne Elliman.

## ERIC CLAPTON BAND 3
August 1978–January 1979
As 2 without George Terry or Marcy Levy. Eric was back to a basic four piece with him as sole lead guitar.

## ERIC CLAPTON BAND 4
January 1979–September 1979
E.C. (guitar/vocals), Albert Lee (guitar), Carl Radle (bass), Jamie Oldaker (drums), Dick Sims (keyboards).

## ERIC CLAPTON BAND 5
September 1979–c. August/September 1982
E.C. (guitar/vocals), Albert Lee (guitar), Dave Markee (bass), Henry Spinetti (drums), Chris Stainton (keyboards).
Gary Brooker (keyboards/vocals) joined in 1980 after the Far East tour and the album "Just One Night".

## ERIC CLAPTON BAND 6
c. August–September 1982 – to date
Hawkins played the first eight dates of the 1983 US tour and was then replaced by Jamie Oldaker for the rest of the US tour, all the European concerts and the final trip around America.

# SOURCES

1. Melody Maker 26/3/66.
2. Greil Marcus, Mystery Train, Omnibus 1977, p. 39.
3. Sunday Times Magazine 1/3/70.
4. Steve Turner, Conversations with Eric Clapton, Abacus 1976, p. 38.
5. ibid, p. 32.
6. Sunday Times 1/3/70.
7. Daily Sketch 30/9/70.
8. Turner p. 11.
9. Time Life 24/9/71.
9a. The Cream Complete, Wise Publications, p. 7.
10. Time Life 24/9/71.
11. ibid.
12. Sunday Times 1/3/70.
13. Quoted in an anonymous and unpublished draft of a Cream biography called He's a Leo and I'm a Taurus, courtesy of Pete Frame. Hereafter referred to as Leo.
14. Turner p. 39.
15. Surrey Comet 25/1/64.
16. MM 23/5/64.
17. MM 31/10/64.
18. MM 7/11/64.
19. MM 13/3/65.
20. Leo p. 7.
21. ibid p. 8.
22. MM 31/7/65.
23. Cream Complete p. 9.
24. MM 23/10/65.
25. Beat Instrumental September 1966.
26. MM 26/3/66.
27. MM 11/6/66.
28. MM 25/6/66.
29. BI November 1966.
30. MM 15/10/66.
31. Turner p. 47.
32. David Henderson, Scuse Me While I Kiss the Sky; the Life of Jimi Hendrix, Bantam, 1981 p. 168.
33. ibid p. 124.
34. MM 26/11/66.
35. BI November 1966.
36. MM 31/5/67.
37. ibid.
38. John Tobler and Stuart Grundy, The Record Producers, BBC 1982, p. 36.
39. Pete Brown relates the story of Sunshine . . . 'Jack and I had been up all night, trying to get something together and it hadn't been going well. In desperation, he picked up his string bass and said, 'well, what about this?', and I said, 'wait a minute' and looked outside – 'it's getting near dawn, when lights close their tired eyes' . . . and that's absolutely how it happened. It was five o'clock in the morning, the birds were twittering and we were feeling terrible'.
Clapton wrote the bridge, 'I've been waiting so long/to be where I'm going/in the sunshine of your love.
40. BI June 1967.
41. Leo p. 31.
42. MM 18/11/67.
43. Music Maker February 1968.
44. Rolling Stone 11/5/68.
45. ibid.
46. ibid.
47. MM 13/7/68.
48. RS 4/1/69.
49. The concert at the Royal Albert Hall was filmed by Tony Palmer in a hamfisted and patronising attempt to endow the music with some intellectual credibility suited to the pretentiousness of the times. The whole impact of the band on stage was lost in a frenzy of pseudo-psychedelic, rapid fire camera work, out of synch with the music, which itself was poorly recorded. The three interviews were quite amusing, particularly Ginger Baker's. With a

look of total incredulity on his face at the reverential tones of the interviewer and the half-assed questions he asked, the master of the monosyllable deflated the whole pompous exercise about technique and practise with "Well, I just 'it 'em" and "Well, I used to, but I don't anymore".

50. Disc & Music Echo 18/10/69.
51. MM 4/5/68.
52. MM 1/2/69.
53. ibid.
54. MM 12/4/69.
55. Musician Player & Listener October 1982.
56. MM 21/6/69.
57. New Musical Express 13/9/69.
58. Daily Mail 9/6/69.
59. Musician Player & Listener October 1982.
60. MM 4/10/69.
61. NME 25/10/69.
62. MM 2/8/69.
63. RS 15/10/70.
64. Disc & Music Echo 26/11/69.
65. MM 22/11/69.
66. London Evening Standard 2/12/69.
67. RS 15/10/70.
68. Turner p. 81.
69. Disc & Music Echo 20/6/70.
70. MM 4/7/70.
71. NME 13/9/69.
72. NME 10/10/70.
73. RS 11/5/68.
74. Jim Miller (ed) The Rolling Stone Illustrated History of Rock & Roll, Picador 1981, p. 295.
75. RS 11/70.
76. MM 5/12/70.
77. NME 13/1/73.
78. Turner p. 87.
79. NME 22/7/72; Sounds 8/1/72; NME 23/9/72.
80. Clapton and Townshend first came together in their mutual admiration for Jimi Hendrix, touring the London clubs together to watch him play in 1966. Townshend was an important figure in Eric's recovery from heroin addiction. "I don't know how to repay him. He was always there to give me faith in myself. It's a very intangible sort of debt I owe him. I did the Tommy movie for him, I must admit. I didn't want to do that at all. Me playing the preacher in Tommy was very, very paradoxical. Especially while I was doing it, 'cause I was loaded at the time. . . . I'm still in debt to him right up to the hilt" (RS 20/11/75). They are still close, but perhaps their differences are becoming more apparent with age as each reaches a crossroads in their own lives. "I don't know what Eric really wants out of life anymore. I know that some of the things Eric finds very important I don't give a damn about. You know he was very hurt when he stopped being voted number one guitar player in various guitar magazines . . . that was important to him . . . he thinks of himself far more as a musician than a star" (RS 24/6/82).
81. NME 12/7/75.
82. Guitar Player 1976.
83. The Record Producers p. 40.
84. 1979 tour programme notes.
85. NME 6/74.
86. Sounds 14/12/74.
87. MM 14/12/74.
88. RS 20/11/75.
89. ibid.
90. 1979 tour programme notes.
91. RS 20/11/75.
92. ibid.
93. 1979 tour programme notes.
94. Daily Express 31/7/76.
95. Enoch Powell is the Official Unionist member of Parliament for Down, South in Northern Ireland. Formerly in the Conservative Party and a Government minister, he has become infamous over the years for his inflammatory speeches on race relations in Britain.
96. Creem 1978.
97. MM 9/10/76.
98. ibid.
99. Sounds 9/10/76.
100. NME 7/5/77.
101. BBC Radio 1, The Friday Rock Show 25/4/80 – interview with E.C.
102. 1979 tour programme notes.
103. Friday Rock Show.
104. A film was made of the tour for RSO by Rex Pike, called The Rolling Hotel. To date it has never been shown to the public.
105. RS 9/8/79.
106. Musicians Only 10/11/79.
107. MM 9/12/78.
108. Quoted in Gary Herman's Rock'n'Roll Babylon, Plexus 1982, p. 59.
109. MM 9/12/78.
110. RS 20/11/75.
111. RS 6/4/68.

# APPENDIX
# "A Little Lick To Play"

This section deals briefly with the more "technical" aspects of Eric's playing over the years, his guitars, amplification, playing style and sound. There are two reasons for collecting this information together in one section. Firstly, many readers would rather read about the chronology and incidents of Eric's life than which make and model of guitar he was using at any particular time. Thus the main body of the text is devoted to the story of Eric Clapton allowing readers to skip this section altogether if they so wish. However, by the same token, guitarists and other musicians would expect to read about the technology and so it is presented in a (hopefully) convenient fashion as a small chronology in its own right, bringing together information from the text and material reserved for this appendix.

It has been written that if Eric Clapton had not played another note after his time with John Mayall's Bluesbreakers, his influence as a guitarist would still have been enormous and his place in rock history assured. There is some substance to this point; Clapton brought to the Bluesbreakers three or four years of hard listening and learning, digesting wholesale the catalogues of Freddie King, Albert King, B.B. King, T-Bone Walker, Otis Rush and Hubert Sumlin. Together with Mike Bloomfield and Johnny Winter, Clapton brought this music to the attention of appreciative white audiences worldwide where it might otherwise have died in the ghettos of Chicago, swamped by the burgeoning soul scene of the northern United States during the early and mid-Sixties. It is the best possible answer to those who have always criticised white blues guitarists like Clapton, accusing him of bastardising a pure musical form, ripping off black blues musicians, emasculating the heritage and so on. Clapton in particular, not only helped popularise the music, but re-kindled interest in the electric guitar as the prime vehicle for its execution.

In the late Fifties and early Sixties, it was a rare thing to see an American guitar in England. The first popular electric solid-body guitar, the Fender Telecaster had been available in America since 1948 and its sister guitar, the Fender Stratocaster was introduced in 1954. Although widely used in America, very few filtered through to England until the beat boom took hold around 1963. The Shadows were the first group over here to be seen with American guitars and the popularity of the group, prompted both Vox and Hofner to produce similar looking instruments for those unable to afford the real thing.

Eric Clapton, in fact, started off slightly closer to the real thing than most semi-pros. His first electric guitar was American, not a Fender, but a Kay "Red Devil", similar in shape to the Hofner Verithin. Intentional or not, both the Kay and the Verithin were copies of the Gibson ES335 first introduced in 1958 as a double cutaway semi-solid guitar with two pickups, and favoured by two major Clapton influences, B.B. King (Lucille) and Chuck Berry.

Clapton marked the start of his professional career with The Yardbirds in 1963 by purchasing his first Fender, a red Telecaster with a white scratchplate. He also got his first taste of a real Gibson ES335, lent to him by Chris Dreja for some gigs and recording session. Clapton still has this guitar, using it now mainly for slide work. The sound and style of The Yardbirds largely restricted Clapton to playing rather wild and undisciplined sheets of power chord rhythm guitar. Only in his early session work with Otis Spann, Chamption Jack Dupree and backing Sonny Boy Williamson on tour with The Yardbirds, was Clapton able to truly demonstrate that his frequent trips to West End import record stores was paying off. On the live Sonny Boy album, one can hear tight economical Texan blues inspired single string lead solos and his own interpretation of B.B. King's famous 'ringing tone'. During his time with The Yardbirds, Clapton's playing evolved from that of a good semi-pro player to a musician with the ability not only to recreate the sound and style of the great blues players, but also with the crucial facility to develop these assimilated "licks" into a more personalised style of playing. Clapton's progression can be traced through three key Yardbird tracks (from a playing point of view), *A Certain Girl*, *Got To Hurry* and *I Ain't Got You*, each with early forms of Clapton signature licks. Even so, something was missing.

In April 1965, Clapton packed up his Telecaster and took it into John Mayall's Bluesbreakers for a 12 month heroic stint. His playing style and sound developed so fast and became so well known that references to "Clapton-style" guitarists appeared in large numbers each week in the Musicians Wanted columns of *Melody Maker*. After a short while with the Bluesbreakers, Clapton cast aside his 'Tele' in favour of that extra bit of magic, the Gibson Les Paul Standard introduced in 1952.

Although initially popular with the dance bands of the early Fifties, the Les Paul fell out of favour among younger musicians, to be replaced by the Fender Stratocaster, a trend which continued as famous musicians like Buddy Holly and Hank Marvin adopted it. The Les Paul was also losing out to Vox, Hofner and Rickenbacker and the model was discontinued in 1961 although the name was still used in 1960–1961 on a double cutaway solid guitar that eventually became the S.G.

In 1965, the old Les Pauls could be acquired relatively cheaply and Eric's first, was a magnificent flame top maple made between 1958–1960.

The trebly, biting sound of the Fender gave way to a rich, mellow, powerful blues sound and coupled with a Marshall 50 watt amp and 4 × 12″ speaker cabinet, produced the unforgettable sound of electric blues guitar at its most expressive. To this, Clapton added his own aggressive blues style developed through competing in a raucous R&B band like The Yardbirds and he served up a cordon bleu delight for blues guitar afficianados, on the album *John Mayall's Bluesbreakers with Eric Clapton*. The rough edges and tinny sound of earlier days was replaced with an approach to playing full of assurance and confidence. In The Yardbirds, much of Eric's playing had been lost in the overall barrage of sound, but Mayall was far more professional, more aware of stage dynamics. He pushed Eric forward as the star of the show and Eric responded by playing as he had never done before.

The solos on the "Beano" album are timeless statements of blues guitar soloing, *All Your Love* (replicating Otis Rush's original), *Hideaway*, *Steppin' Out, Double Crossin' Time* and the pièce de résistance, *Have You Heard*, probably the finest white blues guitar solo ever committed to vinyl. Eric also tried out his voice on this album with Robert Johnson's *Ramblin' On My Mind*. Strained and tentative here, Clapton's vocals developed apace over the years until today, when he rather chillingly sounds like Otis Rush. Ironically, Clapton is able to do what B.B. King could never manage, that is to sing and play lead lines at the same time, although he could never emulate Hendrix's trick of singing and playing different lead lines simultaneously.

Moving on to Cream in May 1966, Clapton continued to play the Les Paul, but boosted the amplification to a 100 watt stack, made up of an amplifier and two 4 × 12″ speaker cabinets. As Cream grew, so did the stack, ending as a triple with a split lead from the guitar. However, at this size and power, Clapton found the volume very difficult to control and he was soon to shun loudness as an aspect of rock guitar playing. As well as producing a classic blues sound, the mellow "bassy" qualities of the Les Paul helped fill out the sound in the absence of a rhythm instrument, while Jack Bruce utilised his EBO bass and its textural and tonal qualities to the same end. Other features of Eric's approach to playing at this time included the removal of the covers from the Les Paul pick-ups, (not actually recommended, as dust and dirt can collect), and the use of light gauge Clifford Essex strings. Playing with Cream, Eric was pushing strings all over the fretboard and so favoured light strings for bending. However, like other guitarists, he soon discovered that what is gained in string flexibility using light strings, is lost in tone quality, so he switched to heavier Fender Rock'n'-Roll strings. Curiously however, Eric later returned to using light strings, Ernie Ball Slinkies, when his playing style did not involve string bending to anything like the same degree as with Cream.

Early in 1967, Clapton appeared for the first time using a Gibson S.G. standard guitar, a small bodied double cutaway guitar designed to replace the Les Paul. Eric's was a Series 1 model made between 1961–1965 incorporating two humbucking pickups. Both Clapton and Bruce had their guitars painted in psychedelic colours by the Fool design team, in keeping with the predilections of the times, although the SG did not differ markedly in tone from the Les Paul. This particular SG, eventually found its way in bits to Todd Rundgren, (possibly via Jackie Lomax), who restored it to its former glory.

By 1967, and due almost entirely to the patronage of Clapton and his contemporaries such as Peter Green, Mick Taylor and Mike Bloomfield, there had been a tremendous resurgence of interest in the Les Paul series. The Gibson company responded to this by re-issuing the model late in 1966 and in various forms, it has been a best seller ever since.

To go with his new guitar, Clapton introduced a new guitar sound, the first of two "trademark" sounds that have made E.C.'s playing immediately recognised by guitarists everywhere. He called this first sound "woman tone" produced by removing all the treble from the tone controls and either turning both pickups full on or just using the rhythm pickup. Good examples of this sound can be heard on the Cream single *I Feel Free* and *SWALBR* and *Outside Woman Blues* on *Disraeli Gears*.

Despite the presence and influence of Jimi Hendrix, Clapton was never heavily involved in the use of guitar effects pedals. The guitar "tricks" on Cream's studio albums were derived from the engineer's control board rather than the guitar. *Sweet Wine* on *Fresh Cream* had no less than six separate guitar lines; 3 lead, rhythm guitar and 2 lines of single note feedback, reminiscent of Clapton's solo on the Bluesbreakers' single, *On Top Of The World*. *Deserted Cities Of The Heart*, to cite another example, contained an out of phase double speed solo.

Clapton did allow himself one effect, the Vox Wah Wah pedal, first used by Hendrix on *Burnin' Of The Midnight Lamp* and used to devastating effect by Clapton on *White Room*, *Tales Of Brave Ulysses* and later with Blind Faith on *Presence Of The Lord*.

By the time the studio tracks for *Goodbye* were recorded, Eric was fed up with playing "the fastest axe in the West" game at maximum volume and was experimenting with his amplification. On *Badge* and *Doin' That Scrapyard Thing*, Eric played his guitar through a Leslie Cabinet normally used in conjunction with an electric organ. The rotary "paddle" located at the top of the cabinet gave a swirling "doppler" effect to the sound.

Clapton carried much of his Mayall sound with him into Cream; if the name reflected the coming together of the world's most accomplished rock musicians, it also symbolised the rich, lush texture of Eric's playing, highlighted by the advent of "woman tone". Clapton's playing achieved a magical quality with Cream; thrilling vibrato and a unique ability to put peaks and climaxes in his licks made his playing more physically exciting than just about anyone else around. The live version of *Sittin' On Top Of The World* on *Goodbye* exemplifies this. But as Cream moved to its inevitable end, Eric began to change his ideas about playing and he was looking for the space and freedom to develop these without feeling driven on by a relentless and (eventually) unsympathetic rhythm section. He played different guitars; the ES335 and a rare 1963 Gibson Firebird with special pickups, both guitars being used for the Albert Hall Farewell Cream concert in 1968. The Blind Faith gig at Hyde Park saw Eric with another unusual guitar, a Telecaster Custom with a Stratocaster neck. This marked the transition point where Eric abandoned Gibsons as his regular guitars and switched to the Fender Stratocaster.

The two year period between the end of Cream and the formation of Derek and the Dominoes was an important period of learning and re-evaluation for Eric as a musician. He played with a more diverse range of people than at any time before or since, during which he laid down some of his best session work, particularly with King Curtis, Aretha Franklin, Jackie Lomax, The Beatles, Delaney and Bonnie and the Plastic Ono Band.

With this re-evaluation of his stylistic aspirations away from power based heavy blues, came a re-assessment of the most appropriate guitar sound. He had said that he left Cream, a rock'n'roll player and undoubtedly the Fender Stratocaster is a guitar built for rock'n'roll. Eric sought a more biting, penetrating sound whereby the trilling of notes could be made even more incisive. Jeff Beck had come to similar conclusions about his own playing style and he too, switched from a Les Paul to a 'Strat'. His comment was that he found the Les Paul too easy to play; to get the best from a 'Strat', you had to "fight it". Part of the reasoning behind this comment is the weight of the 'Strat'. Being lighter than the Les Paul, with a thinner body, the guitarist can physically feel all the vibrations of the guitar and so it is somewhat harder to control. Also the 'Strat' has high frets and a convex fingerboard, so some chords are harder to play than on the Les Paul's flat fingerboard. Clapton also abandoned Marshall amplification for Fender Dual Showman gear, but more significantly, developed a new playing technique which became as much a calling card of his sound in the Seventies as "woman tone" was in the Sixties.

The old Fender Stratocaster that Clapton adopted had a three position pickup switch. Probably by accident, it was discovered that by catching the switch between the first and middle pickups, a thin, hollow reedy sound could be produced further enhancing the rock'n'roll qualities of the guitar. Never blessed with a nickname like "woman tone", this effect was introduced to the guitar world again by Jimi Hendrix on *Little Wing*, and subsequently used extensively by regular Strat players like Richard Thompson, in the wake of Clapton's example. Eric picked up on it in his earliest days of Strat playing, incorporating it into songs like *Yer Blues*, *Slunky* and *Coming Home*.

Brought up initially on the music of country blues artists like Big Bill Broonzy and Robert Johnson, Eric was always interested in slide guitar playing. However, he restricted his efforts to acoustic sessions in private, never on stage or on record, until Duane Allman inspired him to explore the possibilities on electric guitar – and in public. When Eric does stretch out on slide guitar, he uses his Gibson ES335.

In general, Clapton has kept faith with the Fender Stratocaster. Only occasionally do other guitars get an airing; the Gibson Byrdland at the Bangla Desh concert, a white Les Paul for the Rainbow gig and brief outings for his Gibson Explorer. Dobro is featured on many Clapton tracks and his main acoustic is a Martin D-28 with a pickup built into the bridge. Since 1974, Eric has hardly ever been seen on stage without "Blackie" slung round his neck, a mid-Fifties black Stratocaster, a classic of the breed. His other main Fender Strat is a 1956 Sunburst named "Brownie", used on *Money And Cigarettes*. Clapton's favoured amplification is Les Fender's Music Man range, endorsed by Clapton in the catalogue and used in conjunction with either JBL 120 speakers or the Leslie Cabinet.

Eric Clapton's influence on the world's guitar players great and small has been immense. He used to copy Otis Rush and Albert King solos and now the wheel has come full circle. Lynrd Skynrd did *Crossroads* on their live album *One For The Road*. The lead lines and first solo are note for note copies of Eric's playing on *Wheels Of Fire*.